AMERICAN UNIONISM
Fallacies and Follies

The Foundation for Economic Education, Inc.
Irvington-on-Hudson, New York

Published March 1994
ISBN 0-910614-97-0
Copyright © 1994 by
The Foundation for Economic Education
Irvington-on-Hudson, NY 10533

Dedicated to the memory of
J.P. Humphreys
who scorned the union maxim
that "might makes right."

Table of Contents

Introduction by Hans F. Sennholz   1

I. FALLACIES AND ILLUSIONS

The Origins of American Unions   13
    Clarence B. Carson

On Labor Unions   28
    Percy L. Greaves, Jr.

Workers and Unions—How About Freedom of Contract?   35
    George C. Leef

Ideological Roots of Unionism   41
    Hans F. Sennholz

II. CONSTRAINT AND COERCION

On the Right to Strike   57
    Charles W. Baird

Howard Dickman's *Industrial Democracy in America*   65
    Robert James Bidinotto

A Christian View of Labor Unions   73
    Gary North

Adversary Unionism   78
    John O. Nelson

Unions and Violence   87
    Morgan O. Reynolds

The Economics of the Barricades   97
    Antony G.A. Fisher

A Tale of Infamy: The Air Associates Strikes of 1941   100
    Charles W. Baird

Unions Drop Their Mask 116
Charles W. Baird

Unions—and Other Gangs 121
Joan Wilke

III. THE FRUITS OF UNIONISM

The Impact of Unionism 129
Clarence B. Carson

The Redistribution of Wealth—Labor Union Style 143
Robert G. Anderson

Unions and Government Employment 156
Dennis Bechara

Compulsory Public-Sector Bargaining: The Dissolution of
Social Order 167
Sylvester Petro

Unemployment, Unions, and Inflation: Of Causation
and Necessity 183
Sylvester Petro

Employee Ownership: A Rapidly Growing Threat
to a Free Market 200
Dwight D. Murphey

Government's Assault on Freedom to Work 208
Thomas J. DiLorenzo

Do Unions Have a Death Wish? 229
Sven Rydenfelt

Boulwarism: Ideas Have Consequences 234
William H. Peterson

Index 239

Introduction

Many myths surround one of the most important yet least understood institutions of contemporary society—labor unions. They persist not only because the critics are weary of facing and exploding them again and again but also because labor organizations have a vested interest in reinforcing them. The very existence of unions depends on the perpetuation of the myths that comprise the labor union ideology.

The core of the ideology is the notion that the market order does not function fairly and equitably and that it victimizes working people. Adam Smith remarked that workers labor under a disadvantage in their dealings with wealthy employers. Jean-Baptiste Say, J. R. McCulloch, and John Stuart Mill echoed the notion. Alfred Marshall confirmed it, as did A. C. Pigou and nearly all contemporary economists. They all commiserated with laboring people and, therefore, extolled the benefits of labor organizations for the purpose of removing the disadvantage. They often stood shoulder to shoulder with socialistic writers who hailed labor organizations as ramparts against the evils of competition and as mainsprings of social justice.

The union ideology is as animate and alive today as it was at its beginning. Most contemporary economists still cling to the age-old notions of employer holding power and labor inability to wait, or to some aged exploitation doctrine. But in contrast to yesteryear, unionism now is deeply entrenched in tradition, legislation, and jurisdiction.

Labor unions are well-organized and well-financed institutions that do everything in their power to preserve their existence. To ensure their survival, yea, their growth and expansion, they pursue every feasible option along ideological, economic, and political lines. Struggling valiantly for self-protection and self-preservation, they have assumed ambidextrous features and faces, which may predominate differently over time, according to the strength and kind of resistance confronting union efforts. But regardless of the predominant face, the activities of labor unions are always directed toward self-preservation by remaking the union environment, removing disabilities and extending the scope of union opportunity.

1

Labor organizations are among the most effective educational institutions in all matters of economic and social thought. Well-financed, always activist, they engage in systematic propagation of economic doctrines reflecting union views and interests. They energetically work through all media of communication and impart their doctrines on all levels of education. From coast to coast countless union organs make extensive use of historical narratives that tell the union story, of foes and friends, of sacrifices and triumphs. They speak of the worker's noble struggle for recognition and status in the late nineteenth and early twentieth centuries, and of violent resistance by greedy managers and owners. When in desperation workers resorted to strikes and boycotts, management fought back with lockouts, blacklists, and strikebreakers. But in the end, so the unions report, justice prevailed and organized labor became strong enough to bargain on an equal basis with its evil adversaries and call a halt to labor exploitation.

The remarkable success of this union rendition of labor history is built precariously on several subtle and specious pieces of popular reasoning. Every union organization routinely builds on the fallacious notion that labor conditions were deplorably poor in the past, but improved materially when unions appeared on the scene. Union spokesmen routinely echo the primitive syllogism that events coinciding in time must also be related causally. They repeat *ad nauseam* that at the beginning of the labor movement more than a century ago, when few workers were organized, hours were long and wages were low. But the knights and heroes of labor confronted the exploiters and fought them to a halt. Union effort and sacrifice brought remarkable improvements.

The advocates of government regulation of hours and wages usually draw a similar conclusion. Labor conditions were poor before government intervention; they measurably improved after government passed minimum-wage laws and forcibly limited the hours of labor. Consequently, they confidently conclude, the intervention by wise legislators and civil servants materially raised the workers' level of living. Unfortunately, neither the advocates of labor legislation nor the proponents of union organization tell us how the improvement credit is to be divided and attributed.

If it were true that events coinciding in time are, *ipso facto,* connected causally, we could also conclude that acid rain and water pollution in recent years have visibly improved our levels of living, that the roar of jet engines has enhanced our environment, and the increase of heart disease and cancer has added to our quality of life. Of course, no rational observer would draw such a conclusion. But we are urged to believe, and millions of people actually do believe, that labor unions and labor legislators did improve working and living conditions through strikes, threats of strikes, or legislative restrictions.

It is self-evident to economists that labor's phenomenal progress resulted from increased productivity, that is, from more output per man hour. Labor reaped great benefits as labor productivity rose due to increased capital investment per worker. Better tools and equipment provided by investors caused output to double every twenty to thirty years. Moreover, inventors created new products and devised new techniques while entrepreneurs made better use of existing capital as well as manpower. With the rise in the marginal productivity of labor, employer competition in the labor market caused wage rates to rise and labor conditions to improve.

Workers themselves did not contribute to the steady improvement in their working conditions unless they managed to save and invest in facilities of production. In fact, wherever labor unions caused output to decline through strikes, inefficient work rules, labor agitation, or any other reason, they actually kept wage rates lower and working conditions poorer than they otherwise would have been. The visible deterioration of economic conditions in countries with powerful unions, e.g., Great Britain, illustrates the point.

The remarkable sway of union ideology rests on a logical error that confuses coincidence in time with causal relation. Throughout most of union history the spokesmen of labor, voicing crude versions of the exploitation doctrine, made their demands for more, more, and ever more in exchange for ever less labor exertion. In most parts of the world laboring under stagnant economic conditions, such demands would have been simply dismissed as sheer lunacy—the machination of madmen.

In the capitalistic countries, however, entrepreneurs and capitalists in time succeeded in significantly raising labor productivity, thereby boosting wage rates and improving labor conditions. They actually delivered what unions were demanding. But who was acclaimed as the great benefactor of labor? The agitators proclaiming exploitation and profiteering, or the capitalists—entrepreneurs who were quietly building tools rather than consuming their incomes so that there should be more in the future? Unfortunately, public opinion was led to applaud the loud agitators and feature the union leaders.

Labor leaders forever reinterpret labor history. They extol virtues and motives of the agitators of labor unrest such as in the case of the Great Railroad Strikes of 1877 when twenty people were killed in Pittsburgh. Rioting, looting, and burning destroyed millions of dollars worth of railroad property. In the end, Federal troops had to be used to suppress the disorder. Unions commemorate the Chicago Haymarket Riot of 1886 when a bomb was thrown killing one policeman and wounding many others. Seven perpetrators were arrested, four of whom were hanged. Unions treasure the memories of the Homestead Strike of 1892, the Pullman Strike of 1894, the Coal Strike of 1902, and the most bloody Colorado anthracite coal mine conflict leading to the "Ludlow Massacre" of April 20, 1914, when women and children burned to death. Unions cannot forget how slow state and local governments were in coming to the aid and support of labor, and how, in many cases, they actually thwarted the efforts of workers to gain their objectives.

Union thought deeply influences the tone and emphasis of economic writings. There are few textbooks in economics that do not laud the valiant efforts of labor organizations toward improving labor conditions. There are few economic commentaries that do not extol the virtues of labor unions. They pave the way for socialism; in fact, most labor unions actively proclaim, promote, and disseminate the doctrines of socialism. After all, it is difficult to censure the competitive system for its labor inequities without drawing the conclusion that it should be abolished. But even where union leaders cast their lot with the market order, their tacit assumption of labor exploitation tends to pave the way for the command system.

Labor leaders fervently disseminate crude notions of the labor theory of value and the exploitation doctrine, which provide the *raison d'être* of unionism. Without union protection, we are told, most Americans would be laboring from dawn to dusk for pennies an hour. Unions are said to have raised, and continue to raise, the wages of all workers through association and collective bargaining, to have improved working conditions and reduced daily chores and working hours. Because of their great faith in labor unions and labor objectives, the American people continue to endure destructive strikes and threats of strikes, tolerate union coercion and violence, suffer many inconveniences, and credit economic improvements to labor leaders. To many millions of Americans, membership in a labor union is an important social duty and the strike a noble task.

Unfortunately, the exploitation doctrine, wherever it serves as guidepost for human action, engenders disaster. The labor legislation it breeds not only reduces labor productivity and wage rates, but also sows discontent and social conflict. The minimum-wage legislation and other attempts at raising wage rates and fringe benefits above those determined by the market, create unemployment and depression, which in turn calls for ever more government intervention. The labor unions it sponsors not only reduce labor efficiency through a multiplicity of work rules, cause maladjustment and unemployment, especially of junior members, but also reduce economic service generally, which keeps levels of living lower than they otherwise would be.

The basic method of all unionism is restriction of labor competition; the basic effect is unemployment. In an unhampered labor market without labor unions, wage rates, and working conditions are determined by the productivity of labor, which, in final analysis, is the value ascribed to services by consumers, clients, and patients. Competition among employers, together with opportunities for self-employment, tend to lift the wage rate of every worker to this very level of productivity. If, for any reason, someone should earn less than his productivity rate, his employment would be highly profitable. He would become the object of employer bidding for labor, which would lift the price of his labor back to his productivity level. If, for any reason, he should demand more than his productivity rate and claim a share of capital or entrepreneurial income, he is a candidate for unemployment. That business would be more productive without him.

Professional people, too, are subject to these principles of the market. Their incomes are determined by the value judgments of their customers, clients, and patients who are the supreme directors of the production process. Surely, there is deplorable government intervention that makes matters worse. In the health-care industry, government may subsidize and regulate the industry through Medicare, Medicaid, and other schemes, which make it vulnerable to politics. The industry must expand or contract, prosper or suffer, always readjusting to changing political fortunes. A labor union representing doctors would not improve the situation; it, too, would reduce the quality and quantity of the service and provoke ugly confrontations.

Unions restrict competition in their part of the labor market in order to raise the wage rates of their members. They are not concerned with outsiders whom they bar from access to union industries. Nor do they give much thought to their junior members who may lose their jobs as a result of union activity. But they are rather effective in their efforts to raise the employment costs of senior members while inflicting grievous losses on junior members, outsiders, employers, and consumers. Unions restrict the competition of outsiders whom they fight with every available method, even violence on the picket line. The excluded workers must seek other employment or remain unemployed. Their fate is of no concern to the unions.

When, many decades ago, unions were limited to a few industries only, the labor they cast out could find employment in other parts of the labor market that were still free. In them the supply of labor would rise, which would lower the wage rates of unorganized workers. But with the spread of unionism throughout basic industries and the proliferation of labor legislation, e.g., minimum-wage legislation, there is no escape for the victims. Unemployment has become a chronic mass phenomenon that is holding more than eight million Americans in its grip.

Unions favor collective bargaining which, in union terminology, means the substitution of a union's bargaining for the bargaining of individual workers. In reality, it is the bargaining of a select group that asserts the power of the picket line to keep all outsiders from bargaining. *Collective bargaining, in this sense, means the denial of the right to bargain by outsiders.* When some union agents sit down to deal with an employer, other agents and members are guarding his gates and forcibly preventing outsiders from competing. The employer, fearing violence at his site and willful destruction of his property, may have no choice but to deal with the agents.

If union bargaining were truly collective it would give a voice to all workers at the gate, including eager job seekers. In reality, it is confrontation at the point of a gun. The "right to strike," which is sacred to all unionists, is said to be a natural right to abstain from work. In reality, it is the right to force other people to join the strike. It is the right to prevent willing and eager workers from taking the place of striking workers.

During a 1984 strike by some 52,000 hospital workers against 30

New York City hospitals and 15 nursing homes, 1,199 workers were arrested or charged with serious strike-related offenses (*The New York Times,* August 26, 1984, pp. 1, 47). If 1,199 workers were caught in the act and apprehended, it is likely that many more committed criminal offenses and escaped undetected and unmolested. Surely, the New York police, like any other police, are not likely to apprehend every scofflaw in the very act. Moreover, they cannot possibly prevent the violence or threats of violence against reluctant union members who would work rather than strike and against unemployed workers who would love to fill the open jobs. The potential violence committed against fellow workers and their property usually exceeds by far the destruction wrought on employer property. But in the case of hospital workers the greatest harm undoubtedly comes to the patients whose suffering is aggravated by the wanton denial of care.

Labor unions are the product of the ever-changing labor ideology. From their modest beginning nearly two hundred years ago until this very day their words and actions are clearly discernible in the writings of the critics of the private property order. At the beginning and well into the nineteenth century, however, the legal system remained free from labor ideology, which permitted the courts to examine critically union organization and activity. Courts found that trade societies formed either to benefit their members at someone else's expense, or to work harm on workers who did not join the movement, were disturbing the peace and disrupting social cooperation.

In an 1815 decision involving the shoemakers of Pittsburgh, the court ruled that union activity was harmful not only to employers but also to the community at large. Under the influence of English common law, some judges even held that labor organizations, in denying basic rights to outsiders and forcing other workers to join every strike, were conspiracies prejudicial to the public interest. But while the courts may have limited the effectiveness of early labor organizations, they did not prevent the continuation and expansion of the union movement. After all, ideas control the world; they are mightier than the laws of politicians and the prohibitions of judges.

From the very beginning the union movement was also a political reform movement that sought to achieve by political force what it could not attain by economic force. Where trade unions proved powerless in changing the laws and principles of the market, their representatives were more successful in the halls of politics. As political reformers they labored to introduce government intervention in the economic and social order.

Unionism is an offshoot of modern political and economic ideology; the country that pioneered modern political and economic thought, Great Britain, was also the first to give rise to unionism. It was primarily political at its inception, a constituent of a popular reform movement that later took its name from a national charter, the Chartist movement. Concentrating on political demands, it advocated universal manhood suffrage, the ballot, equal districts for Parliamentary representation, annual parliaments, the payment of members of the House, and the abolition of property qualifications for membership in Parliament.

Some two million Chartists expected successful political action to lead also to economic changes, since political representation of the working classes would lead to measures favoring them. Chartist leaders usually urged peaceful methods, but their agitation aroused resentment and often encouraged violent action. Chartism did not bring the revolution its opponents had feared, but it did lead to political reforms and, above all, leave a foundation for future labor movements.

With the decline of the Chartist movement during the middle of the nineteenth century, British unions for a while concentrated on economic issues. Toward the end of the century, however, they turned to politics once again as socialist ideas—although non-Marxian—were swaying the movement. Their renewed interest in politics brought forth the Labour Party, their primary political instrument. In Great Britain as in other countries following the British example, labor unions now are firmly affiliated with the Labour Party or the Social Democratic Party. Union members may be required to pay "political levies" along with their union dues.

On the European continent, unionism typically developed as part of a wider labor movement, with a Marxian political party usually taking the lead. The party organization generally is the intellectual elite of the movement, affording guidance to and often assuming control of the unions. But political control tends to divide the movement, with different political parties establishing competitive unions. The predominant current is socialistic although some unions are affiliated with Christian parties (mostly Roman Catholic), nationalistic or democratic parties. A few Communistic unions are associated with the party of Marx and Lenin.

The American labor movement, throughout most of its history, kept its distance from socialism and partisan politics. It was "trade unionism pure and simple," with the single purpose to engage in collective bargaining in order to raise wages and improve working conditions of union members. It tacitly assumed that, under capitalism, workers may prosper provided they are organized. But the logic of its own ideological base, the labor theory of value and exploitation doctrine, gradually led it to the socialist philosophy that promises lasting relief to labor only by a radical reform of the system. Collective bargaining must take second place to political action.

Since the 1970s the American Federation of Labor and Congress of Industrial Organizations (AFL-CIO) has become a prime supporter of statist remedies for economic problems, real and imagined. With many unionized industries sinking into deep depression and membership unemployment rising to fifty percent or higher, the traditional instruments of union power, collective bargaining and work stoppage, have lost most of their potency. In fact, they demonstrably make matters worse, causing industry to sink ever deeper and unemployment to rise ever further. Of course, labor leaders would never admit any union responsibility; instead, they are quick to point at the administration in power as the maker of depression and unemployment. They become supporters of political action.

The AFL-CIO now supports the enactment of legislation that would protect unionized industries from foreign competition. It advocates such protectionist measures as domestic-content laws and import quotas, and opposes all efforts at lowering trade barriers on imports from developing countries. It calls for a tripartite National Industrial Policy Board, made up of representatives of organized labor, government and business, that would oversee the reconstruction of the nation's sick industries and decaying communities. Labor is backing legislation that would prohibit plant closings or at least make them prohibitively expensive, and would inject grants and subsidies into struggling, heavily unionized industries.

Unlike the AFL-CIO of old, which had no intention of running the country, the new AFL-CIO acts as if its very survival depends on political action. This new perspective is making labor unions a part of a larger, liberal-socialist movement for economic, social, and political reform. In the footsteps of the European movement, the fiercely independent unions of old are turning into vocal institutions of ideological indoctrination and party politics. But no matter what their strategy may be, the only way of obtaining higher wages, shorter hours, and better working conditions for all is, and always has been, to raise labor productivity.

—HANS F. SENNHOLZ

I. FALLACIES AND ILLUSIONS

The Origins of American Unions

by Clarence B. Carson

It is widely believed that labor unions are organized to counter the weight of and contest with employers. In the common parlance, the contestants are unions and management or, according to the older ideological formulation, "labor and capital." Most textbooks which deal with the subject simply assume that this is the nature of the contest and do not regard it as a question worthy of exploration. For example, one history text accounts for the rise of labor unions this way:

> Individual workers were powerless to battle singlehand-edly against giant industry. Forced to organize and fight for basic rights, they found the dice heavily loaded against them. The corporation could dispense with the individual worker much more easily than the worker could dispense with the corporation. The employer could pool vast wealth through thousands of stockholders. . . . He could import strikebreakers ("scabs") and employ thugs to beat up labor organizers. . . .[1]

Another history textbook puts it this way: "As the factory became the only important producing unit, the individuals connected with it were demeaned. An employee could no longer hope to have his grievances heard, for he could not compete with the power of capital and management."[2] That this is the nature of the conflict is simply affirmed by this statement in yet another history book: "Repeated efforts by trade union lawyers to persuade judges that trade societies had a legal right to carry on collective action against employers were finally rewarded in 1842. . . ."[3] Another says, "Organized labor passed through phases of bewildering complexity before it won the power to meet organized capital on equal terms."[4] In short, so far as the present writer's investi-

Dr. Carson, a contributing editor of *The Freeman*, has written and taught extensively, specializing in American intellectual history. This article, which first appeared in the January 1980 issue of *The Freeman*, was subsequently reprinted as a chapter in *Organized Against Whom? The Labor Union in America*. It appears here by permission of the author.

13

gation goes, there seems to be near unanimity in the view that labor unions exist for and engage in contests with management or capital.

Undoubtedly, some portion of the contest or conflict is between unions and management. They are the formally designated contenders. The rhetoric of union leaders is frequently filled with charges against management, and employers have often been at the forefront in contending with unions. If an agreement is reached, it is usually between unions and management. (Unions have often contended with one another also, but agreements do not so commonly arise from these.) Moreover, there is at least one economic basis for the contest to be between unions and management. In their pursuit of self-interest, employers will ordinarily seek to employ the most effective workers for the lowest price (or wage) they can attain. And, on the other hand, workers may be expected to seek the highest price possible for the least amount of their work.

Cooperation with Employers

Even so, the basic conflict of labor unions is not with management (or employers or capital, or whatever it should be called). Belief to the contrary is based on appearances buttressed by propaganda drawn from ideology, a point to be taken up elsewhere. Furthermore, permanent labor union organizations could not have arisen from or been sustained by contentions between employers and employees. The underlying reason for this is that the employers and employees are not competitors. Their basic relationship to one another is one of mutual benefit and cooperation. The employer provides the job, and the employee does the work. To accomplish their common purpose, they must work together, so to speak. An enduring contention which could sustain an organization is practically out of the question.

Of course, employers and employees do sometimes contend. Employees have grievances, and employers have dissatisfactions. On rare occasions, employee grievances may be so general that they will walk out. There have been a goodly number of instances of this throughout American history, usually provoked by the attempt of the employer to lower wages. But this is not the stuff of permanent labor union organization. (Indeed, nowadays such a walkout, if it were to occur among unionized employees, would be called a "wildcat strike," i. e., an improper and unsanctioned union activity.) Such a walkout could only fail in its object or succeed; in either case, the occasion for collective action would be past, and no permanent organization would be called for. Grievances are usually limited in scope and rarely arouse collective action. True, labor unions may establish procedures for dealing with grievances, but that is an auxiliary service, not the basis of their permanence.

Excluding the Competition

What, then, is the basis of the permanent labor union organization? It is this, that the union can and will obtain for its members a larger return for their efforts, when employed, than they could obtain on the open market. There is but one way this could be accomplished on anything like a permanent basis: *By reducing the supply of labor available in a craft, profession, or industry.* There are many artifices, of course, by which this can be done.

This should tell us, too, who labor is organized against, who the basic and underlying contest is with. And it does. Organized labor unions are organized *to exclude from a craft, profession, or industry all competing workmen* who are unorganized or not under the discipline of that particular union. The enduring contest on which permanent labor unions subsist is not unions versus management but union worker versus non-union workers or those who are competitors belonging to a different union.

The union-contest with management is sporadic, temporary, and, even when it is in progress, usually secondary. The enduring contest is with workers not members of the dominant or struggling union. Such union contest with management as there is has as its primary aim the formation of an alliance. The purpose of the alliance is to align management with the union in its reduction of the supply of labor available to employers. The seal of the alliance is the agreement or pact between union and management, or, since management or "capital" is inessential to labor unions, a pact binding those who perform the labor for whatever employer constitutes the seal.

Re-examining the Premises

Each of these propositions runs contrary to what is widely believed about labor unions. Since they do, it may be helpful to restate them serially. When that has been done, we can proceed to the reason and evidence on which they are based. These are the propositions:

1. The premise of the labor union is that it can and will obtain a larger return for its members than they would receive in the open market.

2. The means of accomplishing this on anything like a permanent basis is by reducing the supply of labor available in a craft, profession, or industry.

3. The union acts to reduce the supply of labor by excluding non-members from a craft, profession, or industry.

4. When there is an agreement between union and management, it consists mainly of an alliance by which management undertakes to enforce the union terms.

The price of labor in the market is determined by supply and demand. "Labor is not a commodity," according to a formulation which became a part of the Clayton Antitrust Act, and therefore its price ought not to be determined in the manner of commodities. But that is a semantic irrelevance, for whether labor is a commodity or not, it is offered for sale in the market, either in goods or services or directly to employers. The argument amounts to this, that the price of labor ought not to be determined in the market. That amounts to the position, however, that labor ought not to be offered for sale in the market.

How, then, is labor to be obtained? There are only two possibilities, though there are some variations as to extent. Labor must either be freely offered (and accepted) or it must be compelled. There is no evidence, to my knowledge, that labor unions are animated by the desire to have workers compelled to work, although some labor union leaders have been attracted by totalitarian systems. Their animus runs in the opposite direction, to have less work rather than more performed, less than would be freely done.

Labor unions, then, still rely on labor being offered for sale and bought in the market. It follows, then, that the price must still be determined largely by supply and demand. (There may be elements of extortion involved in union activity, but the means of satisfying human wants are too numerous and varied for outright extortion to succeed for long in any other than a totalitarian system.) The thrust of labor unions, then, is to reduce the supply of labor available in order to raise the price for their members. The thrust is to exclude from availability competing workers.

Discrimination

On rare occasions, union men have stated candidly the nature of their undertaking. For example, when Local 35 of the International Brotherhood of Electrical Workers was hailed before the Connecticut Civil Rights Commission to answer charges that it discriminated against blacks, it attempted to avoid the charge in this way. "Local 35 argued that it had not violated the law because it discriminated against all races!"[5] Young John L. Lewis put the matter forthrightly when he spoke to a conference of union men and coal operators in the midwest in 1901. He was explaining why they were conferring with one another:

> As I understand it, it is for the purpose of wiping out competition between us miners first, viewing it from our side of the question; next for the purpose of wiping out competition as between the operators in these four states. When we have succeeded in that and we have perfected an organization on both sides of the question, then as I understand the real purpose of this movement, it is that we will jointly declare war upon every man outside of this competitive field. . . .[6]

That is the best statement, too, the present writer has ever encountered of the idea of an alliance between unions and management.

Sometimes there is a confrontation between workers which reveals clearly the animus behind unionism. One such took place between Irishmen wanting work on the Chesapeake and Ohio Canal which was under construction in the 1830s. Workers from County Cork organized into a secret society which attempted to keep workers from Longford from working. Pitched battles ensued, and President Andrew Jackson eventually sent in troops to restore order. The ultimate object of the contending parties, according to an engineer who was present, was "to expel from the canal all except those that belong to the strongest party and thus secure for the remainder higher wages." According to an historian, "Laborers from Cork . . . sought to keep interloping Irishmen from competing with them for jobs on the canal."[7]

Why Force Is Used

It should be emphasized, however, that violence is not essential to unionism. It is sporadic and temporary, like the contentions between union and management. What is essential to unionism is the limitation on the supply of labor available and some means to induce employers not to avail themselves of the general supply. Some sort of coercion or intimidation is necessary to the union enterprise, however, for two reasons. In the first place, some means must be available to keep jobs from those who would seek the higher paying union jobs. And, secondly, some means must be used to get employers to accede to acting against their best interest, i. e., to pay more than they would otherwise have to do to get workers. Both experience and reason teach that these conditions are unlikely to prevail without coercion or intimidation.

Be that as it may, the American labor union originated as a means of excluding competing workers from jobs. A brief history of the beginnings will show that.

The notion that labor unions involve primarily a conflict between themselves and management—a contest between employer and employee—introduces confusion from the outset in recounting the history of American labor unions. One historian gives this account of what happened at Boston around 1760:

> The masters themselves sometimes joined forces to protect their interests.... Thirty-two master barbers "assembled at the Golden Ball, with a Trumpeter attending them," and jointly agreed to raise their rates for shaving from 8s. to 10s. per quarter, and "to advance 5s. on the Price of making common Wiggs and 10s. on their Tye ones." It was also proposed that "no one of their Faculty should shave or dress Wiggs on Sunday morning ..."[8]

The writer implies by the phrase, "the masters themselves," that this did not quite qualify as union behavior. On the contrary, it was the quintessence of union behavior. A labor union is an organization of those who perform the work in a trade, profession, or industry to gain a monopoly of such employment in order to establish conditions under which they will work. Whether they work for hire for one employer or serve the general public is irrelevant. There have been, and are, unions throughout the history of them made up largely of self-employed persons—such as barbers, plumbers, electricians, and so forth—who serve the general public. They function, as do all unions, to increase the rewards of their members by reducing the number who may so serve. (They may do so by intimidating non-members, by getting exacting qualifications passed into law, by charging high membership fees, or whatever.)

Unions were of little importance in the United States until well into the nineteenth century. Only in the 1830s did union membership constitute a significant portion of the population. For one thing, most Americans were farmers, and there the situation did not lend itself to unionization. For another, the courts were indisposed to tolerate disruptive tactics which they often described as the product of conspiracy.

Craftsmen Against Unskilled

There were, however, some efforts at organization, and it is important to understand what was involved. At the time of the founding of the United States, most manufacturing done for the public was done by skilled tradesmen. There were shoemakers, cordwainers, ironworkers, sailmakers, hatters, and such like. There were generally three ranks of such tradesmen: apprentices, journeymen, and masters. Apprentices had to and journeymen usually did work for a master craftsman. Masters sometimes formed trade associations, as already noted, and journeymen sometimes organized to effect conditions of employment. These relationships were traditional, however, and did not lend themselves much to what we think of as union activity.

It was the break-up of this mode of manufacturing by the use of machinery and the accompanying specialization that led to many attempts at organization. If I may generalize so broadly, what happened was that craftsmen organized in an effort to prevent the more specialized—and less skilled—workers from being employed. To put the matter somewhat grossly, it was the skilled craftsmen against the industrial workers. One historian has described these early conflicts this way:

The biggest problem faced by skilled laborers was the competition they met from inferior workmen ... whom employers hired in order to reduce their costs. The locals [organizations of skilled workmen], accordingly, sought to create strict rules concerning the number of apprentices to be employed in a shop and to establish a minimum wage; adoption of such a wage would force the employer to pay the same rates for both good and bad workmanship and, it was hoped, would eliminate the poor worker.[9]

Class Warfare

An account by another historian shows also that these unions were organized against other workers:

> ... The attempts on the part of employers to lower standards by hiring untrained workers—foreigners and boys, eventually women—also led to vigorous efforts to enforce what today would be called a closed shop. The New York Typographical Society complained bitterly that the superabundance of learners, runaway apprentices and half-way journeymen undermine the wage rates of "full-fledged workers...." There were many turnouts in this and later periods against employers who tried to take on artisans or mechanics who were not union members in good standing....[10]

In the course of the nineteenth century, workers other than craftsmen were sometimes organized. That did not change the fact, however, that they were most directly organized against other workers. Workers against whom they were organized were frequently classified, and it is not unfair to assert that union people thought of them as classes. The broadest and most basic category of workers against whom unions were organized were categorized as "scabs"—those who would take a union man's job if he vacated it by walking out or going on strike. The first category in point of time was that of unskilled or lesser skilled workers, as already pointed out. Women were another class against which they were organized. One historian points out that the "natural tendency was to regard women solely as competition; accordingly, men alternately deplored, condemned, and bitterly opposed

their use by employers."[11] Negroes constituted another class who encountered opposition. Unions were much less than enthusiastic about
the abolition of slavery,[12] and once they were freed "violent clashes
between white and Negro laborers became frequent in the northern
industrial centers."[13]

Opposition to Immigrants

But the one class that excited the most determined opposition was
immigrants. And, among immigrants, Orientals, particularly the Chinese, were the ones most opposed.[14] The union ire was focused at first
on contract labor brought in from abroad. The nature of the union
effort is illustrated by the following story. North Adams, Massachusetts, had several prosperous shoe factories after the Civil War. Machines were introduced which greatly increased the number of shoes a
workman could produce and reduced the skill required in doing it.
The Knights of St. Crispin succeeded in organizing many of the craftsmen who were fearful of losing their jobs or having their pay reduced
by bringing in less skilled workers. One employer hired an inexperienced workman, and the other workers went on strike. He sent to the
West Coast and contracted for and brought in 75 Chinese to run his
factory.[15] The unions were able to mount such strenuous opposition
that the contract labor law was repealed and a Chinese Exclusion Act
was passed. At about the same time, immigrants began to come, in
ever increasing numbers, from southern and eastern Europe. This
aroused fervor for more and broader immigration restriction. An historian described the impetus behind it this way: "While middle-class
critics of laissez-faire lent dignity, organized labor put pressure behind
it. Indeed, the first concentrated attack on the new immigrants came
from labor leaders."[16]

My point is *not* that union members were guilty of craft status,
gender, racial, or ethnic prejudices. They may or may not have been,
but that is incidental. My point is rather that in opposing unskilled
workers, women, Negroes, Chinese, and Europeans they were doing
what they are organized to do. Namely, they were trying to exclude
competing workers from their undertaking so as to get higher rewards
for themselves.

The most dramatic evidence of this occurs when unions resort to
overt intimidation and violence. Most of this is visited upon other

workers, though the fact is too seldom remarked, or is discussed as if it derived from some norm of human behavior. There have been instances, of course, when supervisory personnel, managers, and owners have been physically assaulted. One organization—the Molly Maguires—even concentrated on mayhem against foremen and managers.[17] But it was exceptional and short-lived. Moreover, the general practice is that in labor disputes owners, managers, and supervisory personnel can go about their affairs unharmed. If the general public are the employers (in the case of plumbers, and such like) they are rarely molested in labor disputes.

Attacking Competing Workers

It is quite otherwise with competing workmen. The whole wrath—at least on the physical side—is usually focused on them. This has been so from the early days to the present. In the early nineteenth century, shoemakers walked out in Philadelphia. Six journeymen stayed on the job. "The strikers kept up a sharp eye for them and when they briefly emerged one Sunday night to visit a near-by tavern, beat them up severely." Moreover, there "was deep resentment against non-union workers who would take the place of strikers and attacks were not unusual upon persons already being called 'scabs.'"[18]

In 1880, when the Leadville Miner's Union struck in Leadville, Colorado, some of the mines tried to stay in operation. These events transpired:

> The managers employed every available man who could handle pick or shovel, hold a drill or swing a sledge. The strikers used every means at their command to keep men from going to work and to pull out those who were at work. . . . Every day, and sometimes twice each day, a "Committee," composed of several hundred strikers, made the rounds of the mines that were working. . . . Fists, clubs, and sometimes pistols, were used, but without fatal results.[19]

Violence at the Herrin Mines

Indeed, for something near to warfare to occur between contending groups of workers, when some workmen persist in working during a strike is not that unusual.[20] Perhaps the most horrendous example in American history occurred at Herrin, Illinois, in 1922. A national coal strike had been called by the United Mine Workers. The Southern Illinois Coal Company decided to operate a strip mine near Herrin. The steam-shovel operators they employed were members of a union, but their union had been suspended by the American Federation of Labor. John L. Lewis sent out a notice that theirs was an "outlaw organization" and that the operators should be treated the same as any other "strikebreakers."

Striking union men armed themselves and surrounded the strip mine. Shooting broke out, and three of the strikers were killed. Finally, a parley was held across the lines, and the workers were offered safe passage if they would throw down their arms and surrender. This they did. They were then lined up and marched toward Herrin under armed guard. The leader who had promised safety to those who would surrender was deposed and another took his place. What then occurred may best be related in the words of the grand jury:

> The surrendered men were then marched some 200 yards . . . to the vicinity of a barbed wire fence, where they were told they would be given a chance to run for their lives under fire.
>
> The firing began immediately, and thirteen of the forty-five were killed and most of the others were severely wounded.
>
> The mob pursued those who had escaped and two were hung to trees, six were tied together with a rope about their necks and marched through the streets of Herrin to an adjacent cemetery, where they were shot by the mob and the throats of three were cut. One of the six survived.[21]

It is only fair to note that the superintendent of the mine was also killed. He had been with the workers at the mine and had been instrumental in the surrender. He was crippled and could not keep up with the marchers. When he fell out, he was shot to death.

Even so, most of the violence and direct intimidation in strikes falls upon those who attempt to continue working or accept employment at a struck plant. Nor is this intimidation of workers simply a tactic for getting at employers. It is that, of course, but it is more. It is of a piece with virtually the whole of the union effort, which is to limit the supply of labor. When there is an attempt to operate a struck plant this attempt to reduce the labor supply takes on flesh and blood and force is often directly applied. At other times, the impact of unions on other workers has to be established by analysis, since it expresses itself in unemployment, employment at low wages, higher prices, decline in production, and underemployment.

Employers have often resisted unionization. Over two centuries, virtually every conceivable device has been used to discourage unions. Above all, most employers resisted the kind of recognition of the union which makes it the bargaining agent for all employees. But once an employer recognized a union, what was in his interest then changed in a significant way. He enters into an alliance with the union, however reluctantly, and the expansion of the union to include his competitors becomes his interest as well as that of the union.

The union aim generally is to organize all competing workmen in a trade, profession, or industry. If only some such workers are organized, their effort will likely come to naught, for the employer whose workers are organized will probably be driven out of business, or tradesmen will lose their clientele to others. It should be noted, however, that the employer's interest even in this respect diverges somewhat from that of the union he has recognized. Whether his competitors unionize or not is no particular concern of his. His main concern is that non-union competitors be removed from the field so that their products not compete with his. In so far as this is accomplished with the proclaimed goal of unionization, the aims of the union and the unionized employer may become as one.

The Boycott

The most direct device for eliminating non-union competitors is the boycott. Sometimes boycotts have been carried out by open agreements between unionized employers and unions. A flamboyant case of a combination between building contractors and union to keep out competition occurred in New York City in the 1930s. In fact, local manufacturers of equipment were also in on it.

> . . . One of the three parties to this combination, Local 3 of the International Brotherhood of Electrical Workers, was interested in broadening the work opportunities of its members, who were employed by the local contractors and the local

manufacturers. The local manufacturers were interested in monopolizing the metropolitan market for their products. . . . The local union contractors were interested in having more equipment built on the job . . . and also in the protection afforded them as dealers by the union agreement to handle only manufactured products that were purchased by the contractor.[22]

Suit was eventually brought against this combination under the antitrust acts. When the case was appealed to the Supreme Court that body affirmed that it was in violation of the antitrust acts, but only because unions had acted in conjunction with business.[23] In the 1940s, when William L. Hutcheson, longtime head of the United Brotherhood of Carpenters and Joiners of America, was brought to court by the government for repeated boycotts in jurisdictional disputes with other unions, the suit failed. The Supreme Court held that he was not culpable because only unions were involved.[24]

In any case boycotts have usually been conducted by unions without overt aid from employers. The Knights of Labor had employed the boycott extensively in the latter part of the nineteenth century.[25] But the most aggressive use of the boycott was by the American Federation of Labor in the 1920s, 1930s, and 1940s. They used it, of course, in jurisdictional disputes with other unions, but also extensively to try to exclude non-union made products from commerce. No unions were more effective in this than the Longshoremen's, for they operated at pivotal points for blocking the transport of goods. One such boycott was undertaken in San Francisco in 1916. Here is a brief account of it:

In total disregard of federal laws the union boldly proposed to interfere with the shipping of commodities which were classed as nonunion or unfair, in order to fasten closed-shop conditions not only upon the port of San Francisco but upon the entire Pacific Coast. Sugar landed on the docks was refused unloading because somewhere on its journey it had been handled by nonunion men. A shipment of shingles was embargoed because the shingles had been made in an open shop . . .[26]

And so it went.

Conclusion

Masses of evidence could be compiled to support the conclusion that labor unions are organized, basically, against other workers. The evidence that they engage in open conflict mainly with other workers can hardly be disputed. Reason clearly supports the conclusion that unions can only succeed in getting higher rewards for their members by reducing the available supply of labor. That when a union is recognized by a company an alliance has been formed is largely an inference, albeit a logical one. Of course, unions have done many things which do not fit closely into this pattern, but when the matter is surveyed broadly the conclusion emerges that unions are organized against other workers primarily.

It is greatly to be doubted that labor unions would have gained much of a following had they flown those colors. In any case, they did not. In fact, unions made little headway for most of the nineteenth century. It was only after they had adopted an ideology which helped to conceal what they were about that they began to gain anything like widespread adherence.

1. Thomas A. Bailey and David M. Kennedy, *The American Pageant* (Lexington, Mass.: D. C. Heath, 1979), p. 501.

2. Charles S. Miller and Natalie Joy Ward, *History of America* (New York: John Wylie and Sons, 1971), p. 432.

3. Henry W. Bragdon and Samuel P. McCutchen, *History of a Free People* (New York: Macmillan, 1978), p. 289.

4. Samuel E. Morison, *The Oxford History of the American People* (New York: Oxford University Press, 1965), p. 768.

5. Ray Marshall, *The Negro Worker* (New York: Random House, 1967), p. 75.

6. Walter G. Merritt, *Destination Unknown* (New York: Prentice-Hall, 1951), p. 151.

7. Richard B. Morris, "Andrew Jackson, Strikebreaker," *American Historical Review*, vol. 55, p. 55.

8. Foster R. Dulles, *Labor in America* (New York: Thomas Y. Crowell, 1960, 2nd rev. ed.), p. 21.

9. Joseph G. Rayback, *A History of American Labor* (New York: Macmillan, 1959), p. 55.

10. Dulles, *op. cit.*, p. 27.

11. Rayback, *op. cit.*, p. 121.

12. See *ibid.*, p. 100.

13. *Ibid.*, p. 122.

14. See, for example, Joseph R. Buchanan, *The Story of a Labor Agitator* (Freeport, N.Y.: Books for Libraries Press, 1971), p. 66.

15. Frederick Rudolph, "Chinamen in Yankeedom: Anti-Unionism in Massachusetts in 1870," *American Historical Review*, vol. 53, pp. 1–29.

16. John Higham, "Origins of Immigration Restriction, 1882–1897: A Social Analysis," *Mississippi Valley Historical Review,* vol. 39, p. 81.

17. See James F. Rhodes, "The Molly Maguires in the Anthracite Region of Pennsylvania," *American Historical Review,* vol. 15, pp. 547–61.

18. Dulles, *op. cit.,* p. 28.

19. Buchanan, *op cit.,* p. 14.

20. For recent examples, see Sylvester Petro, *The Kohler Strike* (Chicago: Henry Regnery, 1961), p. 45 *et passim:* and *The Kingsport Strike* (New Rochelle, N.Y.: Arlington House, 1967), pp. 154–57.

21. Merritt, *op cit.,* p. 154.

22. *Ibid.,* p. 103.

23. *Ibid.,* p. 109.

24. Maxwell C. Raddock, *Portrait of an American Labor Leader: William L. Hutcheson* (New York: American Institute of Social Science, 1955), p. 249.

25. See Norman J. Ware, *The Labor Movement in the United States* (Gloucester, Mass.: Peter Smith, 1959), pp. 334–45.

26. Merritt, *op. cit.,* p. 160.

On Labor Unions

by Percy L. Greaves, Jr.

Unemployment can be a dreadful condition. The inability to find a needed job is a heart-rending experience for anyone. For those with young children to feed and clothe, it is a terrifying predicament. It gnaws at and destroys the spirit and self-confidence of even the strongest souls. With nerves on edge, family harmony too often flies out the window.

In addition to the deep mental anguish, there are also physical and financial losses. An adult's health, as well as his spirit, may suffer irreparably. A child's growth may be permanently stunted. The loss of the family car can reduce both the hope and the possibility of getting another job. The foreclosure of a mortgage on the family home can liquidate the savings of a lifetime. In short, a prolonged period of unemployment can wreck a person's life.

Then, too, the unemployed are not the only sufferers. With millions of able-bodied persons searching for a source of income or twiddling their thumbs in frustrated idleness, the potential quantity of goods and services available in the marketplace is greatly reduced. This means higher prices and lower living standards for everyone. Government programs to provide a floor for the unemployed also mean higher taxes and/or still higher prices as a result of the political creation and distribution of unearned dollars. Actually, mass unemployment and its aftermath is probably the greatest single driving force behind our politically sponsored inflation.

So solving the problem of mass unemployment is a major task of our time. Before we can solve it, we must locate the root cause. There was no unemployment at Plymouth or Jamestown. There was no mass unemployment during this country's first hundred years of existence. What is different today?

Mr. Greaves (1906–1984) economist, lecturer, and author of numerous articles and books, served with the U.S. House of Representatives Committee on Education and Labor during the preparation and passage of the 1947 revisions of the National Labor Relations Act, popularly known as the Taft-Hartley Act. This article appeared in *The Freeman* in December 1983.

Not a Free Market

One major difference is that there is no longer a free market in jobs and wage rates. There are now laws on the statute books that grant certain groups of workers the privilege of demanding and getting higher wages than they could and would earn in a free market. The unemployed are no longer permitted to compete and thus reduce the higher than free market wage rates of the privileged few. So those shut out from the higher paying jobs must compete for work and drive down the wage rates in unorganized occupations. Then, they face the floor decreed by minimum-wage laws which often prevent employment at these reduced market-wage rates.

Employers cannot long pay workers the legal minimum wage rate if consumers cannot or will not buy the resulting goods and services at prices that cover costs. As a result, millions are now legally prevented from taking either high-paying jobs or low-paying jobs. The free market in jobs and wage rates has been legally destroyed.

It should thus be evident that the remedy for mass unemployment is to repeal the laws which prevent people from competing for the higher paying jobs or taking the lower paying jobs—lower paying, until workers acquire the skill and experience needed to climb the ladder to higher incomes.

Historian Clarence B. Carson has written a small book, *Organized Against Whom?*, which tells some of the story of how we strayed from the free market path for jobs and wage rates. It is an ugly story vividly describing the coercion and violence employed by many in the labor union movement in their effort to convince the electorate that they are entitled to special privileges and immunities. They have successfully convinced many that labor unions are the protectors of downtrodden poorly paid workers who are supposedly at the mercy of greedy all-powerful employers who rob them of their rightful earnings.

Today, thanks to socialist and labor union propaganda, there is little understanding of the fact that employers are merely middlemen operating in a heavily taxed and very competitive market place. Actually, employers have very little to say about wage rates. Employers are compelled by market forces to pay employees in accordance with the value that consumers place on the production of their marginal employees, the last hired. If employers pay higher wage rates than they get back from consumers, they suffer losses and sooner or later cease to be employers. If employers seek to increase their profits by paying lower than market wage rates, competitors soon bid away their employees. Thus, the free market competition of employers is the salvation of workers looking for higher wages.

The Voluntary Way

In a free society, labor unions, like other organizations, would be voluntary groups trying to advance the interests of their members. They would abide by the laws and seek no special privileges or immunities. Unions that offered employers the most competent and reliable workers, who were willing to work for competitive free market wage rates, would grow and prosper. Labor unions that offered incompetent workers, insisted on featherbedding, or other unnecessary or costly conditions and demanded higher wage rates than competent non-union members would willingly accept would soon fade away. Certainly, in a free society no group should or would resort to violence, coercion, or special privileges to obtain what it seeks.

The free market operates according to the Golden Rule. The higher values one contributes to the marketplace, as valued by consumers, the more one receives in return. Free market operations are always voluntary transactions by which all parties exchange something they have for something on which they place a higher value. Goods and services thus continually move to persons who place a higher value on them. Barring human error or the use of force or fraud, all parties gain from all such transactions. The prevention of the use of force or fraud is a prime function of government.

Dr. Carson tells us how many labor unions now operate, with the help of laws and court decisions, coercing employers to join with them to grant them a monopoly of certain jobs. Such unions are thus able to shut out the competition of competent applicants for those jobs. Then, by demanding still higher wage rates, some unions further reduce production and employment by pricing some of their own members, those with low seniority, out of their high-paying jobs. In short, labor unionism, as now practiced, is not only the enemy of employers, investors, and consumers, but it is primarily the enemy of competent job seekers who, as a result of union action, must remain underpaid or unemployed.

Unions Gain Monopoly Status

Today, we live in an economy of political privileges with all kinds of lobbies trying to get for their members what they consider their "fair share" of the political largesse. Unquestionably, labor unions have been one of the first and strongest of these political pressure groups. As Dr. Carson narrates, they won their first great political victory in 1914, when they persuaded Congress to decree: "That the labor of a human being is not a commodity or article of commerce." Congress has great powers, but it did not by this legislation alter the fact that labor is one of the factors of production traded in the marketplace.

With this law on the books, union leaders waged a propaganda campaign demanding that government help them raise wage rates above those of the free market, which they maintain, falsely, are set too low by the whims of all-powerful employers. Their propaganda campaign was accompanied with strikes and violence that disturbed the entire nation and contributed to the mass unemployment of the depression period that started in 1929.

As a result of this propaganda and the show of force, Congress and the courts were persuaded in the 1930s to grant these labor union advocates of self-serving coercion most of the special privileges and immunities they sought. Now, we have the results. Employers as a breed are becoming scarce. So are investors willing to place their savings in new or expanded production facilities. The combined result is that the ranks of the unemployed are now reckoned in the millions. Mass unemployment has even caught up with many of the legally privileged union members. The economic laws of the market cannot long be circumvented without eventually producing undesirable consequences.

As Dr. Carson tells us, our constitutionally chosen government has empowered the labor unions to accomplish all this. He may be a bit harder on the unions than they deserve. There can be no excuse for their resort to violence and coercion. However, they can hardly be blamed for taking advantage of the special privileges and immunities from prosecution that Congress and the courts have conferred on them. In taking advantage of existing laws, they are doing no more than many college kids, lots of old folks, and millions of persons in between. Of course, that does not make it right or permanently possible. Neither Congress nor the courts have any power to repeal the laws of economics. They could make us all millionaires, but only by destroying the value of the dollar. A price must be paid for every interference with the inexorable laws of economics.

A Story of Special Privilege

It would seem we are fast losing the freedom for which our Founding Fathers pledged their lives, their fortunes, and their sacred honor. As Dr. Carson writes: "The thrust of the American Revolution was in the direction of removing special privileges and legal supports from groups and organizations." For decades now the courts have supported Congressional grants of "special privileges and legal supports" on a wholesale basis. As Carson writes, this has been "a fundamental departure from the principles of good government," not to mention the principles of sound economics.

Our government has permitted, encouraged, and even underwritten the power of labor unions to coerce all other elements of our society to bend to their will. This small book tells much of the story of how this came about. In doing so, it exposes many of the errors in the popular fallacies, the acceptance of which has permitted labor unions to attain their present position of power. This story is one with which every American should be familiar.

The book is not without its faults and contradictions. Some are only the result of an unfortunate choice of words. For example, lawlessness is referred to as the "state of nature." Or, "An ancient union complaint could certainly be disposed of if governments neither recognized, gave status to, taxed, or otherwise noticed private organizations, except as they might disturb the peace." That would mean no legal recognition or taxation of corporations or any other private organizations. In effect, it would repeal the First Amendment. For no press or religious organizations would have any status or right to be recognized in court. Or when Carson writes, "Congress is empowered to make laws regulating commerce." The Constitution carefully limited that power to "interstate commerce," and that is what it meant until the Supreme Court, in 1937, ignored the key word "interstate" in a 5 to 4 decision which upheld the National Labor Relations Act, popularly known as the Wagner Act.

There are some unfortunate contradictions in the book, as when we read, "Let me confess at the outset that I do not know what labor unions are." Then the author proceeds in chapter after chapter to tell what they are and what they do. At another point we read, "Violence is not essential to unionism." That is true, of course, if they operate within the rules and ethics of a free society. However, the thesis of this book is that labor unions are organized against society in general and against other workers in particular. As the author describes so well, they have for years pursued their policies by resorting to violence and coercion. For decades now the government has given its support to their anti-social actions—actions that impede not only full employment and prosperity but also the legitimate activities of many governmental entities.

Criticism might be made of such statements about labor unions as, "They are not economic organizations," and "Nor is the labor union primarily a political organization." If economics is the science of human actions to attain selected goals, then attaining union goals by boycotts, strikes, and stopping others from working are certainly economic actions. This book presents many incidents illustrating how labor unions have used both economic and political means to attain their present position of power.

Perhaps this reviewer's greatest disagreement is with the author's assertion that "Labor unions are religious, or religion-like organizations and, as I say, once this is grasped they come into focus. Their immediate goals are ethical in character; their ultimate goals are religious. Their economic claims are ethical in character." The latter might be so if they sought their legitimate ends by ethical means. However, there is nothing ethical or religious about the use of coercion, be it legal or illegal.

As for labor unions being religious, many economically ignorant labor union members and Congressmen undoubtedly swallow the propaganda and follow the wishes of the union bosses with a "religious" faith and fervor. We may live "in the age of the divine right of majorities," as the author rightly states, but the fact that labor unions are "supported by compulsory tithes and taxes" does not make them religious or "established churches."

Religion pertains to the supernatural—metaphysics. Except for the fact that reason tells us there must have been a Creator, religions deal with matters which cannot be logically proved or disproved. Religions are concerned with the irrational aspects of human life. Consequently, honest people, who are both sane and intelligent, can and do differ on religious matters. The aims and actions of labor unions are certainly neither heavenly nor irrational. They are earthy and concrete. Labor unions seek more for their members. There is nothing wrong with that objective if they pursued it by ethical means—by voluntary agreements for the mutual benefit of all parties. However, as Dr. Carson has so vividly pointed out, our present problems have arisen from the use of violence, coercion, and special privileges which are neither ethical nor particularly metaphysical.

The mass media, which are largely manned and edited by labor union members, constantly present a one-sided favorable picture of union policies, privileges, and activities. The public needs to know more about the antisocial effects of the prerogatives exercised by labor unions. This book strips away much of the veneer that covers the unfortunate deification of labor union activities, activities which, if committed by individuals or other organizations, would be properly labeled as crimes. We need more books which, like this one, expose the root cause of mass unemployment, a major blight not only on economic peace and prosperity but also on the pursuit of human happiness.

Workers and Unions—How About Freedom of Contract?

by George C. Leef

All but a few diehard socialists now concede that free markets serve the needs and desires of consumers far better than governmentally sanctioned monopolies or cartels. Fortunately, Americans can usually shop for the goods and services they want in more or less free markets. For only a few things must we deal with a monopoly if we want to deal at all, and in those instances, consumer dissatisfaction is high. The Postal Service immediately comes to mind as an example.

This article is about another instance of consumers being deprived of the benefits of a market: representation in dealing with employers. In the United States, the law prevents the emergence of a market for representational services employees would be willing to pay for in matters relating to their employment. Either you represent yourself or you accept representation by a labor union which may or may not be to your liking. Workers cannot shop around and then contract with the organization they believe will give them the best value for their money. It is my contention that this situation ill serves workers and is a principal explanation for the decline of labor unions in America.

The necessary conditions for the existence of a market are simple. Buyers must be free to shop around for what they regard as the best value, negotiating and entering into a contract with the seller whom they believe gives them that. Sellers must be free to offer any product or service or combination thereof which they think might appeal to prospective customers. The actions of the market participants, it must be noted, are voluntary and usually individual in nature.

One of the many services which people may want others to perform for them is the service of representing their interests in dealing with employers. Most professional athletes, for example, have contracted with agents who represent them in negotiations with team owners. And, of course, many other workers desire to have a third

---

George C. Leef is an Adjunct Scholar with the Mackinac Center, Midland, Michigan. This article first appeared in *The Freeman* in December 1992.

party represent their interests in the determination of pay and working conditions, the handling of grievances, the enforcement of safety standards, and other matters concerning their employment. In the United States, labor unions have historically filled that role.

There is no more reason to object to organizations designed to provide representational services that workers are willing to pay for than there is to object to any other kind of voluntary organization. The only test any association should have to pass is the test of the marketplace: Can it pay all of its expenses out of funds given willingly to it? The test of the marketplace compels all kinds of organizations, both those run for profit and those which are non-profit, to search for the most efficient means of providing people with the goods and services they desire.

Unfortunately, labor unions as they exist under U.S. labor statutes are profoundly non-market entities. They are not voluntary associations of individuals who have common interests and willingly contract with an outsider for the rendering of services they desire. Instead, they are involuntary associations of individuals who, on the basis of a majority vote in which they probably did not even participate, are required indefinitely to accept the "representation" of outsiders. It should not surprise anyone that many people shun that type of association, doubting that the benefits will be worth the costs.

How Unions Gain Exclusive Bargaining Power

For those unfamiliar with labor law, here is how the process works. Suppose that the workers at ABC Widget Company have no union and they bargain individually with the management over wages, benefits, and conditions of work. One day, an employee gets the idea that he and his fellow workers might be better off if the International Widget Assemblers Union (IWAU) represented them in collective bargaining with the management. He and some IWAU personnel begin to solicit signatures of workers on cards calling for an election. If they succeed in getting signatures from at least 30 percent of the workers, they will turn the cards in to the National Labor Relations Board (NLRB). Assuming that nothing is amiss, the NLRB will then set a date for a certification election.

In this election, the eligible workers will choose between representation by the IWAU, or no union representation. (Rarely, workers can choose between two unions or none at all. Unions seldom compete against each other.) If a majority votes in favor of the IWAU, then, under the exclusive representation provision of the law, the IWAU becomes the bargaining representative for all the workers, even those who wanted no union or some other union. Furthermore, the IWAU will remain the exclusive bargaining representative indefinitely. There are no periodic re-elections to test the continuing popularity of the union and its contract never comes up for renewal because there isn't one. The IWAU's relationship to the workers it represents is not one of contract, but simply of governmental fiat.

The law does allow for "decertification" elections. These rare phenomena, however, are not nearly sufficient to give workers anything approaching consumer sovereignty. Decertification elections only occur if at least 30 percent of the workers sign cards signifying that they desire such an election. The employer is not allowed to instigate or assist in this process. Many workers do not know that decertification is an option for them, and among those who do know, many are apprehensive about sticking their necks out in opposition to the union. And finally, to win the election, the opponents need a majority. If they get it, those who still want the union's services are prevented from having them. If a majority votes to keep the union, those who think they would be better off without it are compelled to put up with it.

It is unavoidable that a large number of workers will be dissatisfied under these procedures. That would not be the case if we had not collectivized what should be an individual decision.

Given their legal status which shelters them against having to compete to retain the patronage of those whom they "represent," it is not surprising that labor unions are widely perceived as taking their members for granted. The union leaders have a virtually captive market, and act accordingly. (The Supreme Court has ruled that workers may resign from a union at will, but still must pay fees to the union equivalent to their pro rata share of the cost of collective bargaining. Unions usually calculate that this amount is only slightly less than full dues.) The price of union "services" (dues) is subject to no competitive pressure, and therefore is set as high as the leaders think is safe. Nor is there any reason to believe that the revenues thus raised will be used mainly for the benefit of those who pay them. Huge salaries and perks for the union leaders are the norm. Moreover, vast amounts are lavished on political and ideological causes that have nothing to do with the jobs of the workers, and which many of them oppose.

And while union leaders spend money hand over fist on matters which are not germane to the welfare of the members, they find ways to unburden themselves of matters which are. Consider safety. Unions could conceivably render valuable services to their members if they actively sought out unsafe working conditions, held workshops on how to avoid accidents, and took other steps designed to promote safe working conditions. But union leaders lobbied to get the government to take over the workplace safety field, thus simultaneously saving unions money and enabling them to avoid the blame for mishaps. Similarly, the responsibility for assisting workers who have been laid off has been shunted onto the bureaucrats.

We arrive at the conclusion that unions are state-protected monopolies which act just as you would expect any protected monopolist to act. They maximize profits for their owners and poorly serve their customers. They also devote considerable resources to maintaining their monopoly position against any erosion. That is why you find union spokesmen advocating, always under a smoke screen of concern for the "public interest," laws which limit the freedom of Americans to buy from non-union sources. Modern unions are creatures of coercion, and do not hesitate to employ further coercion to protect themselves from other people's desires to have nothing to do with them.

Restoring the Market Process

I suggest that it is time to reverse course. The National Labor Relations Act has politicized the entire field of labor relations. A return to the common law of contract, tort, and property rights as the governing body of law in employment relations would allow each individual worker to decide for himself if he wanted to join or contract with any organization for representation services when dealing with management. In any firm, you might find that some percentage of the workers are represented by Union X, some percentage by Union Y, and some percentage choosing no union representation at all. Unions X and Y would find themselves competing to retain their customers and expand their clientele. They would have to worry about losing business if they charged too much, or failed to satisfy the desires of those whom they represent. In short, unions would become service businesses just like any other.

Defenders of the status quo will argue that this reform would allow workers who decide against any union to be "free riders" on the pro-worker accomplishments of the union(s). This is a proposition which is often stated, but seldom argued for. How can it be known *a priori* that a union will produce benefits for all the employees of the firm, much less that whatever those benefits might be, each employee would regard them as worth the cost?

If Joe Blow, a newly hired and relatively inexperienced worker, fears that union wage demands might cost him his job, and, after weighing the probable gain against the probable loss concludes that the union is not in his best interest, why should others second-guess him and force him to join? Perhaps he gets a raise that he couldn't otherwise have gotten and keeps his job, or perhaps he becomes unemployed. *Ex ante,* it cannot be known whether Joe will be a "free rider" or a victim.

But even more fundamentally, why does it follow that the government should coerce people in order to stamp out "free riding"? All sorts of voluntary activities create what economists call "positive externalities" for others. If you work to keep your home looking nice, your neighbors get a "free ride," but does it follow that they should be taxed to help pay for your desired level of lawn and garden upkeep? If Joe Blow is a "free rider" who benefits to some extent from union endeavors he has not helped to pay for, so what? Those who are willing to pay the costs of the union are not deprived of any benefits thereby.

Of course, the argument might be made that excessive free riding could so undermine the union that it could no longer produce any benefits, but does that remote possibility justify an infringement on employee freedom? I think not. Moreover, I am aware of no instance of a union collapsing due to excessive "free riding" in the many years prior to the passage of the NLRA.

Another argument which would be raised against allowing the market to function in the field of labor relations is that unions would be far less powerful if they did not speak for all the workers. Supposedly, workers must either have monopoly representation or none at all.

Of course, competitive unions would be less "powerful" than are those invested with monopoly status, but power is not necessarily in the best interest of the worker. The power that union leaders cherish has often been wielded with recklessness and arrogance, costing workers their jobs. The good that unions can do for workers, such as improving safety conditions, can still be accomplished even if it requires cooperation among several different unions. In fact, as I have argued above, unions would probably become more effective representatives of the workers whom they serve if they faced the threat of loss of paying customers if they did not do a good job.

Freedom of Contract

The competitive market process is the only way of discovering what goods and services consumers desire enough to pay for. That process requires that consumers be free to contract according to their own values and desires. Unfortunately, we abandoned the individualistic, market-based approach to labor relations in the 1930s. The result has been monopolistic unions which are largely indifferent to the desires of their members.

If we restored the market process to labor relations, workers would be able to contract for just the representation services they wanted with organizations competing for their favor. That would be the most pro-labor piece of legislation imaginable. It would probably lead to an abrupt reversal of those declining union fortunes. It would usher in a new era of cooperation and prosperity. And most importantly, it would restore to American workers a long-lost freedom—the freedom to make their own choices.

Ideological Roots of Unionism

by Hans F. Sennholz

The economic literature of our age is but a mirror of the prevailing economic thought and doctrine. There is a vast literature on the labor movement, usually in full agreement with its many manifestations. Countless books intone the praises of its organization and history, and repeat a few vague old notions on labor's disadvantage and exploitation. But these old notions continue to provide the very ideological foundation of labor unionism and the labor policies of all contemporary governments in the Western world. Refuted and exploded innumerable times in the past, their power and vigor make it necessary to answer them again and again.

It is rather difficult to trace a thought back to its original thinker. Old thoughts may never die. Once formed and uttered, embodied and expressed in fit words, they may walk the earth forever. The notion of labor's disadvantage is usually ascribed to Adam Smith, and has been held ever since by hosts of writers. A number of classical economists, above all, Jean-Baptiste Say (1767–1832), J.R.McCulloch (1789–1864) and John Stuart Mill (1806–1873) repeated the idea, in time embellished it. The Cambridge School of Alfred Marshall (1842–1924) and A.C. Pigou (1877–1959) expanded and popularized it to justify workers' combinations and collective bargaining. The first president of the American Economic Association, Francis A. Walker (1840–1897), added his conception. Countless contemporaries continue to echo the old exercise.

The wage of labor, according to Adam Smith, depends on the contract made between workers and masters. But their interests are not the same. The workmen desire to earn as much, the masters to grant as little as possible.

The labor movement of the early nineteenth century may have

Dr. Hans Sennholz was Head of the Department of Economics at Grove City College in Pennsylvania, where he penned this essay. This chapter is an excerpt from an article which originally appeared in February 1984 in *The Freeman*.

sprung from the following passage in the *Wealth of Nations,* or at least may have received the master's approval and benediction:

> It is not, however, difficult to foresee which of the two parties must, upon all ordinary occasions, have the advantage in the dispute, and force the other into compliance with their terms. The masters, being fewer in number, can combine much more easily; and the law, besides, authorizes, or at least does not prohibit their combinations, while it prohibits those of the workmen. We have no acts of parliament against combining to lower the price of work; but many against combining to raise it. In all such disputes the masters can hold out much longer. A landlord, a farmer, a master manufacturer, or merchant, though they did not employ a single workman, could generally live a year or two upon the stocks which they have already acquired. Many workmen could not subsist a week, few could subsist a month, and scarce any a year without employment. In the long-run the workman may be as necessary to his master as his master is to him, but the necessity is not so immediate.[1]

Say, McCulloch, Mill

The French writer Jean-Baptiste Say did more to spread Smith's teaching in general and Smith's doctrine of labor's disadvantage in particular than any other writer. In his *Traité d'économie politique,* published in 1803, he repeated Smith's remarks and eloquently elaborated the implications. The wants of the masters, according to Say, are less urgent and immediate than those of the workers who without gainful employment would soon be reduced "to the extremity of distress." This circumstance, Say concluded, must have its effect on the rate of wages both parties tend to accept.[2]

J.R. McCulloch, in his 1851 *Treatise On the Circumstances which Determine The Rate of Wages and the Condition of the Labouring Classes* eloquently repeated the Smith doctrine in defense of union organization and activity. Trade union leaders quoted McCulloch and thousands of pamphlets spread his views on the benefits of labor combination. Actually he was merely popularizing Smith's doctrine of labor's disadvantage.[3]

John Stuart Mill, who dominated the intellectual scene in Britain and the United States for nearly half a century, professed two different theories of labor combination. In his younger years he was rather skeptical about labor's ability to improve working conditions through combination. In his *Principles of Political Economy* he spoke of "narrow limits of power" beyond which union activity would keep "a part of their number permanently out of employment."[4] Combinations may be successful only where the work-people are few in number and are concentrated in local centers. They may impose higher costs on employers who will pass them on to consumers in the form of higher prices.

Some twenty years later Mill presented a different theory of the prospects and consequences of combination. Under the influence of his friend, W.T. Thornton, he not only reproduced the doctrine of labor's disadvantage but also invoked his "standard of morals" on behalf of labor unions. He mixed his economic beliefs with his moral convictions and arrived at an ardent labor union doctrine. The laborers' wages, according to Mill, tend to fall within a certain range the higher limit of which is "consistent with keeping up the capital of the country," and the lower limit of which "will enable the labourers to keep up their numbers." Unable to resist even a single employer, and surely the tacit combination of employers, the laborers must yield. Their wages, as a rule are "kept down at the lower limit." When laborers combine in a union that includes "all classes of labourers, manufacturing and agricultural, unskilled as well as skilled" they may achieve the higher limits. Whoever adheres to "a standard of morals" must wish "that the labourers may prevail."[5]

Walker, Marshall, Pigou

Francis A. Walker (1840–1897), the outstanding American economist of his time, justified combinations on the grounds of "impaired" or imperfect competition which may work against the workers. Adam Smith provided his guideposts: "Masters are always and everywhere in a sort of tacit, but constant and uniform, combination not to raise the wages of labor above their actual rate" (*The Wealth of Nations,* pp. 66–67, quoted by Walker, *The Wages Question,* p. 392). In the name of justice and "for the peace of industrial society," labor must be permitted to play the same game. Professor Walker, therefore, concurred with Messrs. Mill and Thornton and all other defenders of trade unions. But he added a reservation that continues to be heard even today, a century later: Labor unions served a useful purpose in the past, but have lost their justification in the present. In his own words, "My difference with such defenders of trades-unions as Mr. Thornton is merely as to the time when these should be put away as an outgrown thing. I find no ground for expecting any benefit to the wages class as a whole, from restricting the access to professions and trades in any country where education is general, where trade is free, where there is popular tenure of the soil, and where full civil rights, with some measure of political franchise, are accorded to working-men."[6]

Alfred Marshall (1842–1924), one of the great names in the development of contemporary thought, had such great influence on his fellow economists that the first quarter of the twentieth century can probably be called the "Age of Marshall." Much of the Marshallian framework remains intact today, in the last quarter of the century.

Marshall elaborated Smith's doctrine of labor's disadvantage and embellished one of Thornton's original thoughts that "labour will not keep." Labor may be at a special disadvantage because it is "perishable" and the sellers are too poor to withhold it from the market. The want of reserve funds is common especially to all grades of unskilled labor, the wages of which leave little margin for saving. Moreover, unskilled workers are most numerous and always eager and capable of taking each others' places, which makes a laborer's disadvantage cumulative in two ways: "It lowers his wages; and as we have seen, this lowers his efficiency as a worker, and thereby lowers the normal value of his labour. And in addition it diminishes his efficiency as a bargainer, and thus increases the chance that he will sell his labour for less than its normal value."[7]

The Economics of Welfare

Arthur Cecil Pigou (1877–1959) was the successor of Marshall as professor of political economy at Cambridge University. He was, it may probably be said, the last member of the Cambridge School, which John Maynard Keynes made his chief target of attack. Pigou's *Theory of Unemployment* (1933), especially, embodied the "classical economics" that was loudly rejected by Mr. Keynes. But Keynes never objected to Professor Pigou's doctrine of labor combination and union activity, or his notion that the pricing process allowed for a margin of "indeterminateness" that was available for collective bargaining.[8]

In his celebrated opus *The Economics of Welfare,* Professor Pigou depended on collective bargaining to prevent the "cutting or nibbling" of wage rates. In fact, he sounded like a socialist who is firmly convinced of the power of employers to "exploit" their weak and defenseless workers, especially through piece-wages. In his own words, "When a bad employer succeeds in 'nibbling' the rates, his success makes it difficult for his competitors to refrain from following his example, and is apt, therefore, to start a cumulative movement. But it is not necessary that piece-rates should be fixed by individual bargaining. In this fact the solution to the problem may be found. For collective bargaining furnishes a guarantee against the kind of nibbling which is really exploitation, and also makes it easy to provide machinery—whether joint committees or jointly appointed rate-fixers to adjust particular rates."[9]

There Is No Margin of Indeterminateness

If eminent economists from Adam Smith down to our age professed such forceful doctrines it cannot be surprising that multitudes of lesser writers joined in the chorus, that nearly every man of public affairs continues to identify himself with the eminent economists, and every union spokesman proudly echoes the doctrines. But no matter who may sponsor the precept, how often it may be repeated, and how popular it may be, it cannot possibly stand a critical analysis. It contradicts basic economic knowledge and clashes with economic reality.

The doctrines of labor's disadvantage and deliverance by collective bargaining are "short-cut doctrines" that promise instant relief and improvement through collective force. They probably spring from sympathy for the hardships of the poor which is a noble passion of the human heart, and from the most beneficial of all the affections—hope—which is the only universal cure. They promise an exciting shortcut to income and wealth without the pain of extra effort and labor and without the arduous task of capital formation that makes human labor more productive. And lest we forget, they bring popular applause for "goodness" and "benevolence" although they pave the way for so much folly and suffering.

There are no shortcuts to economic production and income. Wage rates for any kind of labor, from complex mental labor to simple physical exertions, are determined by the anticipation of the service they render to human well-being. In particular, they are determined by anticipation of the price that can be obtained for the increment of goods and services expected from the employment of the worker. Economists call this increment the "marginal" product that determines the compensation for every kind of labor. It can be made to rise through greater labor exertion and improvements in the quality of labor. It may be raised with the help of more capital and application of more productive methods of production. But it cannot be made to rise through collective bargaining. There is no "margin of indeterminateness" that can be appropriated by militant labor unions. There is no "no-man's land" in which the biggest battalions determine the outcome of the battle.

In a private-property order labor is treated like any other factor of production bought and sold on the market. Employers need to buy materials and supplies, tools and equipment, and all kinds of specific labor. To stay competitive and serve his customers best, an employer must buy the needed factors at the lowest possible prices. But the prices he offers must be high enough to secure the necessary supplies from the sellers, outbidding all other competing buyers. He may make mistakes in his bidding for the factors of production. He may bid to pay more than the going rate, which raises his costs of production and invites offers in excess of his needs. If his bids are lower than the market price, he may not be able to secure the needed supplies. A businessman who continues to make such mistakes, i.e., incurs higher costs than his competitors or fails to obtain the needed supplies will, in time, cease to be a businessman. Someone else more capable of judging prices will take his place.

Employer Combinations Are Ineffective

Even if employers were to combine openly or tacitly to keep wages below the marginal rate, to which Adam Smith alluded, their sinister efforts would be destined to fail. If they would pay less than the full rate, they would render the employment of labor more profitable. New entrepreneurs seeing new opportunities for profits would appear on the market and bid for more labor, which would bring wage rates right back to the marginal productivity of labor. Even if employers would manage to prevent the arrival of newcomers through institutional barriers, such as government licenses and permits, their open and tacit combinations would soon fail because they themselves would be tempted to buy more labor at such bargain rates. They would be tempted to expand their activities, bidding for more labor in any way conceivable. After all, there may be small employers who would like to grow, some who are young and eager, some who are poor and desperate, perhaps on the brink bankruptcy. They all may want to hire profitable labor in order to reap the benefits. If they cannot raise wage rates, they may want to adjust working conditions, improve fringe benefits, or compete effectively in countless other ways, which once again would raise labor compensation to the marginal rate.

Employer combinations designed to restrain wage rates ignore many other factors of labor compensation that remain the objects of competition. In this respect a combination agreement is like a wage "freeze" or "stop" imposed by a fuddled government; it may arrest a single factor of competition, the rate of wages, but tends to stimulate the competition for labor in countless other ways, from generous expense accounts to country club dues. If government cannot effectively enforce a wage stop, using threats, fines, and brute force, it is unlikely that an association of employers, or even a national association of associations, lacking that force, can lower wage rates.

If it is true that employers compete with other employers in countless subtle ways, it is rather futile and unwise to enter into restraint agreements and wage combinations. This fact alone, which undoubtedly is well-known to experienced businessmen, points at the obvious conclusion that the colorful reports on employer combinations, today or from the distant past, are probably overstated and exaggerated.

Comparing employer combinations with worker combinations, that is, labor unions, the basic differences become apparent immediately. While employers tend to compete openly and tacitly to engage the needed labor, labor unions actually prevent the competition of their members. Employers may evade a wage agreement in countless different ways; workers may not be able to escape the union command. They face an agonizing decision: to cross or not to cross the picket line. Employers are virtually free to compete in the labor market; workers are not. They may live under the threat of brutal retaliation not only at the picket line but also at work and at home.

Surely, to be more competitive in the labor market, an employer may openly improve the fringe benefits of his workers without inviting any physical danger to himself or his family. A worker who ignores his union command and actually crosses a picket line may jeopardize all his property and risk bodily harm not only to himself but also to his family. It must be concluded, therefore, that combinations and organizations of restraint are rather ineffective among employers. But they may be highly effective in their design to restrict competition when they consolidate and syndicate the workers.

Workers Can Wait

It is said that workers cannot wait for remuneration and, therefore, suffer a disadvantage in their bargaining position toward employers. "The masters have the advantage," according to Adam Smith. The workers without gainful employment would soon be reduced "to the extremity of distress," according to Jean-Baptiste Say. Thus stated by the mentors their disciples have been repeating it ever since.

This ability-to-wait theory of income obviously is moving in a vicious circle. It ascribes disadvantages to poor laborers who cannot wait, and explains their inability to wait with their lamentable poverty. The masters can wait because they are affluent, and they are affluent because they can wait. Actually, the ability to wait has no bearing on wage determination unless it is the ability to withdraw permanently from the market. Withdrawal of labor raises the marginal productivity of labor just as the withdrawal of capital raises that of capital. But such a withdrawal, if it is conceivable at all, would reduce total output and thus total income. It would aggravate everyone's economic conditions but especially those of workers who chose or were forced to withdraw.

The inability-to-wait doctrine, which lives on in contemporary economic literature, received considerable intellectual support from Thomas Robert Malthus and his theory of population. Nearly all classical economists were convinced that the power of population is indefinitely greater than man's power to produce subsistence. Population, when unchecked, increases in a geometrical ratio. Subsistence only increases in an arithmetical ratio. The disproportion unfortunately condemns the least productive class of population to hopeless misery and poverty.

Malthus and Population

The Malthusian law of population indisputably explains economic conditions in many parts of Africa and Asia where additional quantities of means of sustenance are immediately absorbed by additional numbers of people. But in capitalistic societies with economic freedom and private property in the means of production, with private initiative and entrepreneurship, economic production tends to outpace by far the proliferation of population. Freedom of thought and policy always bring unprecedented economic development together with declines in birth rates and mortality rates, which significantly raise the levels of living and prolong the average human life. If working people no longer hover at the subsistence minimum the Malthusian law of population cannot be made to support the inability-to-wait doctrine.

The doctrine nevertheless lives on, nourishing labor combinations and commending collective bargaining. It never explains why workers acting in concert have greater holding power than workers acting individually and alone. After all, human wants and basic needs for sustaining human life are always individual. It is true, an association of workers may pool member resources and thereby consolidate and equalize the hold-out period. It may save membership dues and accumulate a strike fund for distribution during "waiting periods." And above all, it may concentrate its holding power on a single employer, inflict or threaten to inflict painful losses on him in order to make him submit to union demands. Such tactics of worker combinations leave employers no choice but to form their own defense organizations that can meet the workers' collective power with holding power of their own. Most employer associations sprang from this necessity of self-defense.

Employers organize in self-defense from labor organizations defending themselves from alleged "cutting," "nibbling," or outright exploitation. Both sides are often locked in a bitter struggle of self-defense, which is testing their ability to wait, impoverishing both and hurting the public. Both sides act like pawns in the game of economists who call it "cutting" or "nibbling" with its predictable consequences.

Are employers capable of cutting and nibbling in the absence of powerful labor unions? They are as capable or incapable of nibbling at the price of labor as they are with other prices for materials and supplies, water and electricity, or travel facilities. In the case of labor, as with many other factors, employers may have a choice between many grades and qualities. What may appear like "nibbling" and "cutting" may actually be the purchase of mediocre labor. Workers differ greatly not only in learning, training, and skills but also in dependability, conscientiousness, honesty, cooperation, and goodwill. Some employers may choose to attract only the most productive workers by offering the highest wages; others may try to get along with mediocre labor, paying average wages; others yet who may have special skills in handling difficult labor may try to make do with less expensive labor. They all mean to achieve the lowest costs per unit of output in order to serve their customers best.

"Labor Is Perishable" and It "Will Not Keep"

In its crudest form expressed by Professor Marshall, the inability-to-wait theory calls for collective defense on grounds that labor is "perishable" and that it "will not keep." This startling observation obviously implies that, in contrast to labor, capital is more durable and therefore stronger than labor. Unfortunately, this whole line of reasoning is flawed rather seriously because it compares two incomparable qualities: labor services with the productive life of tools and equipment. It is specious reasoning which would become apparent immediately if employers were to use it: "We are unable to wait, when compared with labor, because corporate profits and interest income are 'perishable,' but laborers are not." If Marshall had compared labor service with capital service, or labor income with capital income, he would have noticed that all types of income are "perishable." During periods of labor strife and idleness, the services of both capital and labor do not "keep"; both lose time, income, and wealth through inactivity.

Contrary to the pronouncements by the eminent economists, many workers can wait longer than their employers. Small employers are no match for laborers organized in industry-wide unions. Many large employers are "marginal," that is, are operating at the margin of profitability covering expenses and earning a going rate of return. Some employers may be "submarginal" earning less than the going rate. Some may even suffer losses. When labor unions choose to test the ability to wait the weakest employers suffer the greatest pain in the form of calamitous losses, which may spell ruin and bankruptcy. All other producers may be forced to curtail operations and reduce output.

Many classical economists were unduly impressed by the economic strength of the masters. According to Jean-Baptiste Say, "There are few masters but what could exist several months or even years, without employing a single labourer, and few labourers that can remain out of work for many weeks, without being reduced to the extremity of distress." Surely, few American corporations could suffer a strike of several months or even years without jeopardizing their economic survival. And few French companies could have suffered through lengthy shutdowns in 1803 when J. B. Say wrote these lines. They, too, had to pay taxes, interest on loans, and high overhead costs regardless of operation and output. They, too, suffered grievously through time wasted, income lost and opportunities forgone.

The classical economists never were "masters" meeting payrolls and interest payments, facing deadlines for tax payments to various government authorities, or suffering frightening losses from sudden changes in market conditions. They probably never confronted labor unions that meant to inflict maximum harm on the owners. The great writers were academicians motivated by genuine sympathy and empathy and guided by deep feelings of good will for the poor.

Inapt Reverence for the Past

In all matters of labor relations public feeling is apt to side with the laborers. Their poverty, presumed or real, is like a badge of courtesy to which the public readily pays homage or at least demonstrates respect. Most economists who are mindful of public opinion are quick to render honor to labor combinations. In want of a labor union rationale, but guided by considerations of courtesy and public opinion, they may dwell on the history of labor and make much of the distant past.

Francis A. Walker was one of the first to question the present and salute the past. He added a thought to the intellectual armory of unionism that continues to haunt us even today, more than one hundred years later. No longer finding any ground "for expecting any benefit to the wages class" from labor combinations, he raised the questions of "when these should be put away as an outgrown thing." In short, he suggested that labor unions may have lost their justification in the present (1876), but that they were most useful in the past. He bestowed honor and prestige on labor unions by imputing a virtuous and glorious past.

Economics as a theoretical science elaborates eternal, inexorable principles of human action. It deals with the means man must apply in order to achieve attainable ends. History is but a register of human efforts and blunders which cannot confirm, refute, add to or subtract from economic knowledge. It cannot uncover benefits of labor combination in the present or the past if economics finds "no benefits to the wages class." History cannot reveal benefits to all workers if economics demonstrates convincingly that union tactics cause unemployment. Historians should not proclaim the benefits of labor combination and collective force if economists can show that such force not only reduces economic output and thereby hurts consumers, but also inflicts serious harm on unemployed workers.

The unhampered market order allocates to every member the undiminished fruits of his labor. It does so in all ages and societies where individual freedom and private property are safeguarded. It did so 2,000 years ago in Rome, in eighteenth-century England, and in nineteenth-century America. The reason our forefathers earned $5 a week for 60 hours of labor must be sought in their low productivity, not in the absence of labor unions. The $5 they earned constituted full and fair payment for their productive efforts. The economic principles of the free market, the competition among employers, man's mobility and freedom of choice, assured full wages under the given production conditions.

Wages were low and working conditions primitive because labor productivity was low, machines and tools were primitive, technology and production methods were crude when compared with today's. If, for any reason, our productivity were to sink back to that of our forebears, our wages, too, would decline to their levels and our work week would lengthen again no matter what the activities of labor unions or the decrees of government.

Most historians are not economists who elaborate the inexorable principles of human action. They like to portray the Industrial Revolution as a disaster that brought untold misery to the working classes. They hail progressive governments and courageous labor unions for having offered relief to the suffering masses. To them the coercive power of both government and labor union is a necessary instrument for balancing the economic powers of the masters. To economists such an interpretation of history is deficient in basic economic knowledge. They view the Industrial Revolution and the phenomenal improvements of labor conditions and income as a great achievement of economic freedom. It set people free to apply science to industry, and to form and use capital in economic production.[10] The rise of unionism during the past two centuries is seen as the result of fallacious economic doctrines about laborers' disadvantage. Labor unions are the bitter fruit of erroneous theory, with a record of abuse far more grievous than the alleged evils the unions were supposed to rectify.[11]

---

1. Cf. Adam Smith, *An Inquiry into the Nature and Causes of the Wealth of Nations*, 1776 (New York: The Modern Library, 1937), Book I, Chapter VIII, p. 66.

2. Jean-Baptiste Say, *A Treatise on Political Economy* (1803), Third American Edition, 1827, "The wages of the labourer are a matter of adjustment and compact between the conflicting interests of master and workman; the latter endeavoring to get as much, the former to give as little, as he possibly can; but, in a contest of this kind, there is on the side of the master an advantage over and above what is given him by the nature of his occupation. The master and the workman are no doubt equally necessary to each other; for one gains nothing but with the other's assistance; the wants of the master are, however, of the two, less urgent and less immediate. There are few masters but what could exist several months or even years, without employing a single labourer; and few labourers that can remain out of work for many weeks, without being reduced to the extremity of distress. And this circumstance must have its weight in striking the bargain for wages between them" (p. 294).

3. "Few masters willingly consent to raise wages; and the claim of one or of a few individuals for an advance of wages is likely to be disregarded so long as their fellows continue to work at the old rates. It is only when the whole, or the greater part, of the workmen belonging to a particular master or department of industry combine together, or when they act in that simultaneous manner which is equivalent to a combination, and refuse to continue to work without receiving an increase of wages, that it becomes the immediate interest of the masters to comply with their demand. And hence it is obvious, that without the existence either of an open and avowed, or of a tacit and real combination, workmen would not be able to obtain a rise of wages by their own exertions, but would be left to depend on the competition of their masters" (New York: Augustus M. Kelley, 1963), pp. 79–80.

4. *Principles of Political Economy* (1848), in "Collected Works of John Stuart Mill" (University of Toronto Press, 1965), Vol. III, p. 930.

5. "Thornton on Labour and its Claims" in "Fortnightly Review" May 1869, *Dissertations and Discussions, Political, Philosophical, and Historical* (New York, 1875), pp. 74, 75.

6. *The Wages Question: A Treatise on Wages and the Wages Class* (1876) (New York: Holt, 1904), p. 406.

7. *Principles of Economics*, (1890), 8th edition (London: Macmillan & Co., 1920), p. 473.

8. *Principles and Methods of Industrial Peace* (New York: Macmillan, 1905), p. 36. Also *The Economics of Welfare* (1920), Fourth Edition (London: Macmillan, 1932), pp. 557, 558: "Insofar, however, as movements of workpeople are hampered by ignorance and costs,

a monopolistic element is introduced into the wage bargain. Consequently, there is created *a range of indeterminateness,* within which the wages actually paid to any workman can be affected by individual 'higgling and bargaining.' The upper limit of this range is a wage equal to the value of the marginal net product of the workman to the employer engaging him . . . . The lower limit is a wage equal to what the workman believes he could obtain by moving elsewhere, *minus* an allowance to balance the costs of the movement. The width of the gap between the workers' minimum and the employers' maximum varies in different circumstances. It is made larger when the employers in a district tacitly or openly enter into an agreement not to bid against one another for labor, since, in that event, the alternative to accepting terms from them is to seek work, not near by, but perhaps in an unknown district."

9. *The Economics of Welfare,* p. 483.

10. Cf. T. S. Ashton, *The Industrial Revolution* (Oxford University Press, 1948); F. A. Hayek (ed.) *Capitalism and the Historians* (Chicago: University of Chicago Press, 1954).

11. Cf. W. H. Hutt, *The Theory of Collective Bargaining* (Glencoe, Ill.: The Free Press, 1954); Charles E. Lindblom, *Unions and Capitalism* (New Haven: Yale University Press), 1949.

II. CONSTRAINT AND COERCION

On the Right to Strike

by Charles W. Baird

Strikes have re-emerged as a political and labor relations issue. During most of the 1980s, private sector unions used their strike-threat weapon very sparingly. Many employers and unions pointed out that if American industry is to regain its competitive strength, the adversarial union relations model of the National Labor Relations Act (the Wagner Act of 1935, amended by the Taft-Hartley Labor Act of 1947 and the Landrum-Griffin Act of 1959) must be replaced by more cooperative labor relations. However, it now appears that many in the union hierarchy have decided to revive adversarial relations in general and strike threats in particular.

Three recent strikes have received a lot of media attention—the Eastern Airlines strike, the Pittston Coal strike, and the Greyhound strike. The thrust of the media coverage has been that the strike-threat weapon isn't nearly as formidable as it used to be. The chief culprit is alleged to be President Reagan. When he fired the PATCO strikers in August 1981 and successfully hired replacements, he created a model that private-sector employers now emulate. It used to be that employers thought it would be bad public relations to hire replacement workers during a strike, but according to the media, Reagan's actions have removed the stigma. Furthermore, during the 1980s the Supreme Court issued several decisions that significantly reduced the economic value of the unions' strike-threat weapon.

Unionists are so upset at these setbacks that they have sought relief from Congress. Legislation has been submitted in the House and Senate that would make it illegal for any employer to hire permanent replacement workers during a strike. William Bywater, president of the International Union of Electrical Workers, asserts that the union hierarchy has adopted this legislation as its principal legislative priority in the present Congress. Moreover, the Supreme Court cases were all decided on legislative, not constitutional, grounds, so Congress can

Dr. Baird, a contributing editor of *The Freeman*, is Professor of Economics at California State University at Hayward. This article is reprinted from *The Freeman*, October 1990.

override the Court by passing ordinary remedial legislation. Some unionists have proposed just that.

Before they rush to do the bidding of the AFL-CIO, legislators ought to examine the nature of the strike-threat weapon and consider in what sense, if any, there exists a legitimate right to strike. That is what I propose to do in this essay.

The Three Strikes

In March 1989 the International Association of Machinists (IAM) went on strike against Eastern Airlines. At first, pilots and attendants joined the strike; but after 164 days they announced they were willing to cross the IAM's picket lines. The IAM is still on strike, but some Eastern mechanics have crossed the picket lines, and Eastern has filled with replacement workers as many other slots as it needs for its current operations.

In April 1989 the United Mine Workers went on strike against Pittston Coal Company. The strike wasn't settled until February 1990. During this long struggle, striking miners ran up $65 million in court-ordered fines for illegal, often violent actions. Part of the strike settlement called for Pittston to try to persuade the courts to drop the fines against the strikers. So far the courts have refused to do so.

On March 2, 1990, the Amalgamated Transit Union took 6,300 Greyhound Lines bus drivers out on strike in an attempt to shut down Greyhound's operations nationwide. The attempt failed because 1,800 drivers immediately crossed the picket lines, and Greyhound hired what it said were "permanent" replacements for most of the strikers. As of mid-April 1990, there had been 30 or more instances of gunfire attacks and a myriad of less serious acts of violence against buses and their drivers and passengers. On April 10 Greyhound filed a $30,000,000 lawsuit against the striking union based on alleged acts of violence and extortion.

What Is a Strike?

When I ask students to define the word "strike," the most frequent answer I get is that a strike is a collective withholding of labor services by workers who do not like the pay and benefits package an employer has offered to them. This is the definition of strike that appears in most textbooks. If this definition were accurate, I would strongly affirm that there is a moral, as well as a legal, right to strike. But the definition is wrong. Section 13 of the National Labor Relations Act gives unionized private sector workers a legal right to strike, but there is no moral right to strike.

A strike is more than a collective withholding of labor services. It is, in addition, an attempt to shut the employer down by denying the employer access to suppliers, customers, and, most important, workers who are willing to work. The picket line is the principal means to this end. As the Supreme Court acknowledged in *American Steel Foundries* v. *Tri City Trades Council* (1921), even peaceful picket lines can intimidate. Moreover, picket lines are seldom peaceful. People who attempt to cross picket lines are routinely threatened and are often subject to violence. The Pittston and Greyhound strikes are merely the most recent examples of the true nature of picketing during strikes. That is why the Supreme Court, in strongly affirming the voluntary exchange rights all participants in the labor market, limited picketing to one picket per entrance in the *Tri City* case. The National Labor Relations Act has changed the law, but it hasn't changed the right.

A Legitimate Right to Strike

There is an awful amount of muddled thinking about rights on college campuses and among the judiciary. According to the jurisprudential doctrine called legal positivism, legislation creates rights. There are no natural rights. It's a matter of counting the votes. For example, if there are enough votes in Congress in favor of creating a right for person A to interfere in a voluntary exchange relationship between persons B and C, then such a right may be created. All that is needed is that the correct procedures for enacting legislation be followed. According to this view, there are no substantive limits on what Congress may enact.

Legal positivism emerged in American jurisprudence during the first third of the twentieth century. Roscoe Pound, Louis Brandeis, Felix Frankfurter, and Oliver Wendell Holmes, Jr., were among its chief protagonists. Legal positivism gained majority support on the Supreme Court during the New Deal, and it has been dominant ever since.

The framers of the Constitution were not legal positivists. They subscribed to the idea that there are fundamental human rights that cannot be just overridden by any act of Congress. Such rights are inherent in human nature. They do not depend on the outcome of any election. Government does not create or grant these rights. They are antecedent to government. According to this view, in order for an alleged right to be a legitimate human right it must be possible for all humans to possess and exercise the right simultaneously without logical contradiction.

For example, does any person have a legitimate right to a job? If person X claims the right to have a job irrespective of the willingness of any other person Y to employ him, then X's job-related rights are different from Y's job-related rights. X is entitled to possess a job, and Y has the duty to provide it. Since such an alleged right cannot be held and exercised simultaneously by all people in the same way, it is not a legitimate human right.

The only job-related right that can be held and exercised by all people in the same way is the right to make job-related offers to others. Sellers of labor services have a right to offer to work for any employer on any terms the sellers wish. They do not have a right to compel any employer to accept such offers. In exactly the same way, employers have a right to offer to employ any worker on any terms whatsoever. They do not have the right to compel any employee to accept such offers. In short, the employment relationship is a contractual relationship based on mutual consent. In the absence of a contractual agreement to the contrary, no employee has a property right to any job.

What about the right to strike? In the absence of a contractual agreement to the contrary, any employee has a right to withhold his labor services from an employer if he doesn't like the pay and benefits the employer offers. If each individual has this right, then a group of like-minded individuals can exercise this right together. In other words, all individuals who want to may withhold their labor services at the same time. If this concerted action induces the employer to acquiesce to the workers' terms, so be it. That will depend on the relative bargaining power of the two sides, and neither side has a natural right to any bargaining power advantage. Each side's bargaining power depends on the attractiveness of its alternatives.

However, and this is the central point, notwithstanding Section 13 of the National Labor Relations Act, like-minded workers who simultaneously withhold their labor services have no legitimate right to interfere in any way with the right of the struck employer to engage in voluntary exchanges with customers, suppliers, and other workers. Workers who are willing to work for a struck employer who wishes to hire them have a legitimate right to do so. Moreover, they may agree to accept the very terms of employment that the strikers consider to be unacceptable. Replacement workers have the same job-related natural rights as striking workers.

Unionists resort to name-calling to imply that replacement workers don't have the same voluntary exchange rights as other workers. "Strike breakers" and, even more pejoratively, "scabs" are typical epithets. Jack London, for example, once wrote, "After God had finished the rattlesnake, the toad, the vampire, He had some awful substance left with which he made a scab." Richard Trumka, president of the United Mine Workers, who led the Pittston strike, thought it sufficient to say, "Replacement worker is a nice refinement in terminology, but a scab is a scab" to make a case against employers who hire replacements. But scabs are human, and as Thomas Jefferson would put it, they are endowed by their Creator with the same unalienable rights as any other human. Notwithstanding the tenets of legal positivism, not even Congress can justly take away unalienable rights.

Replacement Workers and the Law

The National Labor Relations Act became law in 1935. The law guarantees a right to strike and to use picket lines to try to prevent the struck firm from operating. The *Tri City* one-picket per entrance rule of 1921 was overturned. Mass picketing is now legal. So long as overt violence is avoided (or disguised), pickets may threaten and cajole anyone who attempts to cross the lines. Since the National Labor Relations Act pre-empts state law, and since the local police are frequently outnumbered, police are often reluctant to step in even when overt violence takes place. During the Pittston strike, for example, the mines were effectively shut down by violence and threats of violence. Even judicially imposed injunctions and fines were incapable of restoring the voluntary exchange rights of nonstrikers.

Section 2 of the National Labor Relations Act provides that employers may not fire striking workers. Strikers have property rights to the jobs they refuse to perform. However, in *NLRB* v. *Mackay Radio & Telegraph Co.* (1938), the Supreme Court held that struck employers may hire permanent replacement workers in economic strikes, as well as temporary replacement workers in unfair labor practice strikes. An economic strike is one over issues such as pay, working conditions, and benefits. An unfair labor practice strike is one over some alleged illegal act of the employer such as discriminating against union workers or refusing to bargain with a certified exclusive bargaining agent. In an economic strike, the strikers are still employees (they may not be fired), but the employer doesn't have to reinstate them immediately following a settlement. They have first claim on any job that a replacement worker later vacates. In an unfair labor practice strike, striking workers must, upon settlement of the strike, be given the opportunity to take over jobs held by replacement workers.

The Court did not decide *Mackay* on constitutional grounds. The Court merely held that the National Labor Relations Act doesn't prevent struck employers from hiring replacements. The Court, in keeping with its legal positivist doctrine, said that Congress may pass a law banning replacements but until it does, employers are free to hire them.

In *Belknap* v. *Hale* (1983), the Supreme Court acted further to uphold the voluntary exchange rights of permanent replacements. Prior to *Belknap*, some struck employers hired replacement workers and told them that their jobs were permanent. Then, after the strike was settled, these replacement workers were dismissed and returning strikers took their place. In *Belknap* the Court held that if an employer tells replacement workers that they are permanent replacements and then dismisses them when a strike is settled, the dismissed replacement workers may sue the employer in state courts for breach of contract. As the law stands now, during an economic strike employers are legally entitled to hire permanent replacement workers. If they do so they cannot offer those positions to strikers as part of a strike settlement.

Legislation has recently been introduced in the House and Senate that would make hiring permanent replacements illegal in all strikes. Temporary replacements could be hired, but it is very difficult to find qualified workers to take jobs on a temporary basis. The intended effect of the proposed legislation is to make the union strike-threat more credible as an economic weapon against employers. It is an egregious example of politicians attempting to grant special privileges to an organized, and politically active, interest group in exchange for financial and in-kind assistance at election time.

Recent Supreme Court Cases

The Supreme Court has recently issued three decisions that further decrease the effectiveness of the unions' strike-threat weapon. From a unionist's perspective, these cases violate the rights of union workers. From a natural rights perspective, the Court has only partially restored some basic liberties to nonunion workers and employers. Those same liberties had been unjustly overridden by earlier Court cases upholding and interpreting the National Labor Relations Act.

In *Pattern Makers League* v. *NLRB* (1985), the Court ruled that a union member may resign from the union during a strike and cross a picket line without fear of legal retribution from the union. Under existing law, a union may fine a member who crosses a picket line, and the fine will be enforced by government courts. But a nonmember may cross a picket line with (legal) impunity. Prior to *Pattern Makers,* a union member had to give a 30-day notice before he or she could resign, and no one could resign membership during a strike. Now a union member can resign at any time without notice.

Except in the 21 states that have prohibited them in the private sector, union security clauses may be included in collective bargaining agreements. Under a union security clause, every worker who works in a unionized firm must either join the union (union shop) or pay service fees to the union (agency shop) as a condition of continued employment. In *Communications Workers* v. *Beck* (1988), the Court declared that money forcibly collected from unwilling workers could only be used by the union to pay for the costs of collective bargaining, contract administration, and grievance procedures. No such money could be used for partisan or ideological advocacy or union organizing activities. Fees collected from dissenting workers had to be less than the regular fees collected from voluntary union members. In the case of a union shop, any worker can become a "financial core" member at will. That is, membership duties are limited only to paying reduced dues.

In *TWA* v. *Flight Attendants* (1989), the Court held that after a strike settlement, employers need not replace "crossover" workers with returning strikers who have more seniority. A crossover worker is a striker who crosses a picket line to return to work before a strike is settled. Prior to *Flight Attendants,* strikers maintained their seniority privileges after a strike. A crossover worker who was doing the job previously done by a more senior striker would have to give up the job to the returning worker. Now a striker may permanently lose a job assignment to a less senior crossover.

In sum, these three cases have made it more difficult for unions to maintain solidarity. During a strike a union member may resign at will from the union and cross the picket line. Such a worker completely avoids union dues or, under a union security arrangement, at least reduces his or her dues-paying liability. Moreover, as a crossover, such a worker perhaps gains permanent job assignments hitherto reserved for more senior employees. In conjunction with the *Mackay* doctrine, which enables employers to hire permanent replacement workers, these cases make unions less willing to strike. They decrease the economic value of strike-threats to unions, but they restore some voluntary exchange rights to others.

Conclusion

The current Supreme Court appears to be tentatively moving toward supporting the voluntary exchange rights of all workers. But, since all of these cases have been decided on legislative, not constitutional, grounds, all Congress has to do to again promote unionists' privileges over the rights of others is amend the National Labor Relations Act. Moreover, as present justices retire and new ones take their places, the Court itself could easily move back toward promoting unionist privileges at the expense of the rights of others. A constitutional amendment that incorporates the safeguards the Court enunciated in 1921 in the *Tri City* case and makes affiliation with a union a matter of individual choice, not majority vote, is the only (nearly) reliable way to defend the legitimate rights of all participants in labor markets.

Howard Dickman's *Industrial Democracy in America*

Robert James Bidinotto

Of the enduring myths of economic history, few have hung on as tenaciously as the necessity and desirability of labor unions. Consider a recent editorial in my hometown newspaper, typical of the conventional wisdom:

> While unions today have a somewhat tarnished reputation, most historians generally concede that they played a key role in American economic and social advancement. Unions fought for higher wages and improved benefits for workers, allowing them to participate in the American dream. More money also meant workers could purchase more goods, fueling a consumer economy.
>
> Without unions and their system of collective bargaining, the U.S. could have lapsed into labor chaos and class warfare. These conditions in other countries led to the establishment of communist-inspired revolutions. (*The New Castle* [Pa.] *News*, August 14, 1987)

The editorial is correct about one thing. Today, there is general agreement (even from many on the political right) that while unions may be too powerful, back in the days of "total laissez faire" they were a necessary counterweight to the unchecked power of "robber baron" employers. Unions are widely credited with raising the standard of living for millions of workers; with introducing democracy into the workplace; with protecting helpless laborers from being devoured by rapacious businessmen and blind market forces.

Until now, there has been scant literature presenting a systematic, comprehensive challenge to these claims. But some years ago, eminent labor economist Sylvester Petro suggested a project to Howard Dick-

---

Mr. Bidinotto is a staff writer for *Reader's Digest*. This review-essay first appeared in *The Freeman* in February 1988.

man. American trade unionism—especially its economic and intellectual rationales—deserved a dissection comparable to Ludwig von Mises' analysis in *Socialism*.

What were the ideas, the intellectual influences, that shaped today's labor policies? What popular myths and misconceptions gave rise to those ideas? When did they begin—and where have they led us?

Petro obviously had great confidence in his young listener. Dr. Dickman was then only in his mid-twenties; and his specialty was corporate, not labor, history. But he had an impressive familiarity with the theory and history of the free society, and the diligent temperament of a true scholar. He accepted the commission and went to work.

It would be ten years before the results of his labors were published. Now, readers can see for themselves that Petro's trust was not misplaced, with the appearance of *Industrial Democracy in America: Ideological Origins of National Labor Relations Policy* (La Salle, Illinois: Open Court, 1987, $32.95 cloth, $16.95 paper).

Dickman's book is a true landmark—a grand synthesis of history and analysis, an extraordinary *intellectual* account of trade unionism and collective bargaining. In its breathtaking scholarship alone, it rivals or surpasses such standard works as Milton Derber's *The American Idea of Industrial Democracy* and such impressive general intellectual surveys as Sidney Fine's *Laissez Faire and the General Welfare State* or Arthur Ekirch's *Decline of American Liberalism*. And among the distinguished works written by pro-capitalist scholars, it compares with Dominick Armentano's *Antitrust and Monopoly*, Robert Hessen's *In Defense of the Corporation*, and Thomas Sowell's *Marxism*—except that it is far more ambitious, in aims and execution.

Building on the premise that *ideas* are the tidal forces underlying the course of events, the author explicitly avoids a mere "blow-by-blow history of the organized labor movement in America." Rather, he examines the pedigree of "industrial democracy" as a concept, focusing on the thinkers and theories which made unions and strikes possible. Quoting Friedrich Hayek, Dickman makes clear that his aim is to examine ideas which "often have crept in almost unnoticed and have achieved their dominance without serious examination. . . ."

There are several things unique about Dickman's treatment of labor history. First, his own philosophical and economic framework is explicitly laissez-faire capitalism, building on the ideas of Ludwig von Mises, Ayn Rand, W.H. Hutt, Sylvester Petro, and Friedrich Hayek.

This allows him to place labor relations policies within the much broader context of the general rise of anti-capitalistic, anti-competitive doctrines and institutions. And unlike others who have plowed the same field, Dickman begins not in Civil War America, but as far back as fourteenth-century Europe, "in order to track down the intellectual sources of industrial democratic thought to their wellsprings."

From this unusual theoretical and historical vantage point, *Industrial Democracy in America* offers withering refutations of the historic, empirical, moral, legal, and economic arguments for compulsory collective bargaining. The result is a comprehensive case against coercive unionism unprecedented in scope, rigor, and persuasiveness.

For example, Dickman challenges the historical claims typified by the newspaper editorial cited earlier. As he summarized for this writer: "It is not true that unions were indispensable, that without unions workers would never rise. It is not true in history that most industrial violence was the fault of employers. And it is not true that unions were fighting for the working class." To refute these contentions, he traces the history of unions back to the medieval guild system.

The arguments offered for medieval guilds were strikingly similar to those put forth today for labor unions. "The guild monopoly was rationalized as necessary to protect the unsuspecting public from shoddy goods and unscrupulous artisans, on the theory that unrestricted competition would force producers and traders to cut corners to seize one another's business and exploit the hapless consumer," Dickman observes. "Guilds also existed to protect the social and economic status of merchants and craftsmen—probably their true *raison d'être*. In a society which valued security over liberty, the guildsmen were entitled to a customary, secure position in the social order, *a property in their job or way of life*."

"Owning" One's Job

This premise of a property right to one's occupation led inevitably to hostility toward free market competition, and ultimately to violence. Dickman cites accounts of fourteenth-century merchants waylaid for underselling competitors; of guild members hiring thugs to murder non-members who refused to be bound by guild rates; of frequent "bloody battles for the monopoly of work in a particular town," as one historian put it. The premise of a proprietary interest in one's job also led to the rewriting of history. Employers are typically portrayed as *initiating* industrial violence by depriving workers of their "rightful" jobs or wages while workers merely "fought back" for what was "theirs."

Besides corrupt "rights" theories, economic arguments were advanced to buttress the pro-union position. There was the argument (endorsed by Adam Smith) that workers must be at a disadvantage when bargaining with employers; that labor was the cause and measure of all economic value (Smith's "labor theory of value"); that laborers should get "the full product of their labor"; that business recessions occur when workers are not compensated enough to "buy back what they produce"; etc.

Dickman raises and challenges each of these contentions on economic grounds, displaying a formidable grasp of free market theory. Take just one example—the notion of the "competitive disadvantage" of workers bargaining with employers.

This remains a central pillar of the case for labor unions. Even Adam Smith argued that it "is not . . . difficult to foresee which of the two parties must, upon all ordinary occasions, have the advantage in the dispute, and force the other into a compliance with their terms." While in "the long-run the workman may be as necessary to his master as his master is to him, . . . the necessity is not so immediate." Dickman observes that such passages by capitalism's founding father "constituted an important legacy to the radical socialist and syndicalist critics of capitalism—who purported to demonstrate that employers kept wages at subsistence. . . ."

But are workers, in fact, at a true disadvantage? Due to the mobility of capital, Dickman notes, "an above-normal profit *due to a below-normal wage rate* creates a competitive imbalance which employers will exploit by bidding wages up." He quotes economist J. R. McCulloch, who pointed out that:

A discrepancy of this kind could not be of long continuance. Additional capital would immediately begin to be attracted to the department where wages were low and profits high; and its owners would be obliged, in order to obtain labourers, to offer them higher wages. It is clear therefore, that if wages be unduly reduced in any branch of industry, they will be raised to their proper level without any effort on the part of the workmen, by the competition of the capitalists.

Dickman also rigorously examines the even more basic collectivist moral premises upon which such economic theories frequently rest. He points out, for example, that Adam Smith's well-known advocacy of self-interest, natural rights, and laissez faire was qualified and ambiguous; that Smith himself embodied the conflict between the premises of individual rights and social utilitarianism. Wrote Smith:

> The wise and virtuous man is at all times willing that his own private interest should be sacrificed to the public interest of his own particular order or society ... [and] that the interest of this order or society should be sacrificed to the greater interest of the state or sovereignty of which it is only a subordinate part ... [and] that all those inferior interests should be sacrificed to the greater interest of the universe. ...

Similarly, John Stuart Mill's commitment to individual rights had a utilitarian escape clause. "All persons," said Mill, "are deemed to have a *right* to equality of treatment, except when some recognized social expediency requires the reverse."

It is impossible to discern any basic moral distinction between these two statements, and such anti-individualistic slogans as, "Ask not what your country can do for you; ask what you can do for your country"—or, "From each according to his ability, to each according to his needs." Because such collectivist philosophical premises were shared even by capitalism's most prominent defenders, they have remained largely unchallenged to this day. Dickman painstakingly isolates and dissects each of these in turn, as he traces their historical progression through academia, popular opinion and, eventually, into the law itself.

Of course, these isolated empirical, economic, and philosophical premises slowly congealed into full-blown theories, which Dickman broadly categorizes as "socialism" and "pluralism." The heart of the book traces the origins, implications, and consequences of these two schools, both of which profoundly shaped the American union movement.

Socialism and Pluralism

These competing collectivist theories proposed differing forms of industrial organization. Under socialism, all the means of production would be under the *exclusive* control of society, via the central government. Most American unionists, such as Samuel Gompers, did not buy the socialist call for abolition of private property; they feared (correctly, as modern history has shown) that the socialist state can be as repressive of labor as of business. However, they did swallow much of the socialist critique of the competitive marketplace, particularly socialist theories of unemployment and class conflict, and its moral attack on the profit motive.

Competing with the socialists were the so-called pluralists, who were equally hostile to individual rights, but were suspicious of centralized state power. Their solution was to favor the "rights" of *groups*. "Pluralism . . . was a vision of industrial democracy that amounted to what we might dub 'private government'—to a system in which the state would delegate to private social groups the traditionally sovereign legislative power to make rules for all individuals similarly situated in the economy—rules that overrode their contractual liberty," Dickman explains.

Pluralism cut across the left-right spectrum. In its right-wing, or corporativist form, society "would be reorganized into compulsory economic groups that would conduct economic affairs under the supervision of the state—that is, some kind of tripartite entente of government, business, and labor unions." (This, of course, was the form of collectivism that eventually led to fascism, and to modern industrial policy proposals.) "On the left, pluralism sought to eliminate the capitalist class and parcel out control of the economy between guilds or syndicates of workers and the state." (This syndicalist or guild socialist approach led to the contemporary movement for "decentralized, participatory democracy," in both the economy and society.)

One of the book's mere peripheral triumphs is its unmasking the facade of collectivist benevolence. Before the advent of modern public relations techniques, socialists and syndicalists were more forthcoming about their nature and aims.

Thus early German socialist Johann Gottlieb Fichte spelled out the state's ascetic expectations of the individual. "He who thinks *at all* of his own person and personal gratification, and desires any kind of life or being, or any joy of life, except *in* the Race and *for* the Race," he wrote, is "at bottom, only a mean, base, and therefore unhappy man."

French syndicalist Louis Blanc added: "If you are twice as strong as your neighbor it is a proof that nature has destined you to bear a double burden. . . . Weakness is the creditor of strength; ignorance of learning." (Today, John Rawls says the same things, much more opaquely.)

Nor were such sentiments foreign to our shores. American socialist Edward Bellamy, in his famous utopian novel *Looking Backward* proposed dealing decisively with any laborer shirking his work duties: ". . . the discipline of the industrial army is far too strict to allow anything whatever of the sort. A man able to do in both the duty, and persistently refusing, is sentenced to solitary imprisonment on bread and water till he consents."

These few samples from among many Dickman has unearthed suggest something of the animating spirit of modern collectivism, of which the labor movement has played a key part. It is a measure of the richness of his scholarship that these quotations are drawn not from the text, but from his exhaustively detailed footnotes, which are an education in themselves.

An Anti-Empirical Approach

Dickman's methodological approach is as refreshingly unfashionable as are his conclusions. Because he takes ideas seriously, his approach is strongly anti-empirical—if we take "empirical" to mean dwelling on the concrete details of historical events. But if "empiricism" is simply taken to mean exhaustive scholarship, no one can fault him on that score.

Inevitably, his deliberate decision not to wallow in journalistic minutia affects the narrative, sometimes in startling ways. For instance, the book concludes with the effects of the National Labor Relations Act (Wagner Act) of 1935, essentially ignoring subsequent developments. That is because Dickman regards the Wagner Act as an ideological "watershed in American life," which not only "drastically altered the legal framework of the market economy in America," but also "transformed the very meaning of unionism and collective bargaining as they have hitherto been known."

Later efforts to mitigate its onerous consequences—e.g., the Taft-

Hartley Act (1947) and the Landrum-Griffin Act (1959)—were largely cosmetic, he maintains. The ideological war which he chronicles really ended with Wagner. It is that law's basic premises which still dominate conventional thinking on labor unions, and have a continuing impact in such areas as civil rights policies and affirmative action regulations governing the workplace.

The decision not to bring the account "up to date" then, is in keeping with his thematic intent, his focus on ideas—even though it is a decision which more conventional empiricists may criticize. But in any event, Dickman succeeds brilliantly in showing how abstract theories become embodied in the concrete reality of human actions, institutions and, eventually, laws. To supplement his analysis, he appends the text of thirteen pivotal pieces of Western labor legislation, from the Ordinance of Labourers of 1349, to the Wagner Act of 1935. (The Fascist Labor Charter of 1927 is also reprinted, for its unnerving similarities to American labor legislation.) The reader can see for himself the ultimate destination of "mere" theories.

Free market advocates have always been long on theory, but too often short on scholarship. Dickman's formidable work (complete with 158 pages of appendices, footnotes, and index) shows the powerful persuasiveness of a union of the two approaches. *Industrial Democracy in America* is a revolutionary contribution to the literature of industrial relations. Its long-term effects cannot yet be gauged; but for our time, Howard Dickman has provided scholars and thinking laymen with a brilliant interpretive alternative to popular interventionist mythology. And he has exposed, with thundering finality, the fascistic portents inherent in "our quasi-syndicalist system of industrial democracy."

A Christian View of Labor Unions

by Gary North

Why should we speak of a Christian view of labor unions? The best reason is that almost all Christians have some opinion on the place of work in the life of a Christian. Max Weber, the German social scientist, wrote an important book at the turn of the century, *The Protestant Ethic and the Spirit of Capitalism,* in which he argued that the idea of the calling—one's vocation—was a central feature in the attitudes of Protestant laymen who helped lay the foundations of modern production methods and organization. If the idea of work is central to the Christian tradition, and this tradition led to the creation of modern capitalism, then we ought to pay attention to a related topic, the labor union.

Labor unions are not the major part of the total American labor force, contrary to popular opinion. They are important in the large industries such as autos, steel, and television, but only about 25 percent of the American labor force belongs to any union, and many of these are weak, rather insignificant organizations. As I hope to demonstrate, it is almost impossible for trade unionism ever to control over half of a nation's labor force in a democratic country, and where unions control more than this, labor mobility will be reduced markedly.

Do unions raise wages? Unquestionably they do. Do monopolies in business raise prices? Unquestionably they do. Labor unions raise wages in exactly the same way that a business monopoly raises prices: by artificially restricting the supply of a particular resource. Over the long run, with rare exceptions, no monopolist can keep prices raised in this fashion apart from direct government interference into the market. If the government keeps out competitors, then it is possible for monopolists to keep prices above what they would have been in a free market for years or even decades. In the case of diamonds, the DeBeers oligopoly has kept diamond prices up throughout the twentieth cen-

Dr. North is editor of *Biblical Economics Today,* from which this article was reprinted by permission in the July 1978 issue of *The Freeman.*

tury, but it takes the collusion of the South African government to maintain this monopoly (or at least it took such collusion originally).

Monopoly Pricing

The economics of monopoly pricing is the foundation of all modern trade unionism. This is either not understood by the supporters of trade unions, or else it is rejected as irrelevant. You will search your days in vain trying to find a supporter of trade unions who is also a supporter of business monopolies, yet the economics of each is identical. The labor union achieves higher than market wages for its members by excluding non-members from access to the competition for the available jobs. In other words, those who are excluded must seek employment in occupations that they regard as second-best. They bear the primary burden in the marketplace; they are the ones who pay the heaviest price for the higher than market wages enjoyed by those inside the union.

How can unions exclude outsiders from the bidding process? There are many ways, all used effectively by unions over the decades. First, there is raw power. They beat up their competitors. They throw paint bombs (paper bags filled with paint) at the homes of their competitors. They threaten the children of their competitors. Their children exclude the children of the competitors from social activities at school, meaning public (government) school. They shout "scab" from their picket lines. (Strange, isn't it, that those who defend labor unions seldom shout "scab" at Ford salesmen who are challenging the so-called monopoly of General Motors?)

Second, and most effective, trade unionists have been able to convince legislators to enact legislation that excludes non-union workers whenever 50 percent plus one worker vote to choose a particular labor union as the sole bargaining agent in a plant or industry or profession. The skilled trades were the first to get state governments to pass such legislation, and immediately blacks in the South disappeared from the skilled trades. Then professional associations got such legislation passed, most notably lawyers, physicians, and dentists. Then, in 1935, the Wagner Act was passed at the national level. It established the National Labor Relations Board (NLRB), a consistently pro-union bureaucratic federal agency. As far as the favored unions are concerned,

75 percent of all workers are potential "scabs," and the NLRB keeps them in their second-choice jobs.

There is a third, less evident, means of insuring labor union monopoly pricing. This is the minimum-wage legislation. This legislation is always supported by trade union officials, whose members are always earning wages higher than the proposed minimum wage. This legislation sees to it that regions that have less developed unions, such as the South—in fact, primarily the South—cannot attract industry so easily from the more heavily unionized Northeast. The minimum wage was the primary means of warfare by unions against non-union workers after World War II until very recently. It still may be the primary weapon. The primary loser is, of course, the urban teenage male black, who cannot get into the Northern union, or migrate to the South, or offer services to employers that are worth the minimum wage.

Employers pay higher wages than the market would have dictated when their labor force is unionized. Of course, employers outside union domination pay lower wages, since they are not compelled by competitive market forces to bid away labor from unionized firms. Since 75 percent or more of all workers are not in a union, they cannot gain legal access to the labor markets where 25 percent of the workers are employed. They have to work elsewhere. Thus, non-unionized employers are granted a subsidy from government: lower priced workers.

When was the last time you heard a supporter of labor unions argue that the reason why unions are wonderful is because they grant a subsidy to the employers who employ 75 percent of the American labor force? Yet this is precisely the economic effect of compulsory government-enforced trade unionism.

The Law of Market Competition

"Buyers compete against other buyers. Sellers compete against other sellers." Not that difficult a concept, right? Apparently it is the most difficult concept in economics, if we are to judge by the arguments people use in favor of increased government intervention into the free market.

Buyers of labor services compete against other buyers and potential buyers of similar (substitutable) labor services. This means that employers are in constant competition against other employers in the labor markets. They are forced to bid up the price of labor until the point that they can no longer afford to hire any more laborers, or, in the case of the most successful bidder, until all the competition has dropped out of the field. This is the explanation for the curious phenomenon that labor unions subsidize non-unionized industries that are buying labor services from those excluded by law from competing for jobs in unionized industries. The buyers of labor in unionized industries have been compelled by law to depart from the "labor auction" in which 75 percent of American workers are offering their services to the highest bidder.

On the other hand, sellers compete against sellers. This means that those who are harmed by trade unionism are those excluded from union membership. They are denied the right to compete for jobs in certain segments of the economy. They have been denied their right to bid, just as the employers in the unionized markets have been denied their right to bid.

The biblical view of man is work oriented. It affirms that man was placed on the earth to subdue it to the glory of God (Gen. 1:28; 9:1–7). It is not each man's right to work. It is his *duty* to work. What is his lawful right is his right to compete for the job he wants, his right to compete for the labor services he wishes to purchase. No one has a right to my job, including me. Anyone should have the right to compete for my job, including me. And I have the right to compete for his.

Strikes

The striker argues that he has the right not to work, but his employer does not have the right to hire some one to replace him. Modern compulsory trade unionism is based on the wholly immoral premise that the worker owns his job (can exclude others from the position) even though he refuses to work for his employer. To add insult to immorality, most trade unionists also want government food stamps, unemployment benefits (tax-free), and other forms of taxpayer-financed benefits while they are striking. The consumer is supposed to finance his own funeral, and the coercion of law then becomes total.

Obviously, nobody inside the union could reap monopoly wages if everyone were in the union who wanted to compete for the available jobs. The union would then become superfluous. It is only because of the artificial barriers set up against other workers that the union members reap their monopoly gains. This is the reason why, economically speaking, the trade union movement in its present, coercive form will never be more than a minority movement. The union needs the majority of workers outside the union movement, since the union membership has to have victims among the working class in order to reap its monopoly returns.

Once a man's contract has expired, he should have the right to walk off the job if he wants to. He should not have the right to keep his employer from hiring a replacement. Similarly, any employer should have the right to fire a worker, once the contract has expired. But he should not have the right to exclude that worker from competing in other labor markets. Trade unions deny both these premises.

Voluntary unionism is lawful, so long as the civil government does not do more than enforce the contracts agreed to by employers and laborers. A union can help to spread information of better wages or better jobs, thereby helping its members to keep alert to the true value of the services they are offering for sale. Unions can be self-help societies. But when compulsory, under coercive civil law, they are immoral. They must be recognized as such by orthodox Christians.

Adversary Unionism

by John O. Nelson

I should not want to maintain that all unionism is or has been adversary in character. In the past, the unionism of company unions perhaps was not, nor the unionism of the medieval guilds. It may be that Japanese unionism is not. It may be that Russian soviet unionism is not. I shall refer only to Western, "free world" unionism, especially as represented by unionism in the United States.

With those limitations understood, I think it is largely a truism that contemporary unionism is adversary in character and is so recognized to be, not only in the peculiar structure of the various laws (Wagner Act, Taft-Hartley Act) and governmental decrees (NLRB decisions) covering the subject but in the minds of laymen, employers, union members and union leaders alike.

Thus, there had to appear something contradictory in the recent election of United Auto Workers President Douglas A. Fraser to Chrysler's Board of Directors but not in his statement that his new role would "not alter the traditional adversary relationship between the UAW and the auto companies" (UPI, 5/14/80).

The term "adversary" signifies "having an opposing party." As the adjective "adversary" is applied in contemporary references to unions by union leaders, the constitution of unions, those dealing in government with unions, labor relations theorists, and so on, Marxian and related ideologies often play a significant role. The notion of "opposing party" is pretty much merged with that of "enemy." Thus, typically, a union conceives and represents itself as protecting and defending the rights and interests of employees and the same as being necessarily threatened and attacked by employers. It is, for instance, on the ground that employers are intrinsically the enemy of the worker that unions not only justify their existence but the various coercive and war-like practices that they everywhere engages in: forced membership, strikes, the use of goon squads, and so on.

Dr. Nelson is Professor of Philosophy Emeritus at the University of Colorado. This article originally appeared in *The Freeman* in May 1981.

Constitutional Rights Violated

It is on the same ground, with the added one that employers are in a position of unfair strength, that twentieth-century legislation has consistently violated and shelved such basic constitutional rights of employers as those of contracting with whom they please and free speech. Employers, for example, are disallowed by law from saying what they think of unionism to their employees.

We should not, therefore, be unreasonable in describing contemporary unionism as being "essentially" adversary in character, where "adversary" is to be understood in some such strong sense as, for instance, "enemy-related," and "essentially" in its strict philosophic sense. For suppose contemporary unionism divested itself in act and thought of the claim that the relationship between employer and employee was "enemy-related," it should simply not be recognizable as itself.

For our present purposes, however, we need not insist on the whole truth. It will suffice to treat the "adversary relation" defining contemporary unionism in terms merely of "intrinsically opposed," i.e., in objectives, in interests. I can imagine no defender of contemporary unionism either wanting or being able to disagree with this version of the adversary relation.

Given this very weak interpretation of "adversary relation," which hardly does justice to the fierce actualities, I intend to place unionism upon two scales: one measuring the legal coherency of unionism and the other its moral coherency. Somewhat arbitrarily, I shall weigh in the first scale the unionization of government employees and in the second the unionization of private employees (meaning by this: the employees of private enterprises). Probably the two scales could be switched around, though I do believe that the present distribution of scales and weighings has a certain natural appropriateness that will become apparent.

The Unionization of Government Employees

One is vaguely aware that something perverse is going on when municipal, state, or federal employees strike; garbage piles up high; mail is not delivered (during the first Canadian postal strike one even saw mail being burned in the streets of Montreal by postal employees);

firemen refuse to put out fires (or even set them themselves), and so on. The feeling is justifiably present that one is like a person who has been bound and gagged and while helplessly prostrate is assaulted with legal immunity. For whatever the laws themselves may say, it is a commonplace of the contemporary scene that these terrifying activities of government employee unions take place and are allowed to take place.

When the strike that happens to be aggrieving one has ended one's natural inclination is to suppose that everything has returned to a happy state of normalcy. One says, "The unions sometimes go to extremes. There ought to be laws against government employees striking [but there already are]. Then everything will be O.K."

It seems to be seldom realized that as long as government employees may legally band together under the adversary relation of contemporary unionism such grievous violence is bound to take place. For laws to declare both that governmental employees may unionize (I shall consistently use this term in its present connotations) and that they may not strike or employ goon squads or other supplementary violence amounts at one and the same time to sanctioning the view that government employees are a class of persons needing protection against an unfair, stronger party opposed to them (hence the right to coercively organize, to coercively collectively bargain, and the like) and that they may not take certain other coercive action, e.g., strikes, use of goon squads, and so on, necessary to effectuate their protection against that unfair, stronger party which opposes them.

Naturally enough, this incoherent injunction is rejected with a clear conscience by union members and leadership and not insisted on by the public. Even third-party arbitration will seem to offer no effective alternative, unless it is not really third party at all but safely committed to the union side. For in the economic realm there can really be no true third party: there exist but employees and employers. Thus the simple truth is: if government employees are legally entitled to unionize they are entitled to strike, to use goon squads, and so on. This is a practical tautology and in the last analysis everyone recognizes it as such.

Who Is the Employer?

What is not often enough or seriously enough considered is the claim that government employees have a legal right to unionize. But just here the most serious question is in order. For what the adversary principle which underlies and sanctions this unionization dictates is that the employer of government employees is an opposing and even inimical party. But who is the employer? In a republican form of government like our own the sovereign is the people. The school boards, legislatures, city councils, executive officers, courts, various bureaus of government that nominally do the hiring are agents of the sovereign people; thus, they are not the true employer; the sovereign people are (as when I purchase a house through an intermediary I am the true purchaser, not the intermediary). It follows from the adversary principle, therefore, that unionized government employees must be conceived and conceive themselves as being opposed by the sovereign people and consequently themselves as opposing and being aligned against the sovereign people.

Now it is simple legal nonsense to suppose that the agents of a sovereign should be entitled to hire as employees of the sovereign persons opposed by definition and dedication to him. It is compound nonsense to suppose that any group under a sovereign is legally entitled to align itself, much less employ force, against the sovereign. Only another sovereign can claim such a power.

In sanctioning the unionization of government employees, then, legislatures, courts, executive branches of government, and the like either engage in the legal absurdity of sanctioning subjects of the sovereign of which they are the agents in aligning themselves, and even using force, against that same sovereign or they in effect set up a sovereign independent of the sovereign whom they represent which is aligned by definition and dedication against him. In either case, the representatives or agents of the sovereign people do what they cannot legally do: they betray the client whom they represent; and since this is their sovereign, they in effect engage in treason; for in its broad, general sense "treason" denotes a breach of allegiance to one's sovereign.

An Illogical Position

As for the unionized employees of government themselves—I mean those who voluntarily unionize—they too do what they legally cannot do. In aligning themselves against their sovereign they assume the role of independent sovereigns. Indeed, in levying the sorts of demands that they customarily do, saying that unless this or that exaction be granted they will cut off this or that public service, they act as if they were the rulers of their sovereign. Thus, their actions and professions are the reverse side of the legal nonsense engaged in by legislatures and courts that sanction the unionization of government employees. Nor can it convincingly be objected that the sovereign or people have granted their employees these rights and powers by virtue of the fact that those legislatures and courts are their agents. For in a republican form of government the people cannot alienate their own sovereignty.

But shall we want, then, to maintain that unionized government employees engage, like those who sanction their unionization, in treason? One is, I admit, disinclined to render such a harsh verdict. Certainly, for instance, we do not want to say that anarchists and others who oppose the government or the very existence of government are necessarily engaged in treason. And there is some good reason for our not wanting to. The basis of government in a Republic is presumed to be consent of the governed. Presumably, therefore, a person who refuses to give his assent to be governed—say, an anarchist—is not really the subject of a sovereign. Thus, though he may engage in war against our sovereign he cannot be said to be engaged in treason, since our sovereign is not *his* sovereign.

Actually, however, the case of the anarchist and the case of the unionized government employee are entirely different. The anarchist does not in theory and need not in practice avow himself a subject of any sovereign. The unionized government employee in a Republic, and in this argument I am limiting reference to sovereignty under a Republic, cannot possibly claim that he has not avowed himself a subject of the people's sovereignty. He did so when he claimed, as a citizen, the right to unionize. He did so when he voted to unionize and claimed that his vote had a certain status under law. He did so when he hired himself out, under the status of being a citizen, to the government. *One cannot have one's cake and eat it too!*

Thus, a first impression to the contrary notwithstanding, the unionized government employee—again, I mean the employee who has voluntarily unionized—is, just as much as the legislatures and courts that sanctioned his unionization, engaged in a breach of allegiance to his sovereign and therefore, strictly speaking, in treason. But it is, on the face of it, legally incoherent for anyone to claim to have the right to engage in treason. Thus, on all counts, the unionization of government employees has to be legally incoherent.

The Unionization of Private Employees

The common moral and legal objection to the unionization of private employees is that it abrogates the individual's moral and constitutional rights of contract. And patently that is true. It would remain true, moreover, even if unions did not allow themselves the use of strike, goon squads, and other supplementary violence. Their very subscription to coercive membership and coercive collective bargaining (can there be any other species of it?) is both in fact and in intent an abrogation of the right of individual contract.

Persons today are so inured, however, to constitutional and moral breaches of the right of contract by all agencies of government, and in particular its courts, it hardly excites even the batting of an eye to note another occurrence of it. In addition, it has always been recognized that there are certain things that one cannot legally or morally contract; for example, the commission of a crime. With a seeming legitimacy, therefore, government can always make it appear that a restriction upon individual contract is justified by making a certain action illegal.

To be sure, in many such cases a cart is being put before the horse. Mere statutory law is being allowed to in effect amend the constitution and determine constitutional law. It is not, though, always easy to determine just when this switch of cart and horse has taken place. Imperceptibly, merely eccentric viewpoints harden into moral standpoints and then it may seem that a new restriction upon individual contract is the cart following the horse: that it has been dictated by a more privileged concern.

It is my impression, consequently, that attempting to rest the case against the unionization of private employees upon the right of individual contract is not likely to have much success. But even if the attempt were to succeed it seems to me that an attack from our previous direction must be much more conclusive. To be sure, questions of sovereignty and treason are not involved in the unionization of private employees. But the adversary principle is, and once again we shall find it creating insupportable incoherences, though these will now prove to be more moral than legal in character.

How Government Intervenes

The unionization of private employees rests upon the sanction of society and government. These decree that certain conditions having been met—a majority vote of the employees, for example—the employer is required to accept the unionization of his "shop." If he were not required by law to do so and if he were protected by law and government or even society in his refusal to do so his employees would obviously not be unionized. The fact that employers are forced by government and law to accept and hire unionized workers is what we want to keep our eye on.

Now, we have already seen that unionization is based on the adversary principle. Once, then, an employer's working force is unionized we have a body of employees whose aims and interests are conceived as being intrinsically opposed to those of the employer. Even if he is not conceived to be their enemy (and typically he is by union leadership and union principle) he is conceived to be their opponent and vice versa.

As an illustration of the rational absurdity of this enforced condition, suppose that when one hired a certain lawyer to defend one in a suit the lawyer publicly represented himself as having interests and aims opposed to one's own in the suit and acted accordingly. Clearly he would be guilty of malpractice and certainly one should want to dismiss him. Imagine, then, that one could not; that one was forced by law and government to retain and use this lawyer who avowedly conceived his interest and aims to be opposed to one's own and who was acting accordingly! This would be tantamount to forcing a person to sanction his own self-destruction. It would not only constitute the crime of using the law and agencies of an innocent person's own government to injure him but the completely unnatural indignity of making him lend a hand in his own injury. Visibly, this would be a piece of immorality in its most detestable form.

Now the employer who is forced to accept the unionization of his workers is in precisely the same position as the client who is forced to retain a lawyer who is avowedly and in fact pursuing interests and aims opposed to his own. In so forcing him the employer's own government is not only injuring him but forcing him to lend a hand to his own injury. We might add that it is not only government which is guilty of monstrous injustice and immorality in this case but all the employees who are voluntary parties to the unionization in question. They are active and knowing parties to the crime. They would be more honest and excusable if they simply conducted a lynching.

It will be retorted, no doubt: "But the truth is that the employer and employees' interests and aims are opposed. Unionization simply takes account of this fact." But that is wrong. An employer and employee's interests and aims are no more opposed than a client's and his lawyer's. When a lawyer hires out to a client it is mutually understood that while engaged in working for the client the client's interest is the lawyer's.

When a person hires out to any employer it rationally has to be his understanding that, while at work, the employer's interest is his interest. To the objection that the employer wants to pay the employee as little as possible and the employee wants to be paid as much as possible we should want to point out that what we have here is a theoretical picture of hiring phenomena which is based upon a view of persons which conceives of them as economic computing machines: a far cry from actual persons! But even were this in actual practice the case, it would not invalidate the claim that the only moral and reasonable relation obtaining between employer and employee is one in which, for a certain recompense, the latter makes the interests of the former temporarily his own.

Conclusion

If we have been correct in our reasoning, the unionization of government employees stands as sheer legal depravity and the unionization of private employees as sheer moral depravity. In both cases rational incoherency is foisted upon a society of potentially moral and law-abiding individuals and upon some of their most basic inter-relationships. It is no wonder at all, therefore, that in whatever society adversary unionism exists or is allowed to exist that society visibly sickens in proportion as unionization spreads and that pride of work, self-esteem, and production decline in tandem.

What seems to be too little recognition is that while unionization's adversary—whether the public or the private employer—suffers greatly, no one suffers quite such an injury and hemorrhage as the unionized employee himself. We may, I think, state it as an inexorable fact, everywhere confirmed, that he has to find gaining a livelihood changed from a challenge and adventure and accomplishment into a drudgery as meaningless and vexatious as slavery. This has to be, for in the same way that legal incoherency makes whatever it touches difficult and unpleasant so must moral incoherency.

Unions and Violence

by Morgan O. Reynolds

There is a long and violent history of labor disputes in this country. The facts really are not in serious dispute, only their interpretation. Facts always are interpreted within the context of a general theory of human action. One view, popular among Europeans and our industrial relations community to some extent, is that labor violence is simply part of a wider tendency toward violence in the American character. A more influential view promoted by unionists and their academic defenders is that American employers were especially brutal and defiant toward their workers and toward unions, and, therefore, were at least as guilty as unionists in causing labor violence.

Moreover, goes this theory, the violence which sometimes accompanies labor disputes is incidental, and surely is a small price to pay for the benefits produced by unionism. The well-known rationale is that labor must be allowed to combine for its own protection and use "labor's weapons" to offset its inherent bargaining disadvantage relative to capital. Unionism allegedly offsets the excesses of capitalism, a system supposedly stacked against labor and in favor of propertied capitalists who control the means of production. In sum, unionists argue that the benefits of unionism outweigh its modest costs in threats and actual use of violence.

In any analysis of unionism, there are two general issues to confront. The first is to discover the actual effects of unions on economic variables like the level of national output, unemployment, real wages, the rate of inflation, government spending, and so on. The second general issue is to analyze the means unions use to pursue their economic and political ends.

Union men basically argue that their objectives and their effects on the general public justify or excuse the threats and violence which often flare up in union disputes. This argument is familiar among collectivists, who usually argue that it is results that count, not the

Professor Reynolds teaches economics at Texas A & M University. This article originally appeared in *The Freeman* in February 1983.

process. "You must break some eggs to get an omelette," is their contention. Coercion supposedly is all right when exercised on behalf of the good causes that unions seek to promote, or to put it in economic terms, expected benefits supposedly exceed expected costs. Many people would argue, however, that the end does not justify the means, that, indeed, use of the proper means is the real end that we seek in human affairs. Most economists would also object that unions do not, on balance, produce economic benefits.

Useful theories in the sciences and in studies of human behavior are compact yet explain and predict a rich variety of observed and yet-to-be-noticed facts. The theory of monopoly or cartels in economics passes this test because its application to unions yields a tremendous payoff based on a handful of correct statements about unions. The theory explains an impressive array of facts about what unions do. Moreover, there is no competing theory of unionism, no other general theory of unionism available. Even though imperfect, we cling to theories which help us to understand a wide range of behavior until a superior theory comes along. And there is no new theory of union behavior on the horizon.

My purpose here is to briefly recount the theory of unionism, show why *threats and violence are an integral part of unionism,* use the theory to highlight the problem of unionism in the public sector, analyze why the theory is ignored by most of the industrial relations community, and then discuss what to do in terms of public policy.

The Basic Theory

The economist's special insight into union violence rests on the theory of monopoly, more properly, cartel theory, as well as the general notion that people respond to incentives. In economic terms, a trade union is a combination of sellers of labor services who individually have little or no control over the labor market but who seek to control the market through collective action. Unionists have never concealed their ambitions because they often have announced that their purpose was to "take competition out of wages" or to "take wages out of competition." Unionists seek higher wages, shorter hours, and more comfortable working conditions, assuming that the leaders operate in the interests of their members, which I am prepared to concede for present purposes.

There is nothing different in principle between labor unions and combinations of other producers who try to restrict supply and push up the prices of their goods or services. Unions are labor OPECs, concentrated interest groups with interests diametrically opposed to those of consumers. The term consumer is really another name for the general public. Consumers are other producers, so unions represent minority groups of workers who pursue their economic gains at the expense of the majority. In Hobbesian language, the economy would be a war of everybody against everybody else if everyone were organized into unionized blocs.

Labor services are the key input, among the many inputs, that businesses and government agencies use in the daily productive process. Owners and managers of businesses naturally attempt to purchase the inputs they desire as cheaply as possible, given the quality they wish to use. They economize on costs in order to show a profit, an essential condition for survival in the marketplace, or else stretch a given budget further. Households seek low prices too, and therefore behave much like businesses in their buying behavior.

Competition Protects Workers

In a competitive labor market, without unions, what would protect workers from exploitation from "avaricious" buyers? Competition would. The presence of alternative buyers for labor services protects people in their capacity as suppliers of labor services. This protection is one of the paradoxes of a free market. Each person in markets composed of many buyers and sellers of similar services is powerless in the special sense that the prices of services are formed in an impersonal way, beyond the manipulation of any individual. Yet each person is all-powerful, too, because of the many alternatives available and the freedom to refuse or accept various options.

The fictional Irish-American philosopher, Mr. Dooley, said, "This country is ruled by courtesy—like the longshoremen's union." This comment gets at the heart of the continuing controversy over unions, which remain the most controversial private (or quasi-private) organizations in our society. Controversy derives from the fact that unions are departures from a naturally competitive labor market and their power to extract economic concessions ultimately rests on their ability and willingness to use force. Unionists promise to deliver monopoly advantages to their members and their power to deliver on their promises rests on the ability to deny businesses and government agencies access to labor, the crucial input in the production process.

Even when all members unanimously agree to withhold their labor services from an employer in order to enforce demands for more pay and better working conditions, a union controls very little of the available labor in the economy. Simple withdrawal of labor by organized workers is rarely sufficient to enforce their demands, and therefore, they resort to violence or threat of violence to prevent other workers from entering the labor market and "undermining labor standards." Unionized labor markets, to the extent that the unions are successful in their goals, are islands of monopoly wage rates in a competitive sea. These islands can be sustained only by sea walls which keep the rest of the ocean out of their markets, thus forestalling the tendency for prices for similar skills to equalize throughout the economy.

The Power to Strike

Ordinarily, only government can enforce protectionist privileges over the long run, but unions have been granted unparalleled rights of private coercion by government. Unions are a form of restraint of trade because they deny the majority of workers an opportunity to offer their labor services at prices lower than the unionists demand. Successful unionists use intimidation to cut off the labor supply to employers until employers submit to union demands. As Henry George, the nineteenth-century economic writer, put it, "Those who tell you of trades-unions bent on raising wages by moral suasion alone are like people who tell you of tigers that live on oranges."

The presence of violence in labor disputes is not entirely undesirable, however, because it shows that unions do not have overwhelming power. It takes two or more parties for violence to break out. Many workers are willing to defy strikes, picket lines, threats, and suffer violence in order to stand up for their own freedom, and to work at wages that they find to be their best available alternative. This is preferable to the situation in England, for example, where unions have such overwhelming coercive power, and more people are imbued with collectivist ideology, so that few defy union rule in strike situations.

Violence also shows the incomplete power of unions because other organized producer groups like the American Medical Association, tree-pruners, cosmeticians, and so on, do not have to rely on strikes and private intimidation. Instead, they have licensing laws. In the event of encroachments on their market, they merely telephone the government for a policeman to restrain new entrants. If unions relied more directly on the public police force to restrain trade on behalf of worker cartels, the hoodlums and other specialists in violence would be less valuable to union officials. Unions then would look somewhat more respectable and less dependent on "undesirable" elements.

Unions in the Public Sector

Unions have grown rapidly in public sector employment since 1960 and government employees now are more highly unionized than employees in the private sector. About one of every two employees in state, local, and federal government is in a union compared to one of every six employees in the private sector. This creates special problems. Many observers have been inclined to say that unionism is permissible, even desirable in the private sector where it supposedly is a purely private matter, but not in the public sector. I do not share this sentiment, but there is a certain satisfying irony to our recent experience.

The National Labor Relations Act of 1935 specifically excluded government employees from its coverage, no doubt based on the opinion that only capitalists abused their "helpless employees," rather than government as an employer. But beginning in 1962, under President John F. Kennedy's Executive Order 10988 to promote unionism in the federal bureaucracy, there has been a gush of legislation and regulation to promote unionism and collective bargaining in the public sector. Proponents of pro-union legislation claim that government employment is just another industry, and that employees should receive the same "protections" as those in the private sector.

The irony is that the coercive privileges that politicians granted in 1935 to unions in the private sector have now come home to roost and confront politicians with the same defiant, coercive opponent in public employment. Government originally sanctioned union threats and force against private enterprises and non-union workers in the private sector, and now faces unions which are prepared to do the same against government itself. Governments that submit to coercive strikes necessarily govern with the forbearance of union officials, an unhappy arrangement which cannot last in the long run, especially in a democratic society.

A Question of Sovereignty

Special features appear to distinguish government from private industry and the first is the issue of sovereignty. One definition of sovereignty is the supreme and unchallengeable right of compulsion. A genuine sovereign cannot be forced to do something by a private person or a private agency and still be called sovereign. Whoever can force government authorities to submit to his will *is government*.

Government officials of every political persuasion from Ronald Reagan back through our political history have denounced the use of union force against government. Franklin Delano Roosevelt, for example, said in 1937, "A strike of public employees manifests nothing less than an intention on their part to obstruct the operation of the government until their demands are satisfied. Such action looking toward the paralysis of government by those who have sworn to support it is unthinkable and intolerable." A public-sector union, on strike, announces its intention to cut off the government's supply of labor and shut down its operations until its demands are met. This can hardly meet with approval by government officials or by the general community.

A second major difference between government and the private sector is that most government services are paid for through general taxation. Taxpayers are forced to pay, whether they want the services or not. In the private sector, buyers have the option of refusing to pay for a good or service, or else buying it from someone else. No private enterprise, excepting unions, can legally extract revenues through the use of force; they must cater to buyers through voluntary exchange. Union power in the private sector also is constrained by management's incentive to hold down costs and stay competitive in the marketplace. Governments do not face the same intense pressure for efficiency. The issue can be termed taxation without representation. Unionists, in effect, say that the government (ultimately the taxpayers) is not paying them enough and that they intend to force government to pay them more. If there is not enough money, raise taxes. If the government attempts to hire replacements to perform the services at lesser expense, organized workers use threats of force or force itself to prevent the substitution.

The Market Cannot Serve if Competition Is Forbidden

The third issue turns on the necessity of certain governmental services. The marketplace cannot protect the public very well when there are no good, legal alternatives to government-supplied services. In some cases the inherent nature of the services, arguably, can limit competing suppliers, in accord with the concept of so-called natural monopoly or pure public goods. But usually government artificially prohibits or severely handicaps private competitors. Examples are fire protection, garbage removal, schooling, hospitals, public utilities, and even prison-keeping. Private contractors can supply these services and are allowed to do so in some cases. Naturally, they are more efficient than government bureaucracies, generally at 60 percent or less of government costs. The presence of multiple producers vastly reduces the vulnerability of citizens to extortion by public employees who operate in a centralized system of government monopolies.

Most observers argue that protective services by police and courts are unique services which can only be provided by government. In fact, law and order is the basic purpose for the existence of government and only anarchists argue otherwise. If we can get along without public protection from aggression, there is no reason to have government in the first place. No mayor or governor can stand idly by during a police strike while society reverts to lawlessness. A police strike is very much like the aftermath of a natural disaster. Owners are not around to protect their property after a natural disaster and even normally law-abiding citizens find irresistible the temptation to take something. Looting and stealing rise sharply unless something is done. Citizens form vigilante committees or, more often, the National Guard is called up.

Collective bargaining by the police, or any other group of public employees, and strike threats are simply two sides of the same coin, as any realistic person must admit. There are other differences in degree between the private and public sectors which we might discuss, but they need not detain us here.

The Industrial Relations Community

Now let us turn to the industrial relations community. The industrial relations community consists of the thousands of personnel directors, labor lawyers, and industrial relations scholars who write about unions and collective bargaining. Why does this community have so little to say about the economic theory of unions and the role of labor violence? The answer, I believe, is threefold: It consists of one part honest ignorance and confusion, one part class interest, and one part financial self-interest.

Most people in industrial relations are ignorant of the truths of economics, and economists are partially to blame because they have failed to explain things clearly, sometimes because economists have lacked the courage to point out unfashionable truths. But a very important element in accounting for the ignorance of economics on the part of the industrial relations community is willful. The intellectual community fails to look frankly at unionism and labor violence because of an emotional attachment to the view that employees are exploited under free market arrangements, receiving too little of national income, while "fat investors" receive too much.

Union violence is exciting in and of itself for many intellectuals, who generally are bored by stability and gradual material progress. Labor violence also provides intellectuals with support for their view that workers are alienated from the economic system. Workers are not alienated. A minority of employees merely respond to the incentives that they face under a legal regime in which unions are tacitly allowed wide latitude to use coercion. Strikers convicted of vandalism, assault, and other crimes are routinely reinstated in their previous jobs with back pay. This is a formula for irresponsibility. These incentives and immunities account for the commonplace threatening and violent behavior of organized workers, not alienation from their work or the economic system, as the academic and intellectual left typically assert.

Even more important than romantic visions of social change and ferment in accounting for the failure of industrial relations analysts to adopt the correct theory of unionism is the fact that our system of mediating, conciliating, arbitrating, fact-finding, and the whole panoply of machinery often labeled our "system of industrial jurisprudence," provides power and income to the academic community. Industrial relations types perform as expert witnesses, directly shape a turbulent hodgepodge of labor law, and derive handsome fees in the process.

A Vested Interest

Consider arbitration, for example. An arbitrator must maintain his acceptability to unionists, as well as managers, to sustain this source of income; otherwise the parties will choose other arbitrators or settle their differences directly, saving the expense of arbitration. The situation is analogous to a court system in which each judge would derive his income directly from the disputants and would thus take their reactions into account in his decisions.

Concepts like "past practice" and "common law of the shop" were introduced so that arbitrators could decide more grievances for unionists. Employers now are saddled with a kind of arbitration which they probably never expected to pay for. Although arbitrators deny that they are concerned about rendering at least 50 percent of their decisions in favor of union grievances, it is well known that commercial organizations issue ratings on arbitrators and prospective arbitrators, basically in terms of "pro" or "anti" union. The incentives for arbitration and other consulting income help to explain the bland nature of the academic literature in industrial relations, where no scholars are known as "anti-union." It simply pays to be confused. Or, as Thomas Sowell has remarked, "The advantage of intellectuals is that they are not perceived as interested parties." The hard truths of economics are inconvenient in such an environment.

Conclusions

Labor violence is an inevitable side-effect of government-supported worker cartels in an economy that has large numbers of managers and workers who refuse to cooperate with strikes and union coercion. So what can we do about this unsatisfactory state of affairs? There are a variety of competing proposals, many of them excellent, but I want to remind us of what our long-run objective ought to be. Our aim should be to restore the rule of law by repealing the entire muddle of labor laws and regulations which have effectively exempted unions from the rules which apply to everyone else. We should repeal all the laws, statutes, rulings, and regulations which exempt unions from the peaceable behavior expected of everyone else. Unions essentially are immune from contract and tort law and they should be brought back under it. Justice should no longer peek and ask whether or not a union man committed a violent act in pursuit of union purposes. A violent, illegitimate attack is an act of aggression which ought to be punished regardless of its announced purpose.

We cannot declare that this is a free society until everyone is free to accept the best available offer for his or her labor, best in that person's own opinion, free from threat, regardless of how much these decisions supposedly harm the higher-income people represented by union officials. The benefits of unionism do not outweigh the costs of union violence. There are no benefits from unionism for the great mass of working people, only costs. Unions are not public servants that offset the excesses of capitalism, but sectional interest groups with coercive privileges. Peter Wiles' indictment, written in 1955, says it well:

> It is truly amazing that anyone should suppose this crude, selfish, violent and piecemeal process to contribute to social justice. It is, when we come to think of it, incredible that the building up by some salary and wage earners of monopoly power, in greater degree here and lesser degree there, should improve the distribution of income among them all; so incredible that the supposition has only to be directly given utterance to be dismissed.

The Economics of the Barricades

by Antony G. A. Fisher

A few months ago at a dinner party in London, our hostess announced she was quite ready to shoot the hospital workers. She was absolutely sincere, referring to the striking members of a union which had effectively crippled hospitals throughout England, increasing the backlog of patients awaiting surgery by some 60,000. This meant untold suffering, and, in some cases, death for those who could not wait.

At other dinner tables one imagined similar housewives declaring equal fury at the striking truck drivers whose refusal to haul food caused tons of produce to be dumped at sea, making that which dribbled into London shops exorbitantly priced.

It's not a new story. Economic disorder always divides society, pitting one segment against another. Wat Tyler's Rebellion of 1381 was described as "the malice of laborers" refusing to work at the low wages fixed by Parliament. In 1790 the washerwomen of Paris demanded death as punishment for the merchants whose prices of soap had soared, and Marat responded that the people should help themselves by hanging the shopkeepers and plundering their stores. The great German inflation following World War I was first blamed on the balance of payments, then on the speculators, and ultimately on the Jews. Even the Greeks had a word for this: "stasis" or creating hatred between members of society.

What is responsible for this disease of "stasis" from Diocletian down to our hostess last winter? In every instance it is indirectly due to government intervening in the normal course of the market. Wat Tyler's rebels were against fixing of wages after the Black Death had so diminished the labor force the surviving workers could get triple their former pay. There were no unions to blame, no media or communications system (they couldn't even read or write), yet an attempt to cut their pay caused a rebellion or "strike."

_____

The late Mr. Fisher, author of *Fisher's Concise History of Economic Bungling*, was founder of the Institute of Economic Affairs in London. This article first appeared in *The Freeman* in July 1979.

In 1776, American inflation brought despotic controls and punishment to "speculators," evoking this comment by Pelatiah Webster: "we have suffered more from this cause than from any other cause or calamity. It has killed more men, pervaded and corrupted the choicest interests of our country more, done more injustice even than . . . the enemies." The reference, of course was to the enemies of the Revolution.

Few realize the French Revolution came on the heel of France's most appalling inflation and wage and price controls, enforced by the guillotine.

Even the United States and Britain first blamed "speculators" for the inflation of the mid-1970s, then imposed wage and price controls, "guidelines," and "sanctions" intermittently to counteract the inevitable results of government's own inflationary policies.

These controls attempt to hide the rising prices which are the major symptom of inflation. They will not work, any more than breaking the thermometer will cure the flu. In spite of their history of failure, such controls appeal to the politician because they transfer the blame for his own profligacy to scapegoats such as organized labor or capitalists. Yet how could the 5 percent increase permitted by Britain's recent wage restraint policy conceivably compensate the worker whose contract was up for renewal after two years of 10 percent per annum inflation? Add progressive tax rates and the worker is justified in asking 12 to 14 percent per annum increases, or 28 percent, just to stand still!

Unquestionably, British labor unions have entirely too much power, and their members include Marxists intent upon destroying the system. But in the last 50 years British wages have fallen from almost double German or French wages to little more than half their wages. Were the general public to understand this, the current strikes might be considered a justifiable outrage against an unreasonable government, and our housewives might be less anxious to brandish their guns.

Understanding, in fact, is the only possible cure for what history indicates might become a bloody confrontation. It is necessary to understand that inflation is caused by government mismanagement, overspending, and the consequent printing of money, and that controls or sanctions will not mitigate, but will *exacerbate* the ultimate devastation of the economy. It is imperative for people and their political representatives to know that the consequence of such controls is not only a deprivation of human liberty, but a serious inhibition to human productivity which compounds the problem.

But foremost among the evils of inflation, and government's stop-gap measures intended to alleviate it, is the human antagonism, the rancor within a society where each blames another for his plight. Labor versus industry, housewives versus merchants, farmers versus bureaucrats, rich versus poor, and so forth and so on, as society sickens with alienation. Yet the resulting chaos is built on *error:* each individual is reacting naturally to an injustice perpetrated, not by his imagined adversary, but by his government!

It behooves us to get this message across before the misunderstanding destroys us. This is a lesson Americans might learn from the British, if only they will listen.

A Tale of Infamy: The Air Associates Strikes of 1941

by Charles W. Baird

The American labor union movement enjoys much more respect than it deserves. The politicians who, in the 1930s and 1940s, empowered and then kowtowed to the movement have never received enough blame. The following true story is an excellent illustration of these propositions.

Shortly before the Japanese attacked Pearl Harbor, Earl Harding wrote a manuscript for *The Saturday Evening Post* describing the violent 1941 Air Associates strikes and the federal seizure of the firm's facilities. The article, "It Is Happening Here," was scheduled to appear the week following December 7, 1941. In the aftermath of Pearl Harbor, the article was canceled. The galleys and other materials were sent to me by Mrs. F. Leroy Hill, widow of the president of Air Associates. I obtained additional information from microfilm records of *The New York Times*.

Air Associates was a private firm with its main plant in Bendix, New Jersey. It manufactured airplane equipment and parts. The company had five branch plants and two warehouses in Lodi and Belleville, New Jersey; Chicago and Rockford, Illinois; Marshall, Missouri; Dallas; and Los Angeles. During 1941 it employed 600 to 800 people in Bendix and 250 to 300 at its other sites. In mid-1941 it was working on $5 million in War Department contracts. The president of Air Associates was F. Leroy Hill, and its chief legal counsel was Walter Chalaire.

Although the United States was not formally at war, President Roosevelt had declared a defense emergency. American military goods were being sent to England and the Soviet Union, and the U.S. Army and Navy were gearing up for war.

In March 1941, President Roosevelt created the National Defense

---

Dr. Baird is Professor of Economics at California State University, Hayward, California. This article appeared in *The Freeman* in April 1992.

Mediation Board (NDMB). It was a tripartite committee of 11 members—four to represent unions, four to represent employers, and three to represent the federal government. This tripartite structure was modeled after Mussolini's plan for running the Italian economy.

The NDMB was charged with the task of trying to settle labor disputes in businesses with defense contracts. Its power was skewed: It could impose its will on employers, but it could only try to persuade union leaders to accept its recommendations. It rarely was able to do the latter. The NDMB collapsed at the end of 1941 in a capitulation to John L. Lewis, president of the United Mine Workers, in his strike in the "captive mines" (coal mines owned by steel firms that used the coal).

The Air Associates story involves two strikes, two apparent settlements, a threatened third strike with an attempted forced settlement, and the final seizure.

The First Strike

In early June 1941, 12 Air Associates employees formed an organizing committee at the behest of the United Auto Workers-CIO, Aircraft Division (UAW-CIO). The committee met with Leroy Hill on June 17; all voices were recorded. Although the union hadn't collected more than 20 authorizing signatures, the organizing committee asserted that it represented a "vast majority" of the 650 employees at the Bendix plant, and demanded that Air Associates immediately recognize the UAW-CIO as exclusive bargaining agent for all non-managerial workers. After brief negotiations, the committee also demanded that Hill consent to a union shop (wherein all employees are required to become union members as a condition of continued employment) and a higher wage scale.

Hill refused instant recognition but did offer to settle the representation question by a certification election supervised by the local office of the National Labor Relations Board (NLRB). This was a major concession because the 1935 National Labor Relations Act (NLRA) did not require a certification election in the absence of a showing by the union that it had collected authorizing signatures from at least 30 percent of the nonmanagerial employees. The union had not come close to meeting that threshold.

One of the functions of the NLRB in such elections is to determine the appropriate "bargaining unit." That is, it determines who can and who cannot vote in the election.

The NLRB can significantly affect election outcomes by gerrymandering, and it did so in this case. One-third of the non-managerial employees were excluded. The organizing committee tried to identify the pro-union and anti-union workers. (It is legal for unions to do this, but it is "an unfair labor practice" if management does it.) At the behest of its union client, the NLRB then defined the bargaining unit such that a majority of those in it were pro-union. Unit determination had nothing to do with job description. For example, the receiving department was excluded and the shipping department was included. The job descriptions for the two departments were practically identical, but a majority of the shipping department were thought to be pro-union and a majority of the receiving department were thought to be anti-union.

The election took place on July 1. Election campaign rules were then, and still are, rigged in favor of the union. The NLRA permits unions to promise workers all kinds of benefits, but forbids management to make such promises. Moreover, although management is forbidden to contact eligible voters at home or in any other non-public place during campaigns, unions are free to do so.

Many Air Associates employees stated that intimidation and misrepresentation took place during such union contacts. In the end, the gerrymandering and the biased election rules produced a vote of 206 to 188 in favor of the union. The UAW was certified as the exclusive bargaining agent for all bargaining unit workers—those who voted yes, those who voted no, and those who didn't vote. The next step was for the union and management to begin bargaining on the terms of a first contract.

On July 3 management temporarily laid off 12 workers because of a shortage of aluminum. These were not members of the union organizing committee. The workers were told that the layoff was temporary and that they would be recalled as soon as aluminum was procured. They were recalled in two stages, some on July 16 and the rest on July 21. The union did not protest the layoff when it happened.

Under the National Labor Relations Act, it is an "unfair labor practice" to fire an employee because of union activity. This often provides job security for incompetent workers. During the early years of the NLRA, a common union tactic was to get a few known union sympathizers fired, allege an unfair labor practice, and appeal to the government to prosecute the employer. A union would merely threaten to keep management tied up in costly legal defense procedures until management capitulated. This had happened to Air Associates in 1938 before it moved to New Jersey.

A New Tactic

During the 1941 defense emergency, unions added a new tactic in disputes involving companies with defense contracts. Early in the year, at North American Aviation Company in Inglewood, California, and at Federal Shipbuilding and Dry Dock Company in Kearny, New Jersey, unions used strikes that allegedly impeded defense production as a pretext for President Roosevelt to seize the plants and assign the War Department to operate them in accordance with union wishes. These two incidents were not ignored by the UAW-CIO at Air Associates.

On July 8 the union proposed a contract that included a union shop. Mindful of the North American Aviation and Federal Shipbuilding precedents, Leroy Hill wanted to avoid a strike and so was willing to bargain immediately. A UAW-CIO shop committee met with Hill in his office on July 11. Hill, wary of possible allegations of unfair labor practices during bargaining, insisted that the bargaining sessions be recorded. He offered to let the union check the transcripts for accuracy and to post them to keep the workers informed about the progress of bargaining. The union balked. It insisted that bargaining be off the record. Hill turned on the recorder, and the shop committee stalked out of the office and went outside the plant.

Earlier in the day there was a heated verbal dispute between a union organizer and an anti-union worker, and there were rumors that union sympathizers were going to try to blow the quit-work whistle and cut off power in the plant to try to shut it down. To avoid this, management had the steam cut off from the quit-work whistle and had all the unguarded entrances locked.

After lunch, the shop committee returned to the plant through one of the guarded entrances. They asked to go back to Hill's office to resume bargaining. There was a short, recorded meeting wherein, according to Earl Harding, the unionists asserted "that the government had granted them an interest in the business which they were going to protect," and "that the company must prevent other employees from opposing the CIO."

The bargaining seemed to be going nowhere, so the committee left Hill's office and headed back to work. But they assembled near the quit-work whistle and attempted to set it off. When it didn't work, they ran through the plant, turning off power, yelling "strike," and attempting to pull workers away from their machines. At most 50 workers left the plant and began to demonstrate outside. One policeman was sufficient to restore and maintain order.

In the evening of July 11, the union visited employees' homes and urged them to stay away from work the next day, which was a Saturday. Many workers later reported being intimidated during these visits. On July 12 there were about 60 absentees out of approximately 700 workers. The union first claimed that they had been locked out, notwithstanding that management had telegraphed all workers, including those who had demonstrated the day before, that the plant was open and their regular jobs were available.

The plant was routinely closed on Sunday, but on both Saturday and Sunday roofing nails were scattered over all roads leading to the plant. Employees were threatened with "dire consequences" to themselves, their families, and their homes and cars if they showed up for work on Monday.

When the plant opened on July 14, 150 employees were absent. One hundred called in saying that they were too frightened to come to work. There were only 44 Air Associates employees on the picket line. The CIO called in non-employee unionists to bolster the picket line. Inasmuch as the dispute was obviously not a lockout and the company was willing to continue bargaining on the record, the union needed a pretext for its actions. It seized upon the 12 workers who were temporarily laid off on July 3 and asserted that the layoffs were discriminatory anti-union firings. Between July 3 and July 14 it had made no such claim.

On July 15 approximately 600 pickets, at most 50 of them Air Associates employees, wielded clubs, stones, and other weapons. They stoned cars that tried to enter the premises. They pulled drivers and passengers out of cars and beat many of them. Sheriff William Browne said that his forces were too small to maintain order, but he refused to ask Governor Charles Edison to send in state police. Thus Hill telegraphed Governor Edison to ask for help in maintaining order. The approximately 500 Air Associates workers who were eager to work asked Hill to hire private guards to help the sheriff protect them and their right to work. He did so, and on July 16 private guards escorted willing workers in and out of the plant. The unionists were outraged and threatened to bring 1,000 additional non-employee pickets to "clean up" the guards.

On July 17 over 500 employees assembled in nearby Hasbrouck Heights to go to work in groups. A bus was provided, and, together with several cars, proceeded to the plant in a caravan. Between 1,000 and 1,500 pickets stopped the caravan, broke all the windows on the bus, smashed cars, dragged people out of vehicles, and beat them. Finally, Sheriff Browne joined Hill in requesting assistance from Governor Edison. Moreover, Hill threatened to seek help from the U.S. Army "if law enforcement officials are unwilling or not equipped to act."

It is important to understand that there was no legitimate strike. There had been no refusal to bargain, and neither side had declared a bargaining impasse. The union had claimed discriminatory firings, but some who were allegedly fired were already back at work in spite of the union's picket line. Walter Chalaire, Air Associates' legal counsel, met with representatives of the federal government's Office of Production Management on July 14, 15, and 16, where he reiterated the company's willingness to bargain toward a first contract. He did insist that the bargaining be on the record, but he didn't rule out any topic. It was the union that refused to bargain if a record was kept.

Apparently cowed by Hill's threat to call for the Army, the union ceased its violence on July 18 and 19. Willing workers were at their jobs, undeterred by the few pickets outside the plant. Production resumed to 85 percent of normal. For all of July, production was 90 percent of normal.

However, on July 19 the National Defense Mediation Board got involved. The Department of Labor assigned the NDMB to mediate the Air Associates dispute, and the Board ordered management to appear in Washington on July 22 to begin mediation. Irving Abramson, chairman of the New Jersey CIO Council, demanded that the company shut down until the mediation was complete. On July 20 the union asked President Roosevelt to seize the plant "in the interest of national defense." On July 21, 350 Air Associates employees petitioned the NDMB demanding protection for their right to work and asking for a new election.

Mediation began on July 22. On the next day, the NDMB recommended a three-part solution. First, all workers were to be allowed to return immediately without discrimination. Hill already had made this offer. Second, all questions involving back pay were to be submitted to an arbitrator. Third, negotiations toward a first contract were to begin immediately. If agreement were not reached by August 9, the contract would be set by binding arbitration.

On July 27 Leroy Hill accepted all the Board's recommendations except for binding arbitration on the first contract. On July 28 the NDMB issued a statement that Hill's response was a "substantial acceptance" of the Board's recommendations. On July 29 picketing ceased and all Air Associates employees went back to work. The first apparent settlement had been reached. However, Loren J. Houser, UAW-CIO Eastern Regional Director, demanded that Hill ultimately submit to binding arbitration.

The Second Strike

Bargaining sessions under the auspices of the NDMB took place on July 30–31, and August 1, 4, 5, 7, and 8 at the Hotel Pennsylvania in New York City. Anthony Grimaldi, a member of the original union organizing committee and now leader of the UAW-CIO local at Air Associates, was the chief union spokesman. Leroy Hill and Walter Chalaire spoke for the company. The union demanded a union shop, mandatory dues checkoff, a grievance system that prohibited workers from working out even small misunderstandings directly with supervisors, and binding interest and rights arbitration. The company agreed to accept binding arbitration if the union would accept binding arbitration on the questions of compensation for union-caused property damages during the first strike and the legitimacy of the July 1 certification election.

On August 8 a formal impasse was declared. Harry P. Shulman, a Yale University law professor, was appointed arbitrator, and he undertook an investigation of the dispute toward the end of recommending the terms for the first contract. Both sides were notified that the

Shulman report would be made available before the NDMB made its final recommendations.

On September 19 the union voted to authorize a strike if the Shulman report, the NDMB, or Air Associates didn't give in to its demands. No date for the strike was set. On September 30, before the Shulman report was made public, the strike was called.

We don't know for sure why the union did this. Chances were that Shulman would have made recommendations that the union would have liked, and the NDMB would have backed them up. My own conjecture is that by this time the union was resolved to bring about a War Department seizure of the company. Whatever Shulman and the NDMB would recommend would not be as favorable as the unions at North American Aviation and Federal Shipbuilding had won by plant seizure.

There were approximately 400 pickets on the morning of September 30. At most only 70 of them were Air Associates employees. At least 180 employees called in to explain they were absent due to intimidation. Rocks were thrown, and police, workers, and strikers were injured. Hill immediately advertised for replacement workers. The advertisement brought in 2,500 applications, and all striking workers were replaced. Production at the Bendix plant increased to record levels.

In 1938 the U.S. Supreme Court, in *NLRB* v. *Mackay Radio and Telegraph Company* (304 US 333), upheld the right of employers to hire permanent replacements for strikers in economic strikes. An economic strike is one called for any reason other than illegal acts by the employer. Air Associates had committed no illegal acts which caused the September 30 strike. Indeed, it was, in accordance with the law, waiting for an NDMB recommendation when it was struck. Hill was clearly within his rights to hire the replacement workers and to consider the jobs vacated by the strikers to be filled.

Frank P. Graham, chairman of the NDMB, summoned Hill and Chalaire to Washington, and between October 6–8 Hill and Chalaire negotiated with the Board to try to find a reasonable settlement. The NDMB, however, following the now available Shulman recommendations, insisted that Hill sign a contract that gave the union all it wanted. Most important, the NDMB demanded that Air Associates put all striking workers back in their regular jobs even if that meant firing replacement workers. According to Earl Harding, Hill and Chalaire were told that a contract acceptable to the union must be signed "whether the company agreed or not . . . and the Mediation Board proceeded to frame one itself."

Hill and Chalaire left Washington without an agreement, and on October 10 the NDMB announced its final recommendations—complete capitulation to the union, including immediate reinstatement of all strikers. In its official statement the Board said that it "feels obliged to observe that this company has not exhibited toward either the certified union or the NDMB that attitude of cooperation to which the public is entitled on the part of a company whose operations are essential to the defense of the nation."(*The New York Times,* October 11, 1941)

It is important to note that defense production had not been impeded by the September 30 strike. The replacement workers were more productive than the strikers. As to cooperation, in a last ditch attempt to settle the dispute, Hill agreed to all the union's demands except for a union shop, and he agreed to place strikers on a preferential re-hire list and reinstate all of them within 30 days. He continued to refuse to fire replacement workers to make room for returning strikers. The NDMB stated that this amounted to a "rejection" of its recommendations.

On October 11 the NDMB declared that the case was out of its hands, and threatened to turn it over to the executive branch of government. This was code for recommending War Department seizure. On October 18 the NDMB appealed to the Air Associates board of directors to force Hill to capitulate. The directors refused. On the same day the UAW threatened mass picketing of Air Associates by 21 union locals and also threatened to shut down all aircraft plants in the eastern United States unless Hill acquiesced.

On October 17 Sheriff Browne declared that only 45 pickets would be allowed at the Bendix plant, and that only striking Air Associates employees would be allowed to picket. Only 25 pickets showed up, and the plant continued normal operations.

The next day the union called for 250,000 pickets to assemble at Bendix and gave Hill until October 20 to yield or face the consequences. The NDMB asserted that the union would be able to assemble at least 20,000 to shut the plant down. Sheriff Browne made plans to deputize World War I veterans to maintain the peace.

On October 19 Leroy Hill issued a public statement:

> Now it remains to be seen whether the Defense Mediation Board is out to get production or universal compulsory unionization. If it pursues its recent policies it can, of course, force the company to capitulate to the private army of 8,000 or more pickets which the CIO proposes to mobilize to close the plant unless its terms of unconditional surrender are met. Or the Defense Mediation Board can call on the State of New Jersey, and if need be, the Federal Government to protect the right to work of the 800 employees who fully man the plant and have it in full production. If we are let alone and if our employees are protected in their right to work, our defense production will mount steadily and the strikers who want to work can be reemployed long before the thirty days expire. (*The New York Times,* October 20, 1941)

On October 21 the *Times,* in an editorial entitled "One Way Compulsion," referred to the North American Aviation, Federal Shipbuilding, and Air Associates cases and declared, "The conclusion is inescapable that the Government has deserted its true function as an impartial arbiter and become more and more frankly partial to 'labor.'"

On October 22 the union announced that there would be mass picketing the next day. Hill issued a bulletin to all employees warning them of potential violence and explaining that the police had requested that no one try to enter the plant until the police had cleared the roads. He requested that all willing workers assemble at the Bergen County Court House in Hackensack, check in for work, and wait until the police said it was safe to try to enter the plant.

On October 23, 2,000 pickets tried to shut down the plant. Sheriff Browne declared that because he was unable to guarantee the safety of the workers he would cooperate with the *union* to keep workers away from the plant. Some workers sneaked in through a rear entrance. The workers who had assembled at the court house sent a telegram to President Roosevelt asserting that "Lawless CIO picketing is keeping us from work. Do your duty and protect our constitutional right to work." (*The New York Times,* October 24, 1941)

When the sheriff discovered the unguarded rear entrance, he shut it, leaving some workers blockaded in the plant. The next morning the sheriff asked the *union* for permission to allow the workers in the plant to send out for food. Anthony Grimaldi, the local union boss, acquiesced, but when the messenger returned with the food, pickets refused to allow him into the plant. The police protested, but, according to Earl Harding, Grimaldi exclaimed: "Who the hell is running this show? I'll say who'll go in and who won't go in." The food delivery was never made.

Hill and non-striking workers sent a telegram to Governor Edison requesting assistance from the state police. Edison responded by sending a telegraph to Air Associates wherein he blamed *Hill* for all the trouble. He recommended that Hill resign as president and that the New Jersey Chamber of Commerce nominate a successor. The Chamber demurred, stating that the governor had no right to determine who should be president of a private company. The *Times* editorial of October 21 was right. Government had "deserted its true function as arbiter." The state government, at least, had become an agent for the union.

Meanwhile, in the evening of October 24, Hill and Chalaire held a six-hour meeting in Washington with Robert Patterson, Undersecretary of War, and William S. Knudsen, Director of the Office of Production Management. In that meeting Hill gave even more ground. He agreed to place the 50 to 60 remaining strikers immediately on the payroll. That is, the strikers would be paid their normal wages even if they didn't work while waiting to be reinstated. Hill repeated his promise that all of them would be back at work within 30 days.

The next day *The New York Times* ran a front-page story with the headline "Strike Is Settled at Air Associates: Plant Officials Accept NDMB Formula After 6-hour Talk With Knudsen, Patterson." According to the *Times,* Patterson and Knudsen "expressed their appreciation of the company's cooperative attitude and request all returning employees to cooperate with the management in order that full production can be maintained in the interest of national defense." The second apparent settlement had been reached.

The Threatened Third Strike and Forced Reinstatement

On October 27 the union threatened to call for a general strike throughout the eastern United States unless Hill agreed to immediately reinstate all strikers to their regular jobs even if some replacement workers had to be fired. The union's alleged reason for this new threat was that although the 50 to 60 strikers were being paid full-time at their normal wage rates while they were waiting to be reinstated, they weren't being paid overtime. Replacement workers were getting overtime pay. Justice, therefore, required immediate reinstatement.

In my judgment this was a smoke screen. The union didn't want a settlement. It wanted a seizure. It realized that the dispute had to be kept going to get President Roosevelt to seize the company.

As *The New York Times* editorialized on November 25, "[W]hile it has been demonstrated—as the cases of the Federal Shipbuilding Company and Air Associates so vividly illustrate—that no employer may reject a Mediation Board 'recommendation' without being immediately cracked down upon, it has also been demonstrated that if a labor union leader does not like the board's decision the Administration will get him another board."

The captive mines strike later proved the *Times* was right. On November 15 John L. Lewis initiated the strike. He wanted a union shop in the captive mines, as he already had in the commercial mines. The NDMB recommended a settlement that did not include a union shop, whereupon President Roosevelt dismissed the NDMB from the dispute and appointed an arbitration panel which, on December 7, gave Lewis all he wanted. The Air Associates union had good reason to expect that Roosevelt would give it much more than it could get from negotiating with Leroy Hill. On October 28 Richard T. Frankensteen, National Director for the Aircraft Division of the UAW-CIO, threatened to use his "economic strength" to shut down all UAW work in New England, New York, New Jersey, and Pennsylvania unless Hill gave in to the union's demand for immediate reinstatement. Frankensteen explained, "We are not interested in any back door agreements of Mr. Patterson or Mr. Knudsen." *(The New York Times, October 29, 1941)*

Walter Chalaire explained his view of the new strike threat in the same *Times* article: "If the call for the general strike is met, there is a real question of 'who is the government.' We had wasted day after day with the Mediation Board. Its principal concern in our case was not defense production but promotion of compulsory unionism. We found a different atmosphere in the office of Undersecretary of War

Patterson. In that conference we soon reached an agreement. Naturally the CIO wants to throw the controversy back to the Mediation Board."

On October 29 President Roosevelt repudiated the Patterson-Knudsen agreement and ordered Hill to reinstate the strikers immediately. The War Department issued a statement:

> The Undersecretary of War announced today that the War Department was sending a representative to the plant of Air Associates at Bendix, New Jersey to supervise the reinstatement of the strikers there.... The War Department expects that ... the strikers will ... be immediately placed in the jobs which they formerly held, regardless of the fact that new employees have been hired by the company to fill such jobs. New employees displaced from the jobs which they presently occupy as a result of the foregoing reinstatement of the strikers may be given other jobs if the company so desires, or the company may make such other disposition of such new employees as it sees fit. (*The New York Times,* October 30, 1941)

So much for equal protection under the law. All workers are equal, but some are more equal than others. Frankensteen called the Patterson-Knudsen agreement a "thing of the forgotten past" and left to "exchange felicitations" with President Roosevelt at the White House.

On October 30 Anthony Grimaldi looked over the shoulders of Colonel Roy M. Jones and Major Peter Beasley as they supervised the forced reinstatement of the strikers. Hill was ordered to stay in his office and out of the way. The chain of command was embarrassingly obvious, but the nonstrikers would have none of it. W. C. Morton, a spokesman for the non-strikers said, "If these men are returned to work and the men on the machines are displaced by strikers everyone in this plant will walk out, not with the idea of going on strike, but for the purpose of a demonstration." (*The New York Times,* October 31, 1941)

And so they did. The non-strikers undertook a 30-minute work stoppage and two separate one-hour sit-down demonstrations. There was some physical violence. A striker confronted a nonstriker with a lead pipe, and several other nonstrikers grabbed the striker and punched him.

The forced reinstatement settlement had failed. Late at night on October 30 President Roosevelt, certainly with the concurrence, and probably at the urging, of his White House guest, Richard T. Frankensteen, ordered the War Department to seize the Bendix plant of Air Associates.

The Seizure

On October 31, 2,100 to 2,500 fully armed troops took over the Bendix plant. Colonel Roy M. Jones was ostensibly in charge, and he declared that the Army had "reopened" the plant. Actually it never had been closed except on October 24 when Sheriff Browne helped the union close it. President Hill and Executive Vice President Harold I. Crow were ordered off the premises. Union leader Anthony Grimaldi was allowed to stay.

Only Air Associates' Bendix plant was involved in the dispute, so Hill naturally assumed he was still in charge of all the branch operations. He was wrong. On November 5 the Army seized the seven branch plants. The excuse given was that the branch operations had to be coordinated with the Bendix plant. Colonel Jones claimed, "The Army is in here to get out production and until the labor situation is cleaned up, Hill and the others are not in the picture at all." *(The New York Times,* November 6, 1941)

It got worse: On November 18 the War Department instructed the board of directors of Air Associates to fire President Hill. Undersecretary Patterson, who had helped produce the Patterson-Knudsen agreement on October 14, said, "We will return the company to private management just as soon as we figure that they have a management there that will not have labor problems." *(The New York Times,* November 20, 1941) In other words, a management that would take its orders from Anthony Grimaldi.

The board of directors was instructed to submit all names of potential successors of Hill to the War Department for its approval. On November 26, with the permission of the War Department, the Air Associates Board elected Frederic G. Coburn, then chairman of the board of McLellan stores, president of Air Associates.

To add insult to injury, on November 26 the War Department tried to depict Leroy Hill as an incompetent businessman by asserting, "On taking possession the Army found that the company did not have the means to meet maturing obligations to banks and to trade creditors." The government advanced $500,000 to the company, and a spokesman said: "When it agreed to extend financial aid to the company the War Department took the same measures that any bank would take under similar circumstances. It insisted that the company give assurance of satisfactory management and continued production." (*The New York Times,* November 27, 1941)

However, as Hill explained, $500,000 was the standard down payment the War Department made on new contracts. He had been expecting it. Moreover, since the company's inventory had been seized and its ordinary customer receipts had been impounded by the War Department, it was no surprise that banks and trade creditors were complaining about the lack of payments since the end of October.

On November 30, 502 out of 800 Air Associates employees petitioned President Roosevelt to reinstate Hill. According to the petition: "[The] takeover was a capitulation to the dictates of selfish labor union leaders against the wishes of 85% of the Air Associates employees. We further believe the stipulation of the government that the former management be replaced as a condition for the return of the property to its rightful owners is an act of governmental coercion threatening the destruction of free enterprise." (*The New York Times,* December 1, 1941)

On December 26 President Coburn signed a contract with the UAW that included a union shop and everything else Anthony Grimaldi demanded. Only 250 out of 800 employees participated in the contract ratification vote. They all voted yes. On December 29 the War Department turned Air Associates back over to its board of directors and President Coburn.

Postscript

F. Leroy Hill moved to Rockford, Illinois, in 1942. There he founded the Aircraft Standard Parts Company and Aero Screw Company, both of which supplied parts for military aircraft during World War II. After the war he formed Hill Machine Company, which later became Hill-Rockford Company, a manufacturer of assembly machinery. He became a member of the Mont Pelerin Society. Although he retired in 1975, he remained an energetic defender of the right of every person to work free of compulsory unionism. He died from a heart attack at his summer home at Francestown, New Hampshire, on July 7, 1981.

After the war Air Associates specialized in electronics. In 1957 company headquarters were moved to St. Petersburg, Florida, and its name was changed to Electronic Communications. It became the ECI Division of E-Systems, a subsidiary of NCR, in 1976.

Unions Drop Their Mask

by Charles W. Baird

The New York *Daily News* strike that began on October 25, 1990, has been characterized as "an old-fashioned labor-management blowout, the likes of which are rarely seen anymore."[1] Extreme overt violence and threats of violence by strikers and union hooligans against replacement workers, news vendors, newsstands, and delivery trucks have attracted national and international attention, including that of London's *Economist*. Elaborate and expensive strike preparations by the Chicago-based Tribune Company, owner of the *Daily News,* which included secret training sessions for management personnel in Florida, a fenced and guarded "phantom newsroom" in New Jersey, and a nighttime guarded caravan transporting editors to the New Jersey site along a roundabout route designed to foil union types, have added intrigue and even some entertainment value to the tale. But the level and character of violence in this strike give one pause. It is unique in recent history. It is a return to the tactics of the bloody union battles of the late nineteenth and early twentieth centuries.

Violence in Labor Disputes

There is nothing unusual about violence in labor disputes. For example, in the recent Pittston coal strike, which lasted from April 1989 to February 1990, $65 million in fines were levied against the United Mine Workers for such activities as obstructive mass sit-down demonstrations, "rolling roadblocks" to stop coal trucks, spreading spikes on roads, and occupying a production plant for four days. Although the strike settlement included amnesty for all union acts of violence, the Virginia judge who imposed the fines has thus far refused to lift 80 percent of them.

Violence against buses and replacement drivers has been widely reported in the ongoing strike by the Amalgamated Transit Union

---

Dr. Baird is Professor of Economics at California State University at Hayward. This article originally appeared in the March 1991 issue of *The Freeman*.

(ATU) against Greyhound. In May 1990, National Labor Relations Board General Counsel Jerry Hunter authorized a complaint against the ATU in which he cited specific acts of violence, mass picketing for the purpose of intimidation, and miscellaneous picket line misconduct.

In 1983 the Wharton School published Armand Thieblot's and Thomas Haggard's massive study of union violence in contemporary labor disputes. The 20 unions most frequently involved in violence had a total of 1,844 cited incidents from 1975 through 1981.[2] The authors state that "Labor laws and their interpretations by the courts have failed to curtail or circumscribe overt violence, and application of criminal law is hampered by the collective nature of much of it and the inability to fix blame on particular individuals. The end result is that violence continues, and can occur in a modern strike or organizational drive just as easily as it did at the turn of the century."[3]

Unionists would have us believe that a strike is merely a collective withholding of labor services in the face of unacceptable terms of employment offered by an employer. But that is not all there is to it. A strike is a collective withholding of labor services, but it is also an attempt to shut down an employer by cutting off his access to replacement workers, suppliers, and customers. It is one thing for a group of like-minded workers to withhold their own labor services from an employer. It is quite another thing for them to attempt to force other workers, suppliers, and customers to refuse to do business with the struck firm. Such attempts are acts of trespass—in broad terms, acts of violence—against the voluntary exchange rights of non-strikers and the strike target.

Yet the *sine qua non* of every strike is the picket line, whose only purpose is to interfere with exchange activities between non-strikers and the strike target. As the United States Supreme Court recognized in the 1921 *Tri City* case, even a peaceful picket line is inherently intimidating. The Court's solution to protecting the rights of non-strikers in that case was to limit picketing to one picket per entrance. This may seem to be merely a particularly benighted ruling by a pre-New Deal Supreme Court, but the activities of the *Daily News* strikers demonstrate where the opposite view can lead. If "peaceful" acts of interference with the exchange activities of non-strikers are permissible, then strikers cannot be blamed if recalcitrant non-strikers must be convinced of the folly of their ways by using more "persuasive" tactics. The 1940 *Apex Hosiery* decision shows that even the Supreme Court can be seduced into approving acts of extreme overt violence on the grounds that the offenders are pursuing legitimate union objectives.

The Norris-La Guardia Act (1932) and Wagner Act (1935) gave unions legal privileges and immunities that were specifically designed to eliminate violence in labor disputes. Congress reckoned that if employers couldn't fight back, there would be peace. As it turned out, violence didn't abate, but it did become largely limited to the picket line, and it seldom involved third parties. With the passage of the Taft-Hartley Act (1947) and Landrum-Griffin Act (1959), unions lost some of their privileges and immunities and were forced to adopt a mask of civility and reasonableness.

Daily News Violence

In the *Daily News* strike, however, violence took to the streets to an extent unheard of in recent memory. The striking unions dropped their mask. News vendors have been intimidated, beaten, bombed, and shot. Newsstands and their inventories have been looted, bombed, and trashed. Delivery trucks have been bombed and torched, and their drivers have been beaten. Members of the general public who have been imprudent or unlucky enough to be close to acts of sabotage have been injured, and even more of them have been endangered. As Michael Gartner has aptly pointed out, this no-holds-barred attack against the newspaper amounts to thugs' attempting to tell us what we can and cannot read.[4]

James Hoge, publisher of the *Daily News*, has alleged that there had been, as of November 26, some 700 serious acts of violence. The New York Police Department claimed knowledge of only 229 such incidents, and discounted any union conspiracy behind them. Apparently the police don't want to antagonize the unions in one of the most pro-union towns in America. The *Daily News* had to hire protective services from private security companies.

On November 14, at a union rally in front of *Daily News* headquarters, AFL-CIO president Lane Kirkland blamed all of the violence on the newspaper. According to him, "the economic violence of stealing people's jobs—that's the root of anything that might be called violence."[5] If anyone other than a union spokesman had made such a claim he would have been laughed off the stage. To suggest that hiring willing workers to do the jobs that strikers refuse to do is justification for violence against people and property is ludicrous. Strikers do not have property rights to jobs they refuse to do. The employment relationship is one of contract between willing employees and willing employers. If one group of employees is unwilling, the employer has a moral and legal right to make contracts with others. Yet Brooklyn Assemblyman Frank J. Barbaro, in response to the *Daily News* strike, has introduced a bill in the New York State Legislature to outlaw the hiring of replacement workers. Only unions can practice violence with the blessing of politicians.

It Has Happened Before

The *Daily News* strike is very reminiscent of the 1892 Homestead strike. Today there is a 10-foot high gray slab monument in Homestead, Pennsylvania, that commemorates "the iron and steel workers who were killed . . . on July 6, 1892, while striking against the Carnegie Steel Company in defense of their American rights." In fact, the Homestead strikers were violently attempting to deny the "American rights" of non-strikers.[6]

Like the Tribune Company, Carnegie had undertaken elaborate preparations for an expected strike. There had been a violent strike at the plant in 1889, during which the strikers drove out the Allegheny County sheriff and his deputies who were trying to maintain order. In preparing for the 1892 strike, Carnegie manager Henry Frick had a nine-foot board fence, topped with barbed wire, constructed around the perimeter of the Carnegie property. Mindful of the impotency of the sheriff three years earlier, he also arranged for 300 Pinkerton guards to be brought in, should the need arise, to protect plant property and non-striking workers.

On July 6, 1892, after the strike began, Frick tried to land the Pinkerton men at the fenced-in Carnegie dock along the Monongahela River. The strikers tore down the fence, charged the dock, and fired on the tow boat and barges that were carrying the Pinkertons. At least one Pinkerton guard as killed. The tug escaped, leaving two barges filled with Pinkertons behind. They fell under siege, complete with cannon and dynamite. There were additional deaths on both sides. At one point there was an unsuccessful attempt to burn the barges to drown the occupants. In the end, the Pinkertons surrendered. They were savagely beaten and incarcerated in a local theater. The strikers' advisory committee then proceeded to usurp all the governmental functions in the town. Like Robespierre's Committee of Public Safety in the French Revolution, the Homestead Advisory Committee policed all movement and activities of people in the town, especially members of the press. The press was censored, and several people were incarcerated simply because of what they had to say about the strike. The only thing missing was the guillotine. On July 10, Governor Robert E. Pattison activated the National Guard and took the town back from the strikers, who offered no resistance. Peace was restored, replacement workers went to work, and eventually striking workers crossed the picket line. On November 20 the union officially called off the strike. The strike was lost.

In Conclusion

History has been kind to the Homestead strikers. Their actions have been excused by most labor historians as extreme but necessary measures of self-defense in a just war against an oppressive and exploitative employer. But there is no romance left in such a view. Today, most people recognize that the employment relationship is not one of exploitation, it is one of contract. In today's competitive environment, if mutually acceptable collective bargaining contracts cannot be implemented, mutually acceptable individual contracts—i.e., union-free operation—will take their place.

1. *The Wall Street Journal*, November 2, 1990.
2. Armand J. Thieblot, Jr., and Thomas R. Haggard, *Union Violence: The Record and the Response by Courts, Legislatures, and the NLRB,* University of Pennsylvania, The Wharton School, Industrial Research Unit, 1983, p. 55.
3. *Ibid.* p. 4.
4. Michael Gartner, "Nation Shrugs as Thugs Firebomb Freedom," *The Wall Street Journal,* November 29, 1990.
5. *The New York Times,* November 15, 1990.
6. This section is based on my "Labor Law Reform: Lessons from History," *Cato Journal,* Spring/Summer 1990, pp. 175–209.

Unions—and Other Gangs

by Joan Wilke

There are thousands of gangs across the country today. You may belong to one or more of them yourself. And maybe without knowing it.

There are parent and teacher gangs. And consumer gangs. And racial gangs. Women's gangs. Voters' gangs. Religious gangs. Gangs of professional men. Gangs of farmers. Gangs of businessmen. The law even recognizes "one-man gangs". . . individuals claiming to represent thousands of others through the device of class-action suits.

Their goals are often laudable. There's certainly nothing wrong with a higher standard of living with which so many of them are concerned. But it's how that higher standard is attained that separates responsible citizens from gangsterism.

A gang is a bullying group of individuals that draws its strength from numbers for the purpose of pushing other people around. It operates at the expense of others. Any such group deserves to be called a gang. And when it receives legal acceptance and approval, it deserves the title of dictatorship.

The first gang that succeeds becomes the excuse and impetus for the formation of all the others. The first privilege granted to groups by law becomes the justification for all the rest, creating a gangocracy or mob society.

Among the most notorious and successful gangs today are the labor unions. Hardly a day passes that we don't pick up a newspaper and read that "they've struck again."

Back in the old days, when Jesse James got his gang together, held up a train and took the payroll, it was generally considered a robbery. In fact, there was very little doubt about it. Sometimes they might have joined up with other gangs like the Daltons for greater force and surer success. And it was all very beneficial to their standard of living. But then, right during a holdup . . . (TRUMPETS!) . . . the Cavalry

Ms. Wilke, an advertising writer, wrote this article for the December 1975 issue of *The Freeman*.

121

arrived! And they didn't say, "We're here to protect the right of the engineer to get into his cab and for the conductor to go down the aisle." They said "Y'all stop that!" They recovered the loot and put the bounders in jail. Never once did they toss the money bags to Jesse and wish him well. That would have been incredible.

It is just as astonishing to me that today's union activity is protected by law and defended as a "right."

Unions are usually defended on the basis of freedom of association . . . the right to join together for bargaining.

Actually, unions are in violation of others' rights to freely associate. And compulsory arbitration is no bargain.

If unions were simply groups of workers getting together for a better bargaining position with their employer on the terms of their employment, they would be within their *legal* if not their moral rights. They would also probably be fired. And maybe blacklisted among employers. At least, no employer in his right mind would hire someone he thought would cause trouble with his other employees and try to force demands beyond the original hiring agreement.

Unions couldn't exist for very long without the protection of biased laws.

The Law Requires . . .

It is the law that forces employers to bargain, to accept decisions by labor boards, to pay back-wages for time spent in idleness or striking, to make raises retroactive, to prohibit firing and regulate hiring while allowing all kinds of welfare financing of strike activities paid out of the taxpayers' pocket and the employers' production costs. Everyone is the ultimate victim of union extortion.

It all happens under the protection of the law. It couldn't happen any other way. Extortionate power is monopoly power. It can only exist under government protection or establishment. The government has granted labor groups monopoly power over industry.

But union activity is defended as peaceful.

So was Al Capone when he offered "protection" to some little business. But if the businessman refused, you know what happened. That's about what happened in Kohler, Wisconsin, over a period of some ten bloody years. The Kohler strike, complete with bombings, burnings, and brutality, clearly demonstrated the violent gangsterism of union extortion. The law no longer tolerates such courageous refusals to capitulate to unreasonable demands. Bargaining is compulsory. Unions just can't stand such bad publicity. It shows the essential nature of their activity.

It is argued that unions are a bulwark against Communism and we're reminded that unions are not allowed in Russia.

Russia is nothing but unions—with all the bosses in Moscow. Independent unions aren't allowed in Russia because they represent political power and one dictator just doesn't like another dictator in the same country any more than one mobster likes another moving in on his territory. Of course, that's also why U.S. union bosses don't want Communism here. To an ever increasing extent, they are the ones telling the government what to do. They don't want it the other way around.

Dubious Arguments

It is argued that union members are among the staunchest defenders of our American way of life. We all have blind spots, but anyone who thinks he has the right to join with others to use the law as a bludgeon to tell other people how to run their business has no understanding of the American concept of freedom.

There are many people who have joined unions not because they wanted to, but because they had to in order to get a job. That's slavery. It's certainly not freedom of association.

There are many more who will argue that unions are essential in a capitalist society to get the workingman a decent wage. To support their claims, they invariably refer to conditions during the earliest days of industrialization. Actually, union leaders have simply taken credit for the natural and inevitable increase in wages coming from increased productivity.[1] Union demands beyond the market's real wage level stifle the production upon which future raises depend, increase unemployment and price marginal workers out of the market altogether.

Unions further add to unemployment lines and social disruption by limiting and controlling memberships, with priority for entry going to favored friends, relatives, and racial groups.

The law encourages union activity in the private sector but considers it illegal in the public sector.

Irony abounds. Along with a lot of garbage.

Such areas of industry as garbage collection and sanitation were preserved as government's public responsibility for the reason that interruption of such services would be too dangerous or disruptive. So government monopoly of public services was tied to laws making strikes illegal. The laws are simply being disregarded and it is the monopoly position established by government that gives the public workers their striking power.

In San Francisco where illegal strikes have occurred, street cleaners are now making $19,000 a year.

We need to relegate all services other than peace-keeping, law enforcement, and judicial activities to the competitive market and then enforce laws against strikes in those areas of public safety and order reserved as government responsibility.

Strikes and union activity in the private sector serve to justify and incite demands in the public sector and are in themselves disruptive and dangerous.

In the gas crisis some months back, the impact of the truckers' strike was felt in a very short period of time, causing critical food shortages in some rural communities and giving some truckers a very heady feeling about their power.

Any nationwide strike in our interdependent society is bound to have quite an impact on every business and everybody.

While compulsory public-sector bargaining gives union leaders un-due and unconstitutional power over elected government leaders and thus all members of society, union activity in the private sector is equally dictatorial and deleterious.

Industry-wide union standards and dictates act to stifle and cripple the competition between private enterprises upon which efficiency, progress, and continuous service depend.

Leave It to Competition

The only way outside of slavery to make sure services won't be interrupted is open competition. That means competition in labor as well as the rest of industry. It means employment by private arrangement.

Unions need never be outlawed. All that is needed is to abolish privileged status under the law.

Individual bargaining would end the artificial war between employers and employees created by labor bosses for their own benefit. And it is only fair and honest dealing. It means substituting individual efforts in competition on the basis of ability for the shakedown demands of group force. It is everyone getting the best bargain he can without holding up someone else. It is nothing more than honoring one's agreements instead of going back on them.

What an opportunity was missed just recently when the post office employees threatened a nationwide strike. All offices could have been closed down immediately and permanently. Virtually overnight, new systems would have started, with competition working to bring down prices and improving services beyond anything imagined at present. We could have been rid of one of our biggest and most expensive political fiascos. Instead, the criminal action of an illegal strike was rewarded by acceptance of extortionate demands.

The only proper response to job dissatisfaction is: "I quit." Try to take that right away from anyone!

And correspondingly, the response to strikes and union demands is the response only competition can give: "Okay, we'll get someone else."

It is the response of freedom to tyranny. But it is a response that is forbidden by law in a country we still like to call free.

---

1. F. A. Harper, *Why Wages Rise* (Irvington, N.Y.: Foundation for Economic Education, 1957).

III. THE FRUITS OF UNIONISM

The Impact of Unionism

by Clarence B. Carson

Unionism is not a theory of economics, nor does it have one. It is, as I have said, an ethical theory, buttressed by a religion-like ideology. Its theory is that individual workers cannot get their just deserts in an open market, that they must combine and use coercion to get their due. Yet the primary impact of unionism is on the economy, though it extends outward to have effects on all social relations. Underlying the thrust of unionism, then, there must be at least an implicit economic theory.

So there is. It is a theory that is uncovered by positing what it is necessary to believe in order to explain doing what unions do. What unions do is to act to reduce the supply of workers available. They organize some of the workers against the other workers and attempt to monopolize the available jobs. Now it is sometimes supposed that the labor theory of value provides the unionist contact with economics. But the labor theory of value does not provide an economic explanation for the unionist effort to reduce the supply of labor. If labor were the source of all value, it still would not follow that it would be socially desirable to reduce the supply of labor. On the contrary, it would appear that it would be socially desirable to use every smidgeon of labor to the fullest extent possible.[1] It is doubtful, however, that the labor theory of value should be considered as an economic theory; it makes much more sense as a partisan, or sectarian, ethical theory. In short, it is best understood as a claim that labor should have all the product of industry. In any case, it does not explain actual union behavior which aims to monopolize jobs rather than to take the whole proceeds of industrial activity.

Dr. Carson has written and taught extensively, specializing in American intellectual history. This article was originally published in the February 1981 issue of *The Freeman* and subsequently was reprinted in Dr. Carson's book *Organized Against Whom?* It appears here by permission of the author.

Economic Goods Are Scarce

The economic theory necessary to unionism comes into view when we turn the major premise of economics upside down. The major premise of economics is that all *economic* goods are scarce. (Not all economists acknowledge this, but it is nonetheless the premise required for their study.) They are economic goods because they command a price, and they command a price because they are scarce. The minor premise which follows from this, in syllogistic form, is that labor commands a price in the market. Therefore, it is an economic good which is scarce. The scarcity of labor is axiomatic, then, and it is this that makes it a subject of concern for economics.

The major premise of unionism is that *there is a surplus of labor*. Looked at more broadly, the major premise of unionism is a conclusion derived from a major premise of socialism or interventionist economics, namely, that there is a surplus of goods generally. This statement is not made as a universal by its advocates, that is, they do not claim that there has always been a surplus of goods or that it is everywhere the case. Rather, it is described as an historical condition and attributed to industrialization. (Not, it should be noted, as a worthy development, but as a problem, because the goods are not evenly distributed.)

This major premise of socialism—that there is a surplus of goods produced, or producible in highly industrialized countries—was stated dramatically by Karl Marx and Friedrich Engels in 1848. They said, "In these crises there breaks out an epidemic that, in all earlier epochs, would have seemed an absurdity—the epidemic of over-production.... Because there is too much civilization, too much means of subsistence, too much industry, too much commerce."[2]

Over-Production a Problem

This concept of a surplus of goods has had vigorous proponents among Americans of the historical school of economics, usually called institutionalists. The leaders of this school have included John R. Commons, Stuart Chase, Thorstein Veblen, and John Kenneth Galbraith. Stuart Chase, for example, declared that the United States turned the corner and achieved a condition of abundance in 1902. "Abundance," he said, "is self-defined, and means an economic condition where an abundance of material goods can be produced for the entire population of a given community."[3] Rexford G. Tugwell maintained, in the 1930s, that "there is no scarcity of production. There is, in fact, a present capacity for more production than is consumable, at least under a system which shortens purchasing power while it is lengthening capacity to produce."[4] Chase offered documentary evidence for what he conceived of as the capacity for over-production (written in 1931, note, when they may have been more convincing):

> American oil wells are capable of producing 5,950,000 barrels a day, against a market demand of 4,000,000 barrels, according to the figures of the Standard Oil Company of New Jersey.[5]
>
> The real problem [in coal] is excess capacity. The mines of the country can produce at least 750,000,000 tons a year, while the market can absorb but 500,000,000 tons.[6]
>
> American shoe factories are equipped to turn out almost 900,000,000 pairs of shoes a year. At present we buy about 300,000,000 pairs.... Yet if we doubled shoe consumption ... one-third of the present shoe factory equipment would still lie idle....[7]

Three decades later, in different conditions, Vance Packard stated the position of the surplus of goods succinctly:

> Man throughout recorded history has struggled—often against appalling odds—to cope with material scarcity. Today, there has been a massive breakthrough. The great challenge in the United States and soon in Western Europe—is to cope with a threatened overabundance of the staples and amenities and frills of life.[8]

If there were a surplus of goods generally, it would follow that there is a surplus of labor. As early as 1893, John R. Commons held that there was a "chronic excess of labourers beyond the opportunities for employment."[9] Stuart Chase spelled out the position in the 1930s:

> What threatens to continue unabated, in good times and bad, is technological unemployment.... In four years oil refineries

increased output 84 percent, and laid off 5 percent of their men while doing it. Tobacco manufacturing output climbed 53 percent in the same period, with 13 percent fewer men at the end . . .

It can mean only one thing. An equivalent tonnage of goods can be produced by a declining number of workers, and men must lose their jobs by the thousands—presently by the millions.[10]

Emphasis on Consumption

The general premise of a surplus of goods leads to consumer or consumption economics, i.e., to measures promoting the consumption of goods. The premise of a surplus of labor provides the basis of an implicit economic theory for unionism which is nowhere spelled out but which is everywhere practiced by unionists. It is the theory under-girding the practices of reducing the available supply of labor.

The unionist theory of a labor surplus is a self-fulfilling prophecy when it is put into practice. That is, labor unions tend to create the very conditions they posit, namely, labor surplus, or, more precisely, unemployment, underemployment, and low-paid work for non-union workers. But before explaining why, it needs to be made clear that labor is scarce. This has been affirmed already in terms of economics, but there is a more basic axiom than the one cited. It is this. Human wants are insatiable, but the means for satisfying them are limited (scarce). Human labor can be used in innumerable ways to satisfy human wants. Therefore, labor is scarce—essentially and permanently.

I can make the same point in a much more homely fashion, one which brings us in the vicinity of everyman's experience, and one which will get us much closer to the effects of labor unions. There is more work to be done than there is ever time or energy to do. It is certainly true around my house, and from all I have ever learned it is true for others as well. As I write this, there are dozens of tasks I can think of that need doing. The roadway to my house needs some repair; the lawn needs mowing; the lawn needs fill in places, reseeding, and fertilizer generally; the trees will need pruning when the time comes. The place where the water pipe enters the house from the well needs blocking up, because it freezes in very cold weather. I have been in-tending for more than two years to paint the exposed concrete blocks in the foundation of my house. Several rooms inside the house need a new coat of paint. It is time to spread lime on my garden in preparation for next year. My car would benefit greatly not only from being cleaned and washed but also from a good waxing. And this list only scratches the surface of all the work awaiting either my own attention or that of someone whom I could afford to employ. More broadly, there are numerous goods I would like to have for myself or my family—ranging from a yacht and swimming pool to clothing and exotic foods—if I only had the means to pay for them. And every one of my wants would require more or less labor to satisfy it.

In short, I have a *surplus* of wants and a *scarcity* of means for satisfying them. That condition is sufficiently near universal that no one has ever bothered to make a survey to determine if it is unanimous.

Price a Crucial Factor in Satisfying Wants

Equally important, we do not feel all our wants with equal intensity. We have priorities as to which of them we would satisfy with what outlay of our limited means. For example, my desire for a yacht is of such low intensity that I am by no means certain that I would rush to buy one if 50-foot yachts were selling for $100. On the other hand, if new automobiles were selling for $25 each, I would stop what I am doing and lay in a stock of them immediately. *Price,* then, is a crucial factor in my decisions about satisfying my wants. And, the price of labor is a factor in the price of virtually all the goods I want.

What this means, practically, is that all who can work so as to satisfy some human want can find employment—somewhere, at some price. The full employment of all who are willing to work is the norm for human societies. Price is the crucial variable, however, for full employment. This is so both because of the great range in intensity of wants and the range of human capacity, ability, and skill in satisfying wants. Indeed, individuals differ from one another and vary as to the extent to which they can perform all the tasks which have an effect on the quantity and quality of their output. That is, they differ in temperament, power of concentration, intellectual penetration, endurance, strength, skill, and so on. The basic means for making adjustments for differences in intensities of wants and different individual abilities are in price and working arrangements (not "working conditions," for as that phrase is ordinarily used it is simply an aspect of price).

The thrust of unionism is to establish downward price (wage) inflexibility and to raise ever higher the level below which wages cannot go. This means that wages cannot be adjusted to changing demand (intensity of want) or to the lower productivity or different work patterns of some workers. More directly, it means that unions cause unemployment, and the more widely they are established the greater the unemployment. They price workers out of the market, thus causing endemic unemployment.

It might be supposed that the connection between labor unions and unemployment could be easily demonstrated empirically. All that should be necessary would be to match the figures of increasing union membership and recognition with unemployment figures. That it is not so simple will become apparent by examining an instance, and the reasons for its complexity will lead us to the broad and sustained impact of unionism.

Unions and Unemployment

Perhaps the best period for an historical case study of the effect of unions on unemployment was 1935–1939. The Wagner Act was passed in 1935. In 1936, there was a 10.1 per cent increase in union membership over the preceding year. In 1937, the greatest jump in membership for a single year in the twentieth century occurred; it was a whopping percentage increase of 53.9.[11] The main thrust for this increase came from the CIO under the leadership of John L. Lewis. As one writer describes this surge:

> At the end of two years of activity, in December, 1937, the CIO boasted a membership of 3,700,000—composed of 600,000 miners, 400,000 automobile workers, 375,000 steel workers, 250,000 ladies' garment workers, 175,000 clothing workers, 100,000 agricultural and packing house workers, 80,000 rubber workers. The day of labor giants had dawned.[12]

There followed a drastic increase in unemployment. According to one compilation, unemployment stood at about 7 1/2 million in 1937. In 1938, it rose to 11 million, and in 1939 was still lingering around 9 1/2 million.[13] A stock market crash of considerable dimensions occurred beginning in the middle of 1937. One economic historian explains these events in this way. There had been an increase of aggregate labor income at the expense of profit income. This had resulted primarily from the unionization which increased wages of manufacturing laborers rapidly. "A main factor," he says, "on the industrial side in bringing the revival of 1935–1937 to a close was this startling increase in wages, due . . . to a tremendous burst of activity by trade unions under the Wagner Act—a rise in wages unmatched by a corresponding rise in the productivity of labor."[14] Or, technically, in terms of marginal utility theory, the higher union wages made many workers marginal who had been employed, and they lost their jobs.

Described in this way, there appears to be very nearly a *prima facie* case that unions caused the unemployment. Unfortunately, there were other developments during the same period which may have contributed to the unemployment and which certainly muddy the waters of causation. Many were leaving the farms seeking industrial employment, such as, from the Dust Bowl, and some of these added to the rolls of the unemployed. There were changes in governmental fiscal policies which probably had some effect. Here is a succinct summary by an historian: "In June, 1937, Roosevelt . . . slashed spending sharply. He cut WPA rolls drastically and turned off WPA pump-priming. At the very same time, Washington collected two billions in new social security taxes. The government had not only stopped priming the pump but was even 'taking some water out of the spout.'"[15] Benjamin Anderson has challenged this explanation,[16] but it is plausible that the higher wages combined with a slacking off of inflation would have contributed to the unemployment.

Minimum-Wage Laws

Government further aggravated the situation in 1938 by the passage of the Fair Labor Standards Act. This established minimum wages and maximum hours in many industries, resulting in higher wages and shorter hours for some workers. The effect of the minimum wage is the same in kind as a union wage. So far as it works to raise wages above the market level it will result in unemployment.

These latter developments illustrate the point that now needs to be made. Unions are not simply empowered by government, they are aided and abetted by a host of government programs which, on the one hand, conceal or confuse the effects of unionism and, on the other, aggravate them. Union contracts, plus government enactments, would—in fact, do, when viewed from the angle of potential employment—cause massive unemployment, but most of these effects are concealed from public view by a host of other programs. Most, if not all, of this should be attributed to unionism, for governments generally act on unionist premises and the public at large tends to accept union goals, even when they may deplore certain union tactics.

To grasp the full impact of unionism, it may be helpful to view it in the light of the Greek fable of Procrustes. It is said that the countryside was inhabited by assorted petty tyrants and marauders. "One of these evil-doers was called Procrustes, or the Stretcher. He had an iron bedstead, on which he used to tie all travellers who fell into his hands. If they were shorter than the bed, he stretched their limbs to make them fit it; if they were longer than the bed, he lopped off a portion."[17]

The Cost of Fringe Benefits

The thrust of unionism is to make a Procrustean bed, into the confines of which all who would work must fit. The most obvious of the confines is price. By making prices of labor (wages) downwardly inflexible, only those who can produce at a level that would make it worthwhile for an employer are likely to find work. This price inflexibility extends much beyond what is ordinarily called wages. It includes employer contributions to retirement plans, Social Security, unemployment compensation, hospitalization plans, workmen's compensation, and so on. Indeed, these "fringe benefits" have become so expensive that many employers find it less expensive to pay overtime to those already employed than to take on new people. (This is so because there may be little or no fringe benefit payments for the overtime work.) "Overtime" has become a way of life for many industrial workers. Indeed, it is sometimes considered one of the "perks" of the job, and some workers make obligations based on the expectation of it. The supreme irony of this is to be seen in all the verbiage that historians have lavished on the supposedly horrible conditions of work in earlier times when people worked long hours and six- and seven-day weeks.[18]

The thrust of unionism to make a Procrustean bed in which all who would work must fit is much broader than is suggested by downward price inflexibility. Unions and government exert pressure for uniform pay scales, for raises in pay according to seniority, and for objective job definitions. Indeed, the pressure of unionism is to have work as highly structured as possible, to have it done under managerial supervision and control, to have payment based on time worked, to have it performed within factories or factorylike surroundings, to require of every worker within a job classification that he do as much, or as little, as all others, in short, to have it done under conditions that are optimal for unionization.

Home Workshops Opposed

This pressure may best be illustrated, perhaps, by unionist opposition to work being done in the home. Unionists and their sympathizers attached odium to such arrangements by characterizing it as a "Sweating System." In the argot of Americans, a "sweatshop" is a factory where intolerable working conditions prevail. That is not at all the origin of the idea of "sweated labor." It originated as a term of derogation, or was so used by unionists, for work done in the home.

The *Encyclopedia Britannica* describes the "Sweating System" as being closely "associated with contracting. Individual workers or groups of workers contract to do a certain job for a certain price." The work is then performed in the home, home workshops, and the like. The same source says that the "sweating system grew in the United States during the Civil War, when soldiers' wives were employed to make uniforms with the relatively newly developed sewing machines." Unionists attacked the system with all the energy they could muster. The *Britannica* says that "In the United States most of the pressure to eliminate sweating was applied by.organized labor."

Industrial homework has long since been virtually eliminated in the United States by a combination of union and government effort. Unions had considerable success in getting it eliminated in such undertakings as clothing making and cigar making. It became virtually illegal in some states, for Jack Barbash notes that when the New York legislature considered a bill for "partial legalization of industrial homework," it was vigorously opposed by the New York Federation of Labor.[19] At any rate, much homework was made impractical by minimum-wage prescriptions (based on an hourly rate, as they were, employers would be unwilling to pay when they could not check), prescriptions as to working conditions, by zoning laws, and such like.

Problems of Organizing

The unionist motives for opposition to home work are not difficult to surmise. It would probably be nearly impossible to organize such workers. The conditions of proximity and association would not exist for developing class consciousness among them. They could do the work less expensively than it could be done in the factories; thus making it difficult to organize factory workers engaged in similar pursuits. Thus, unionists stigmatized such work arrangements as inhumane and oppressive.

Though there are many other aspects of it, the above examples suggest the outline, at least, of the Procrustean bed made by unionism. It is a bed far short of the size that could accommodate the potential work force of the country.

Those workers who do not fit within its confines are lopped off. For one thing, most workers who cannot fit into factory-like requirements as to hours of work are largely eliminated from consideration for employment. Many who have small children to attend to and household tasks to perform would undoubtedly like part-time employment in the home. An employer who sometimes had large numbers of letters to be individually addressed told me that the first time he advertised for such help applicants tied up his office telephones for days. The next time he had occasion to advertise, he gave only a box number, but he still received hundreds of written applications from people wishing to do work in the home.

Governments Intervene

Governments have assisted in numerous ways in lopping off potential willing workers. Compulsory school attendance and child labor laws largely eliminate children from most employment. Prolonged schooling much beyond the ages of 16 to 18 has kept many young people off the labor market. States subsidize technical and college education on a vast scale. The community and junior colleges founded in unprecedented numbers in the 1950s and 1960s were the most dramatic instances of such an effort. The G.I. Bill of Rights was the largest of the federal efforts along this line, but it has in more recent times been supplemented by both federal and state scholarship and loan programs.

Social Security and other retirement programs enable many at the other end of the age scale to stay off the labor market. Aid to dependent children and other welfare programs provide support for many mothers and older children without their holding jobs. Social Security provides such support, too, in cases where a covered mate has been disabled or died. Unemployment compensation relieves some of the pressure from union- and government-induced unemployment. Indeed, ingenious workers can cut their work time by perhaps as much as one-half or more by working from time to time, getting laid off or having the job discontinued, and drawing unemployment compensation. Some do, but in the nature of the programs there is no way to determine how much of it is deliberate.

My concern is not with the motives which led legislators to enact these and other such programs. The effects are the same whatever the motives, and the effects are the reduction of the available labor supply. And there is bountiful evidence that both unions and governments act upon the premise that there is a surplus of labor.

Even all the efforts that are made at reducing the labor supply by lopping it off do not succeed in reducing the supply so that it will fit into the Procrustean bed for jobs. There are usually still millions looking for employment, or claim that they are. There is a major effort, then, to "stretch" the jobs to fit the available labor supply. Unions are famous, or infamous, for job stretching. It is sometimes called "featherbedding." The way this is usually done is in work rules in union contracts. Here are some examples:

1. Limitations on supervisory personnel performing production work—for example, a Rubber Workers' union provision: "Members of factory management shall not perform work which is normally assigned to direct workers. . . ."

2. Limitations on assigning work outside of an employee's classification, as for example a Meat Cutters' union provision that weighers and wrappers may not "platter" meat cuts in self-service counters.

3. Requirement for minimum number of employees on a job: for example, the Motion Picture operators demand for two men in projection booth.

4. Rules regulating the use of labor-saving methods and machinery. . . .

5. Rules protecting union's jurisdiction: in New York theatres "Carpenters will build a platform, but the covering is prop man's. A

hat (worn) is costume but the same hat (unworn) is a prop. A table is moved by prop men, but the lamp on it is sacred to electricians. . . ."[20]

Governments, too, have made efforts to "stretch" jobs, provide temporary jobs, and "stretch" the money supply to fit the Procrustean bed higher monetary wages on which they have helped to create. The most general effort by the United States to "stretch" jobs has been the mandated 8-hour day, 40-hour week. That effort has met with mixed success, however, as already noted, because overtime pay is often not a sufficient penalty to prevent longer hours, in view of the effective penalties involved in hiring other workers. Thus, government programs are often initiated with the idea of providing more jobs. The role of the unions in this is suggested in the following:

> Unions seek to enlist the aid of government in providing more jobs in the industries in which their members are employed; or to protect job opportunities from being impaired in their industries. . . . [Among these] are the interests of the building trades unions, which have been among the most energetic supporters of government action for a major low-cost housing program; and the metal trades unions for a shipbuilding program.[21]

Inflation to Offset Impact of High Wages on Employment

The most prolonged effort at "stretching" has been in stretching the money supply—i.e., inflation, to offset the impact of high union wages on employment. It is doubtful that most unions could survive for long without progressive increases in the money supply. The continually higher monetary wages on which their success depends would produce such levels of unemployment (even if all other programs to reduce labor supply were in effect) that union workers would no longer be employed.

Further, Friedrich A. Hayek has pointed out that if government is committed to full employment, "current union policies must lead to continuous and progressive inflation. . . . If labor insists on a level of money wages too high to allow of full employment, the supply of money must be so increased as to raise prices to a level where the real value of the prevailing money wages is no longer greater than the productivity of the workers seeking employment. In practice, this necessarily means that each separate union ... will never cease to insist on further increases in money wages and that the aggregate effort of the unions will thus bring about progressive inflation."[22] He has ably described the process of "stretching" that goes on.

Unionist policies flow from a misconception of reality. Labor is essentially scarce in reality. Unionists operate on the premise that there is a surplus of labor. The result is an apparent contradiction. Unionism produces both a labor shortage and unemployment (a labor surplus?). The reason for this is before us. Many potential employers cannot find workers to do the work they would hire done at a price they are willing to pay. (It is commonly observed today, "You can't find workers to do this, that or the other.") Wages are too high to pay for low-priority and low-productivity work. On the other hand, many people cannot find employment at the artificially established high wages.

Institutional Unemployment Plus a Shortage of Labor

The impact of unionism is as broad as the economy over which it holds sway, and even broader than that. It leads to institutional (or structural) unemployment and an endemic labor shortage. It requires massive government intervention to conceal the worst of its ravages. Unionism—labor unions plus accommodative government action—intervenes in the market at its most sensitive point. It makes rigid what needs to be most flexible to meet continually changing conditions. It causes unemployment, labor shortages, promotes inflation, higher prices, less productivity, and leads to fewer goods and services for everyone.

Who are labor unions organized against? They are organized against all who work, and all who benefit from work. They are organized against non-union workers most obviously, for these are often turned away from the gates, may not be able to find employment, and, if they do, may have to accept lower wages. In some respects, unions are organized against their own members, some of whom may be compelled to join or pay dues, the most industrious of whom may be held back to the level of the less productive, and some of whom lose their jobs when the union wage prices them out of the market. They are organized against employers. They are organized against consumers. Above all, they are organized against the weakest members of society, those who cannot fit into the structure of employment—the young, the old, the lame, the halt, and the blind.

1. Marxists, however, are not necessarily being inconsistent in promoting unionism. They are making warfare on capitalism by obstructing production generally. Once in power in a country, they regularly subdue the labor unions.

2. *The Communist Manifesto* in Eugen Weber, ed., *The Western Tradition* (Boston: D. C. Heath, 1959), p. 609.

3. Quoted in Charles S. Wyand, *The Economics of Consumption* (New York: Macmillan, 1937), p. 54.

4. Rexford G. Tugwell, *The Battle for Democracy* (New York: Columbia University Press, 1935), p. 7.

5. Stuart Chase, *The Nemesis of American Business* (New York: Macmillan, 1931), p. 88.

6. *Ibid.,* p. 89.

7. *Ibid.,* p. 79.

8. Vance Packard, *The Waste Makers* (New York: David McKay, 1960), p. 7.

9. John R. Commons, *The Distribution of Wealth* (New York: Reprints of American Classics, 1963), pp. 84–85.

10. Chase, *op. cit.,* pp. 15–16.

11. Irving Bernstein, "The Growth of American Unions," *Readings in United States Economic and Business History,* Ross M. Robertson and James L. Pate, eds. (Providence: Brown University Press, 1965), p. 363.

12. Joseph G. Rayback, *A History of American Labor* (New York: Macmillan, 1959), p. 355.

13. Gilbert C. Fite and Jim E. Reese, *An Economic History of the United States* (Boston: Houghton Mifflin, 1965, 2nd ed.), p. 599.

14. Benjamin M. Anderson, *Economics and the Public Welfare* (New York: D. Van Nostrand, 1949), pp. 444–46.

15. William E. Leuchtenburg, *Franklin D. Roosevelt and the New Deal* (New York: Harper & Row, 1963), p. 244.

16. Anderson, *op. cit.,* pp. 439–44.

17. Thomas Bulfinch, *The Age of the Fable* (New York: The Heritage Press, 1942), p. 154.

18. There is a factory near where I live in which many of the workers work 7 days one week and 6 days the next by regular alternation. In another factory, it is not unusual to work 12 or 16 hours (called "working a double") some days. It would be an error either to suppose that workers resent the long hours or that the decision to work overtime is voluntary. Often enough, the willingness to do so is a condition of continued employment.

19. Jack Barbash, *The Practice of Unionism* (New York: Harper & Bros., 1956), p. 261.

20. *Ibid.,* pp. 167–68.

21. *Ibid.,* p. 247.

22. Friedrich A. Hayek, *The Constitution of Liberty* (South Bend, Ind.: Gateway, 1972), p. 280.

The Redistribution of Wealth— Labor Union Style

by Robert G. Anderson

The redistribution of wealth as well as the creation of wealth is a natural development of the market process. Voluntary exchanges among individuals as producers and consumers constantly bring about the creation and redistribution of wealth.

The advancement in the material well-being of individuals that results from a developing social division of labor is one of the great blessings of a free market society. The specialization of individuals producing goods and services for trade in the marketplace has enhanced labor output far beyond anything that was attained by individuals who produced exclusively for their own direct consumption.

With the market price system as their guide, entrepreneurs respond to their assessment of consumer desires by bringing together capital and labor in the production of goods and services. The future behavior of the consumers in the marketplace ultimately rewards or penalizes these entrepreneurs for their decisions. If the entrepreneur's judgment in the productive employment of capital and labor is correct, as evidenced by subsequent consumer buying, profits result. A lack of consumer buying, however, reflects losses to the entrepreneur for his erroneous employment of these productive resources.

The natural market process is the motivating force for all productive effort, and countless daily activities of this type result in an orderly market price system. Such voluntary behavior by producers and consumers responding to market prices not only creates new wealth but results in the constant redistribution of wealth within a free society.

Competitive Allocation

There can be no reasonable objection to such redistribution of wealth when it results from voluntary exchange in a competitive mar-

Mr. Anderson was vice president of The Foundation for Economic Education until his retirement in 1992. This article first appeared in the July 1979 issue of *The Freeman*.

144 / Robert G. Anderson

ketplace; quite the contrary, such market processes are continually directing productive resources to their highest use and thus bringing about the greatest material progress.

The redistribution of wealth by labor unions, however, differs profoundly from the market process. Unlike the transfer of wealth in a voluntary exchange between a producer and consumer, the shift of wealth by labor unions is accomplished involuntarily, by force and intimidation. Furthermore, the magnitude of the wealth transferred by labor unions as well as the extent of the burden upon those deprived can never be calculated. These are unseen effects of the labor union's impact on the market.

An understanding of this distinction requires an awareness of labor's role in the marketplace. Contrary to the popular misconception that conflict prevails between labor and capital in productive employment, these independent factors of production actually complement one another. A joining together of capital and labor by the entrepreneur stems from the exercise of his foresight in the anticipation of future consumer behavior, and the two factors work together for the benefit of consumers.

The Active Force

It is competition among entrepreneurs for capital and labor, not competition between capital and labor, that is the active force in the free market. Within the context of a particular productive effort, capital and labor join together in producing the output of goods and services for the benefit of consumers. The ultimate valuation of these goods and services by consumers in turn establishes the value upon the specific productive factors employed.

It is true that capital frequently displaces labor in productive activity, as new and better machinery is invented. But far from a destructive, competitive force harming labor, such labor-saving devices are the primary ingredient for material progress. Increases in both the quantity and quality of productive capital—tools and machinery—contribute to an increase in labor's productivity.

The value of labor is dependent upon "getting more goods out of the woods in a given period of time." When capital is employed in production the output of labor is enhanced. While greater work effort can increase production, the history of man's material progress has primarily occurred through the use of capital—more efficient tools. It is an obvious truism that a man working with a machine can produce more than a man with his bare hands, and on a greater scale the observation that the great consuming nations are the great producing nations is directly related to their abundance of capital.

It is equally true that labor competes with labor. Just as entrepreneurs bid against one another for productive labor, so too does worker bid against worker for productive employment. This competition among entrepreneurs, and among workers in the labor market, is a continual force that directs productive resources to their highest and most efficient use. Competition therefore, rather than being destructive, can thus be seen as a guiding force toward the attainment of efficiency in the employment of productive resources. The substitution of capital for labor, which increases the productivity of labor, makes the labor correspondingly more valuable to competing entrepreneurs. This combination of greater capital employment coupled with competing entrepreneurs seeking competing workers, results in ever-increasing benefits for labor.

The Exploitation Theory

The historical evolution of the union in the labor market had its intellectual roots in Marxian theories of exploitation. Arguing from the defunct labor theory of value as its premise, the exploitation theory held that an inherent conflict existed between labor and capital. The labor theory of value erroneously assumed that the source of economic value was labor input. The returns paid to capital and the entrepreneur, therefore, were necessarily assumed to come from an exploitation of the labor employed in production. Interest and profits were considered "unearned," and the increment paid to them created "surplus value," a capitalist accumulation of productive resources in fewer and fewer hands.

Modern marginal utility theory as well as actual experience in the labor market has totally demolished this fallacious labor theory of value and its erroneous conclusions. It is now well-recognized that the true source of value is subjective, that it is the individual tastes, preferences, likes, and dislikes of consumers which give economic value to productive resources. The reason that productive resources have value is because of the contribution they make in satisfying the desires and demands of consumers.

Entrepreneurs try to anticipate what these future consumer values will be and to direct market resources into productive activity to ultimately meet these values. The pursuit of profit is the motivating force for this risk-taking activity. This return of profits to the successful entrepreneur results from his bringing together independent factors of production into a complementary state, *today*. To this end, the factors land, labor, and capital are drawn together for the present benefit of consumers.

Contributing Factors

While labor is an important part of productive activity, it is certainly not the sole contributing factor to productive output. Compensation to the entrepreneur and to the owners of capital and land for their roles in bringing about desired goods and services for the consumer must also be paid. What this payment will be to each contributing factor of production is consumer-determined by the resources they willingly exchange for the end-product of the productive enterprise.

The rent for land, the interest for capital, the wages for labor, and the profits for entrepreneurs are determined by market forces. That is, the given supply of each factor of production relative to the demand for this factor determines its market price. And since it is the final judgment of the consumers on the worth of the productive output which gives value to these productive resources, the greater the quality and quantity of output that these productive resources can generate, the more valuable they are in terms of market prices.

It is for this reason that an increasing abundance of land, capital, and successful entrepreneurs improves the returns to labor. As the total supply of these other productive factors increases, relative to the supply of labor, the greater will be labor's share of the total returns. The higher and higher wages earned by labor, therefore, have evolved from the greater productive output made possible by a declining cost of interest, rent, and entrepreneurial expertise as the supply of each of these has increased.

While the concept of labor unions originated in a labor/capital conflict theory that has long since been refuted, and the advancement of living standards can be directly identified with the market process, the labor union continues to exist today as an imposing force.

The historical growth of unions to their present influence in the labor market has little, if anything, to do with their economic role. An understanding of labor union growth requires an understanding of how the power of legal, government-sanctioned monopolies can displace the market force of competition.

The role of law in a market society is to protect life and property. This function is vital to the preservation of peace and harmony among the members of society. Such a role demands equality before the law if legal justice is to prevail. To violate this principle of universality guarantees injustice.

Special Powers of Coercion Promote Growth of Unions

It is an historical fact that the growth and presence of labor unions can be traced directly to violations of these legal concepts. Prior to 1930 fewer than four million members of the labor force were unionized in the United States. Beginning with the passage of the Norris-La Guardia Act in 1932, and the National Labor Relations Act in 1935, unions acquired special-interest legal advantages denied to any other institution or individual. There is no question that a definite correlation can be found between the preferential legal treatment accorded unions at that time, and the twenty-one million union workers in today's United States labor force.

The growth of union membership during the past forty years would never have been possible without these special powers of coercion. Competitive free-market labor long ago would have displaced this inefficient structuring of unionized labor had not unions possessed their legal advantages. Modern unionism has been the offspring of a statist society of legal privileges.

It must be pointed out that modern unionism is not synonymous with a voluntary association of workers. It is frequently argued that unions are simply a cooperative arrangement of workers engaging in collective negotiation with their employer or employers. To believe that this is *all* that constitutes modern unionism would be exceedingly naive because it ignores reality.

Certainly there can be no moral objection to workers creating a voluntary, private association as their representative in employment negotiations with their employers. From an economic viewpoint, however, such a collective approach can never serve the individual worker's interests as effectively as he can serve himself. The collectivization of individual workers is not consistent with the competitive conditions that exist between workers for available jobs offered by employers. The establishment of a union of workers must subordinate the interests of the individual worker to the group.

It became obvious very early in the history of the labor union movement that the competing threat from workers in the free labor market would lead to the demise of unionism. The survival of labor unions in a competitive labor market would prove impossible as long as freedom of entry by new workers was allowed in the union labor market. Furthermore, the more productive workers within the union itself would inevitably discover the price they were paying as members of the collective group.

Violence and Privilege

The survival of unions was dependent upon the use of both private and legislated favoritism. It is no accident that the entire history of union growth has been marked with examples of violence. To survive and grow, unions systematically resorted to physical attacks on persons and property. Efforts at retaliation by employers led to mass conflict. Public opinion, swayed by a belief in labor/capital conflict theories, passively tolerated and sanctioned this union violence.

As long as the general belief was that outbreaks of violence were caused by employers fighting to preserve their power over exploited workers, the political climate was established for the creation of pro-union legislation. Union propaganda had successfully molded public opinion into believing that unions were the means by which working conditions were improved.

It is a simple truism that ideas determine actions. While truth will ultimately prevail in the intellectual battle of ideas, the belief in fallacious ideas meanwhile will chart our directions, and lead us to the disastrous consequences of these erroneous ideas. And so it has been with the labor theory of value and its concomitant conclusion of exploited labor under capitalism.

Arguing from these intellectual errors, the union was seen as a device to combat socialism and preserve capitalism from its inherent, self-generated defects. Believing that the individual worker was defenseless against the exploitation of the employer, the union has presented itself as a "progressive friend" of labor. By banding together, the workers would be a "countervailing power" within the labor/capital conflict environment that was believed to exist.

Such fallacious beliefs have, indeed, caused needless turmoil among men and destruction of property. Armed with passive support of public opinion and enabling legislation, unions have inflicted massive violence upon persons and property in their attainment of monopoly power in the labor market.

It is imperative to recognize the true nature of modern unionism. The union today is a legal cartel. It is as reactionary an institution as the guild of medieval times, but more insidious in its violence. Its violence against competing workers (scabs), and its intimidation against employers (strike), are matters of historical fact. The ominous presence of union labor today is mute testimony to the triumph of monopoly violence over peaceful competition.

The economic impact of the union as a legal cartel is no different from that of any other monopoly. Its preservation of power is dependent upon government legal protection, and/or private violence. The power of the labor union is particularly significant because it relies on both of these sources—all the power the law allows plus what can be usurped through private violence.

Granted legal immunity from the judicial injunction, and exempted from jury trial in the United States, the legal power of the union against employers is awesome. By the execution of the strike and the illegal use of private violence to restrict replacement of striking workers, a union can effectively enforce its monopolistic wage demands against an employer.

A Progressive Force?

The redistribution of wealth by legal plunder or private violence is nothing new in the history of mankind. What is new, however, is to refer to unions as a "progressive" force as they engage in the destruction of the peace and harmony of the capitalist order. The growth of union power in the private labor market was in direct proportion to its effective use of the law and private violence. The abdication by professional managers of responsibility to corporate owners of broadly held stock companies made the task of unions even easier. Rather than resist and risk bad publicity by replacing striking workers with new workers, the professional managers of large corporate employers yielded to union demands for higher wages. The unions thus succeeded in acquiring for their workers a wage rate higher than would have been attainable under conditions of a free, competitive labor market.

This situation can be clearly seen wherever labor unions are present in a labor market. Union wage rates are significantly higher than the wages paid for similar labor that has not been unionized. The tragedy has been to ascribe this differential to the union's ability to raise the general wage rates of *all* labor, rather than to the use of their monopoly power in raising the wages of just some of the union workers in the labor force.

The direct economic impact of a legal cartel is clearly visible. By forcefully preventing entry of any competitive supplier, the cartel is able to command a monopoly price for its services. The result is that the consumer of goods and services offered by a cartel is prevented from acquiring alternative goods and services from competitive sources.

This is precisely the case with employers acquiring union labor. The supply of workers bidding for the jobs offered by employers is restricted by the union. Furthermore, no individual is permitted to negotiate directly for himself with an employer of union labor. The employer is forced to negotiate exclusively with the union for his labor requirements. Irrespective of market labor supply factors that would contribute to the determination of a market wage rate, the employer is forced to negotiate fixed wage rates with the union.

Above-Market Wage Rates

The legal advantages and private violence of the union are exercised in acquiring wage rates higher than would be paid by the market. The employer, in the interests of short-run peace and a return to productive activity, is intimidated into accepting the wage demands of the union. Regardless of any changes in the market forces of supply and demand, the employers are bound to their fixed wages with the union.

While the union, in the exercise of its powers as a cartel, succeeds in acquiring the payment of wage rates above the prevailing market rate, it cannot insulate itself from the inexorable forces of economic law that must follow from such action. Other consequences, less visible and unseen by many, inevitably result from such forceful intervention in the market.

The most obvious market response is that the quantity of labor demanded, as with any economic good, will be less at a higher price than at a lower price. Many consumers will be unwilling to voluntarily exchange the greater resources required at the higher price. How many consumers will refuse to exchange is dependent upon the subjective valuations of the consumers for the particular economic good. While this knowledge can never be known with certainty, the magnitude of the marginal consumers is the determining factor in establishing what the economist calls elasticity or inelasticity of demand. Economic theory can only inform us, however, that all things being equal, fewer consumers will exchange at a higher price than at a lower price. The quantity of the change is dependent upon the price change and the values of the consumers.

The Employer as Consumer

In the labor market it is the employer who is the consumer. When the price of labor (wages) is increased, the quantity of labor demanded by employers will decline. The extent of the decline, as with any economic good, is determined by the amount of the increase in the price of labor and the number of marginal employers (consumers) in the particular labor market. The higher that wages are forced above the market rate, the greater the decline in demand for the labor by these consuming employers. President Calvin Coolidge put it well, "as more and more workers lose their jobs, unemployment results!"

The surplus labor, unemployment, is an inevitable result when employers become unable to recover from consumers the higher cost of their productive output. The force of the unions can increase wage rates, but that same force cannot be imposed upon the buying decisions of the consumer. As employers raise their asking prices to cover the union-imposed labor costs, many consumers will cease to buy the goods and services offered. The resultant decline in consumer buying requires a curtailment of production from the level that had prevailed.

For some employers, this necessity for reducing production levels may prove fatal. At lowered levels of production the employer may be operating so far below his break-even point that he has no alternative but to cease production entirely. More typically, it will mean a reduction in unit efficiency for employers, as the more efficient employers are transformed into less efficient employers. The decline of their efficiency in production means that fewer workers are required.

At the higher wages acquired through union force, both the unemployed and those within the free labor market are attracted to the higher paying jobs in the union labor market. However, this additional supply of labor can have no competitive impact on the union labor market. The employers are bound to their fixed union wage scale and are forbidden to employ competing labor at lower wages.

Unemployment

The failure of the union-imposed wages to adjust to the competitive conditions of the market leads to both unemployment and a distortion of labor allocation. The magnitude of the unemployment and distortion is dependent upon the difference between union-imposed wages and the market wage. The unions are well aware of this consequence and their propaganda constantly seeks to conceal their role as its cause. Their public image as the "friend of labor" forces them to perpetuate the myths that unemployment and the misallocation of labor is caused by the capitalist business cycle and greedy, profit-seeking employers.

While the rhetoric of the union claims no limit to what it can accomplish for the worker in terms of higher wages, the economic limitations of massive unemployment from exorbitant wage demands is understood. The long-term survival of the union depends upon a large membership, and the preservation of a large membership of workers requires the economic survival of the employers. It is a constant balancing act, therefore, as the union demands wages above the market, but not so high as to destroy the entire market for the union labor, and with it, the unions themselves.

A Free Market Sector

The capacity of the union to accomplish this feat, almost with impunity, lies in an institutional requirement that is essential to union success. The union must have a concurrent free labor market existing beside it. A competitive labor market that responds to changing forces of supply and demand is needed to absorb the unemployed that are driven out of the union labor market.

Less than one-quarter of the labor market is unionized in the United States today. Furthermore, not all union labor is earning above-market wage rates. It is probably a safe assumption that fewer than twenty percent of those in the United States labor market are receiving wage rates above what could be acquired under free market conditions.

It is this small minority of union workers receiving above market wage rates that generates the insidious redistribution of wealth in the labor market. The Tanstaafl principle (There ain't no such thing as a free lunch) has no better demonstration than by this example—*somebody* pays.

There are two groups that pay directly—those who are employed in the free labor market, and those who consume union labor market goods and services. Ultimately, everyone pays indirectly in the form of a lowered standard of living resulting from the disruption of the productive system and reduction of the incentive to the accumulation of capital.

Workers who would be employed in the union labor market, if freedom of entry prevailed, have no choice but to compete in the free labor market where supply and demand forces still determine wages. Their bidding in competition with the existing supply of free market labor causes the wages of free market labor to fall. The result is that wages in the free labor market are lowered because of the entry of the unemployed workers forced out of the union labor market.

This shift of wealth, higher wages to union workers at a cost of lower wages to free market workers, is a subtle, but nevertheless very real, redistribution of wealth. It is, indeed, an exploitation of labor by labor, that is, a forced transfer of wealth from the free labor market to the union labor market in the form of differing wage payments.

Also harmed are the consumers of goods and services produced by union labor. The law of costs ultimately requires that the higher union wages must be borne by these consumers if production is to continue. Future production at the above market labor costs imposed by unions, exacts its toll in the form of consumer prices higher than would prevail in a competitive market. Once again, a forced redistribution of wealth occurs as the consumer must pay the higher costs of union labor, but of what magnitude can never be known. The competitive market price in the absence of union labor is unknown.

While such redistribution of wealth by the force of union power represents exploitation and injustice, the capacity of unions to transfer wealth to themselves is limited by the ultimate consumer. If union wage demands become too excessive, employers are destroyed by the failure of consumer buying. In the so-called private-sector labor market it is a continual balancing act that is pursued by the union.

There is, however, a new and far more effective labor market that unions can exploit. This is the so-called public-sector labor market, the labor market composed of government employees.

Unlike the private labor market that survives by its capacity to produce goods and services that are voluntarily acquired by consumers in willing exchange, the public-sector labor market is supported by the taxing power of government. The law of costs does not apply to government activities as it does to private employers in a competitive free market. As a matter of fact, cost has nothing to do with the price of government activities. More often than not, government-provided services are offered free of price to the consumer. The costs of these government services are generally imposed upon the taxpayer.

Monopoly, Bureaucracy, and Union Power in Public Sector

Union power in the public-sector labor market is further enhanced by the monopoly structure of government-provided services, and the bureaucratic system of government management. Market competition in the form of freedom of entry in supplying alternative sources of goods and services to the consumer is generally prohibited by the force of law. Unlike the private labor market where higher union labor costs invite competition from free labor market employers, the public-sector labor market is protected by legal monopoly. Competitive alternatives to the consumer are denied by the force of law. Whether it is policemen, firemen, teachers, sanitation workers, or clerical government workers, the determination of public-sector wages is more a political or bureaucratic decision than a market determined decision by consumers.

Resistance to union wage demands in the public sector stems more from political considerations than from productivity considerations. It is usually the vocal outcry of the constituency, not the bureaucratic manager, that objects to the excessive wage demands of the unions in the public sector. After all, the bureaucratic manager himself is a worker in the public-sector labor market, and any union gains for his subordinates accrue to him as well. The bureaucratic manager has even less incentive to resist union demands than his counterpart in the private sector market—the professional manager of the large corporation.

The wage costs of public-sector workers, like any and all costs of government, ultimately are borne by the taxpayers. Whereas the union redistributes wealth to its workers from expropriating the resources of consumers and free market labor in the private sector, the redistribution of wealth to the public sector worker comes primarily from increased taxation.

Not confronted with the problems of competitive workers or unwilling consumers, the public-sector union can significantly increase the magnitude of its wealth redistribution. The only effective limitation to such union power is the same force that limits the whole of government—the private wealth of the citizenry that can be seized by government taxation.

Government labor unions have been quick to observe this massive increase in their power to redistribute wealth, and naturally have urged an expansion in public-sector unionization. To this end, the growth of government in economic affairs has opened a new source of labor union power in the forced redistribution of wealth.

It is a sad commentary of our age that the combination of economic ignorance and man's blind pursuit of power has brought us to this point. Any reversal in this state of affairs can occur only if we improve our economic understanding and structure our legal institutions to safeguard our lives and property from such private power abuses.

The hope of the future is in changing ideas. Unions exist today as a monument to intellectual error. They are the product of a statist society that permits the private abuse of power in the forcible redistribution of wealth. Any return to a free society demands the realization that competition and freedom, not legal privilege and violence, are the way to general prosperity for all.

Unions and Government Employment

by Dennis Bechara

September 9, 1919, was a date that altered government employment and the duties associated with it. For this was the time the Boston police force went on strike, causing an alarming state of violence, riots, and looting previously unheard of in the country. The Boston police strike marked the beginning of a long and protracted struggle aimed at the unionization of government employees.

The strike at that time was doomed to failure, for public opinion was against it. The policemen who participated in the strike were discharged, with public approval. When Samuel Gompers, head of the American Federation of Labor which had called the strike, petitioned Governor Calvin Coolidge to reinstate the strikers, the Governor replied: "There is no right to strike against the public safety by anybody, anytime, anywhere." This statement enjoyed almost unanimous approval, and helped Coolidge attain national recognition which ultimately catapulted him to the vice-presidential nomination in 1920. The Boston police strike occurred as the economy was readjusting from the severe pressures of the First World War. During the war, a War Labor Board was formed by the federal government, which encouraged the organization of labor unions. This was the first time the government created conditions favorable for the unionization of employees. So, it is not surprising that as many as five million employees were union members by early 1920.

The Boston police strike was only one of many strikes that took place during this time. It has been estimated that over 3,000 strikes occurred in 1919 involving approximately 4 million employees. Yet, the difference between the Boston police strike and the others was that the latter were aimed at private industry whereas the former was directed not only against the government but against the entire Boston population. People instinctively knew the unfairness of such a strike

Mr. Bechara is an attorney. This article originally appeared in the March 1984 issue of *The Freeman*.

since it touched everyone in Boston, whether or not they wanted to be involved in the controversy. The stark differences between public and private employment became clearer, and people generally agreed that there could not be such a thing as a right to strike against the public safety.

Compulsory Union Bargaining Began in Private Sector

In order to understand the full measure of compulsory public-sector bargaining, it is instructive to study the origins of private collective bargaining and its effects on the unionization of employees in the private sector. The unionization of government employees took place after the principles of majority rule, exclusive representation and collective bargaining were entrenched in private labor relations.

After the abolition of the War Labor Board when the war ended, union membership declined from its all-time high of 5 million members in 1920 to 3 1/2 million members by 1923. During the depths of the Great Depression, union membership hovered around 3 1/4 million members, and it was not until the passage of protective Federal legislation that union membership substantially increased. Under the Norris-La Guardia Act of 1932, the jurisdiction of the courts to issue injunctions was severely restricted in cases involving labor disputes. Similarly, under the National Recovery Act in 1933, collective bargaining was encouraged. Although this statute was later to be found unconstitutional, its encouragement of collective bargaining was enshrined in the Wagner Act of 1935. The effect of this legislation was substantial. The Department of Labor has stated that:

> The 2-year expansion of total union membership brought about a rise from less than 3 million in 1933 to 3 3/4 million in 1935. In the following 2 years (the first 2 years of the Wagner Act), membership almost doubled, advancing to 7 1/4 million. The largest gains during the latter period were made in the automobile, rubber, and aluminum industries, in which workers were organized on an industrial basis. Many of the older organizations, including such unions as the International Ladies' Garment Workers' Union, the International Association of Machinists, and the International Brotherhood of Teamsters, Chauffeurs, Warehousemen and Helpers, also reg-

istered substantial membership increases. The extent of these gains is even more impressive when it is realized that the total labor force increased only 2 percent between 1935 and 1937, and that nonagricultural employment, the main source of union membership, increased less than 15 percent.[1]

Union membership continued to increase during World War II and peaked in 1953, when 25.5 percent of the private sector work force was unionized. Membership decreased thereafter to approximately 16.2 percent by 1978.[2] It is not surprising that although recent labor leader pressures have failed to amend the National Labor Relations Act, other efforts aimed at the same goal of increasing unionization of employees have met with startling success. President Kennedy signed Executive Order 10988 on January 19, 1962, whereby collective bargaining was recognized as a right of certain federal employees. Although the terms of the Executive Order prohibited strikes and mandated that all agreements entered into must meet civil service regulations, the stage was set for further inroads. As one commentator put it: "Kennedy's Executive Order triggered a series of bargaining laws in states with substantial private sector unionism like Michigan, New York, Washington, and Pennsylvania. Only a dozen state governments, mostly in the South and West, do not have some kind of mandatory bargaining law to promote public employee unions today."[3]

The situation in the federal government has been substantially altered by the passage of the Civil Service Reform Act of 1978 which enshrined the principle of compulsory collective bargaining for most federal employees. Membership in public-employee unions has soared during the twenty-year period between 1960 and 1980. By 1960 eleven percent of government employees were unionized, whereas by 1980 the figure had increased to 50 percent of a total of over 15 million government employees.[4]

The recent surge in the unionization of government employees is in marked contrast to the decline in the unionization of the private sector. With government employment becoming more significant in the economy, it is essential that we understand how this differs from employment in private industry.

Market Guidelines

Perhaps the most salient distinction between the private sector and the government is the fact that private enterprise is guided in its behavior by the market and especially by the demand for its services. Businesses base their decisions on the market price for goods and services, and the consumer ultimately has the power to decide whether or not to purchase the items offered. There is always the incentive to be efficient in the provision of goods and services since real or potential competitors may offer a better price.

Government, on the other hand, has no such guidelines. Revenues are based on the taxes collected from the population. Efficiency in the provision of goods and services has no effect on revenues. Nor is there danger of losing the market to the private sector because in most instances competition is forbidden. The Postal Service, for example, has a monopoly in the delivery of first class mail. Regardless of the efficiency of the Postal Service, there is no danger that a private entity will offer alternative modes of delivering such mail. Even where competition is not forbidden, it is impractical in many cases because the government has the power to tax and may offer its services at below-cost prices. Public schools, for instance, have the advantage that no direct charges are imposed on the users of their services, whereas those who attend private schools not only have to pay for the private schooling but must sustain the public school system as well.

Since there is no incentive to economize or lower costs, and since there is no possibility of effective competition, government has considerable leeway in the assignment of priorities to provide goods and services. And since there is no market price for government services, its actions are in a sense arbitrary. Ludwig von Mises elaborated this point:

> A police department has the job of protecting a defense plant against sabotage. It assigns thirty patrolmen to this duty. The responsible commissioner does not need the advice of an efficiency expert in order to discover that he could save money by reducing the guard to only twenty men. But the question

is: Does this economy outweigh the increase in risk? There are serious things at stake: national defense, the morale of the armed forces and of civilians, repercussions in the field of foreign affairs, the lives of many upright workers. All these valuable things cannot be assessed in terms of money.[5]

These facts tend to complicate the employer-employee relationship in the public sector. There are no objective standards by which to judge and reward the productivity of government employees. In a private enterprise, the profit and loss system provides an objective framework upon which to judge the contribution made by each employee. It is true that arbitrary actions on the part of the employer may take place in the private sector. It is conceivable that an employer may act rashly and may in fact discharge his most efficient employees, retaining the least productive. But if he acts in such a fashion, he will do so at his peril.

Non-Economic Factors

The public employer, lacking a market method of judging his employees, turns to other non-economic considerations. At one time partisan politics played the most important role in the employment of government employees. The spoils system became so much a part of political reality that it took President James A. Garfield's assassination in 1883 by a disappointed office seeker to initiate the enactment of the first civil service law. This statute, known as the Pendleton Act of 1883, "created a Civil Service Commission to administer a new set of rules which required appointments to be made as a result of competitive examinations and prohibited assessments on office-holders for political purposes. By law these new rules were applied only to some 14,000 positions, about 12 percent of the total, but the President was empowered to extend them at his discretion. At the turn of the century there were not far from 100,000 in the classified civil service; at the end of Theodore Roosevelt's administration the number had more than doubled, and when Wilson left the White House it had increased to almost half a million. At the same time most states were passing civil service laws."[6]

The situation has changed even more dramatically; the Supreme Court has held that patronage dismissal from government employment violates the U.S. Constitution. The Court stated in *Elrod* v. *Burns,*[7] that patronage dismissals could only be justified in policymaking positions so as to guarantee that the policies which the electorate has mandated may be implemented. In yet another case, *Branti* v. *Finkel,* the Court indicated that patronage dismissals may only be justified if "the hiring authority can demonstrate that party affiliation is an appropriate requirement for the effective performance of the public office involved."[8] It may reasonably be said that the spoils system is no longer an important factor in the employment relationship in the government. However, this does not alter the fact that the public employer has no objective measure by which to judge the efficiency and productivity of his employees. Even in those government agencies where there is a provision of services for which there is a market price (like railroads and the provision of electric power), the agency is operated with other than a profit motive and thus lacks an objective standard.

The Power to Abuse

There is no question that government employees have the constitutional right to form and join unions. This is a part of the freedom of association guaranteed by the Constitution, and is as it should be in a free society. However, to extrapolate from that right of association a concomitant right to engage in collective bargaining is a quantum leap.

The theory of collective bargaining, which is embodied in our national labor policy, confers upon unions the exclusive right to engage in bargaining with an employer over the terms and conditions of employment, in behalf of certain employees. This exclusive right is in itself a very broad delegation of power, as each individual employee correspondingly loses his right to deal with his employer over those terms and conditions. The union that enjoys this exclusive right to engage in collective bargaining has the economic self-interest to raise the wages and other conditions of employment of those employees it represents at the expense of the rest of the work force. Such collective bargaining has had various effects. Some companies have not been able to compete as a result of the high wages exacted by the unions they must bargain with. Others have not been able to hire as many employees as they would have preferred. When we take these effects of collective bargaining, not to mention the consequences of prolonged strikes, it becomes obvious that unions in government will tend to exert an inordinate amount of power over the budgetary decisions of the government. As Sylvester Petro pointed out:

> So long as taxpayers remain a diffuse, unconcentrated group, while public-sector unions enjoy the compact political power derived from the laws granting them the privileges of exclusive bargaining statutes and of compulsory collective bargaining, the taxpayers must fight a losing battle.[9]

Although it is difficult to estimate the actual income generated by public-employee unions, an expert recently estimated that $750 million a year is a conservative figure.[10] Clearly, public-employee unions have an acute interest in promoting compulsory public-sector bargaining.

Essential Differences

Among the many other differences between the government and private employers is the economic advantage enjoyed by the government. Taxpayers must subsidize the government's expenditures regardless of their demand for the services offered. As previously noted, the possibilities of private competition are curtailed. All of these factors enhance the entrenched power of public-employee unions. Besides, since government is usually the only supplier of many services, a strike, however short its duration, can inflict tremendous damage to the population. This in turn causes the politicians to yield to exorbitant union demands so as to lessen the public outcry caused by the strike.

The politicians responsible for maintaining labor peace in the government must reconcile two conflicting demands. On the one hand they must pacify the concerted efforts of public-employee unions to raise labor costs while on the other hand they must stem any outcry that may surface on the part of the population at large to avoid profligate spending. This effort at reconciling these opposing demands is usually resolved in terms favorable to the public-employee unions since these organizations have formidable lobbying power. Public employees have an economic interest in voting for candidates who will be more generous in settlements with public-employee unions. It is not surprising that "public employees participate in elections at substantially higher rates than the general citizenry does, thereby forming a more potent voting bloc than their share of the work force might suggest."[11]

A Political Process

The easiest way for politicians to reconcile the conflict between the general taxpayers' clamor to reduce spending and the strong pressures exerted by public employee unions has been to grant many of the benefits demanded as long as they are to be financed over the long term. There is no short-term need to raise taxes, and both the unions and the taxpayers are satisfied. This development is similar to the so-called "uncontrollable" items in the federal budget where benefit increases have been mandated over a number of years. Since the legislation took place in the past, no politician needs to suffer the consequences of being singled out as responsible for the increase in spending. Public-sector bargaining is part and parcel of the political process since its outcome directly influences the budgetary decisions of the government. This becomes even more acute whenever a strike takes place: "A strike designed to get for the strikers more than the legislative appropriation calls for is thus a political act, not an economic one; its purpose is to supplant the budgetary decisions produced by the political processes of representative government with a form of action which can only be called an act of political aggression or extortion."[12]

Although most public-employee collective bargaining statutes contain prohibitions against strikes, government officials have become reluctant to impose any sanctions on the strikers. In 1980 there were 536 work stoppages involving 224,000 government employees.[13] It seems safe to assume that the reason few sanctions have been taken has been due to the powerful political influence enjoyed by public-employee unions. Yet, one must consider that during the 1981 Professional Air Traffic Controllers Organization (PATCO) strike the government took an unusually strong stand and proceeded to discharge all those strikers who refused to return to work. This severely strong action was politically acceptable and shattered the myth that it is impossible for a government official to deal effectively with the issue of strikes in the public sector. But the issue posed by public employee unions goes beyond whether or not public employees should have the right to go on strike. The question that should be addressed is whether or not compulsory collective bargaining should be the guiding principle for labor relations in the public sector.

The clear differences that exist between a private and a public employer demonstrate the vulnerability of both the government and the taxpayers to the pressures exerted by public-employer unions. Compulsory public-sector collective bargaining will increase government spending inordinately with the consequent adverse effects on the budgetary and policy-making process. It should be remembered that the costs of collective bargaining include all the disputes that may arise during the term of the collective bargaining agreement. Clearly, collective bargaining in the public sector is not the most appropriate mechanism to handle labor relations in government.

Mandatory Arbitration

There are some who share a negative opinion about compulsory public-sector bargaining but feel that the ideal solution is to refer all disputes to compulsory arbitration. In this fashion, it is argued, arbitrators will decide the fairness of the union demands as well as the reasonableness of the employers' position. Yet, this argument overlooks an important consideration. By empowering independent arbitrators to impose contract settlements mandating new terms and conditions of employment, the people at large will have given up their capacity to hold anyone accountable for the particular settlements. Instead of bringing about a solution to the problems posed by the public-sector bargaining, mandatory arbitration will only aggravate them.

If the government were to change its policies and refuse to engage in collective bargaining, would this open the door for arbitrary treatment of government employees? The fact is that government employees have rights protected by the Constitution which are not open to employees in the private sector. We have already seen that the spoils system has been effectively curtailed as a result of recent Supreme Court decisions. In addition to this, the Supreme Court in *Perry* v. *Sinderman*[14] granted public employees who face dismissal the right to a hearing so that they may establish whether or not they had a "property interest" in their jobs.

The instances in which public employees have been dismissed are minimal. In 1978, for example, "only 300 of 2.8 million federal employees reportedly were dismissed or terminated for incompetence."[15] In addition, public employees may not be disciplined for their exercise of First Amendment rights. As all of this reveals, government employees enjoy certain rights that guarantee that they will not be subjected to arbitrary actions on the part of their employer. In addition, of course, public employees enjoy economic security since the government does not run the risk of going out of business. All in all, government employees enjoy greater job security than do employees in the private sector.

Government should rededicate itself to the purposes of the original civil service statutes. A pay scale cognizant of the realities of the market, along with the constitutional and statutory protections afforded public employees, assure them fair treatment without subjecting the government to the shackles of public-employee union pressures. If we continue to pursue the policies of compulsory public-sector bargaining, we will lose further control over the behavior of the government and its spending decisions. As Sylvester Petro has said:

> Compulsory public sector bargaining dilutes governmental sovereignty by transferring the loyalties of public employees from their government employers to their union. It dilutes popular sovereignty by pitting public employees as a group against taxpayers as a group. Instead of serving taxpayers, government employees and their unions extort from them.[16]

It is in our power to change those policies which have brought forth compulsory public-sector bargaining; if we do not, the events of September 9, 1919, may no longer be incidents of the past.

---

1. United States Department of Labor, *Brief History of the American Labor Movement,* 1976, p. 23–24.

2. Myron Lieberman, *Public-Sector Bargaining* (Lexington, Mass.: D.C. Heath and Company, 1980), p. 2.

3. Vol. 4, *Government Union Review* (1983), p. 6–7.

4. *Ibid.,* p. 3.

5. Ludwig von Mises, *Bureaucracy* (New Rochelle, N.Y.: Arlington House, 1969), p. 50.

6. S.E. Morison, H.S. Commager, and W.E. Leuchtenburg, *A Concise History of the American Republic* (New York: Oxford University Press, 1977), p. 414.

7. 427U.S.347 (1976).

8. 445U.S.507 (1980), at 518.

9. Vol. 10, *Wake Forest Law Review* (1974), p. 134.

10. Lieberman, *op. cit.,* p. 13.

11. Vol. 4, *Government Union Review* (1983), p. 14.

12. Vol. 10, *Wake Forest Law Review* (1974), p. 101.

13. United States Department of Commerce, *Statistical Abstract of the United States* (1982–83), p. 411, table 685.

14. 408U.S.593 (1972).

15. Vol. 4, *Government Union Review* (1983), p. 13.

16. Vol. 3, *Government Union Review* (1982), p. 23.

Compulsory Public-Sector Bargaining: The Dissolution of Social Order

by Sylvester Petro

The question of all questions in political economy not too long ago was: what should the functions of government be? Today it is: *will government be?*

Among the numerous, grave, and perhaps critical threats to the survival of civil order in the United States, one more ominous than the rest stands out: the movement in all the states and in the federal government to compel collective bargaining between our governments and unions acting as representatives of government employees. Although this movement rests upon a series of incredible distortions and misrepresentations of fact, it is propelled by premises, theories and arguments which cannot withstand serious examination, and creates chaos in every branch and sector of government where it takes hold, it is nevertheless gaining ground year by year, even day by day, in all our governments—federal, state, and local.

My thesis here is that this movement must be stopped if decent social order and effective representative government are to survive in this country. The nation, the states, the cities large and small, are already besieged by a horde of other destructive threats. Everyone knows this. Because understanding of these other threats is so widespread, however, there is at least room for hope that they will be dealt with more or less effectively. But profound ignorance at every level prevails on the issue of compulsory public-sector bargaining, and the powerful forces determined to inflict it upon the country therefore meet almost no resistance at all, let alone informed, determined, and effective resistance. My purpose is to stimulate such resistance, to inform it, and thus to contribute to its effectiveness. For if such resistance fails to appear, the virtually certain emergence of compulsory public-sector bargaining *universally* in this country—especially when this destructive institution combines with the other crises which are

Dr. Petro is Director of the Institute for Law and Policy Analysis, Winston-Salem, North Carolina. This article first appeared in *The Freeman* in August 1975.

167

breaking the country apart—is bound to bring about chaos, anarchy, and, ultimately, tyranny.

Factual Distortions and Misrepresentations

The first thing we need readily at hand is hard and accurate information concerning the condition of public employment in this country, the status of our public servants, the way they are treated, the rights, powers, privileges, and immunities which they already possess. For among the most serious misrepresentations fueling the drive for compulsory public-sector bargaining are the contentions that our public servants are underpaid and mistreated, that they are denied the rights of "freedom of association" which prevail in the private sector, that they will never be satisfied till they have those same "rights," and that until they do there will be serious "unrest" in government employment, strikes, and all the other bad things which, the leaders of organized labor say, union representation magically causes to disappear.

The fact of the matter is that public servants in this country have always enjoyed the right of free association when that right is properly understood as meaning the privilege of joining any lawful private association. It is true that till recently in some states a person wishing to retain civil-service status might have to forgo joining labor associations not composed exclusively of civil servants of the same governmental unit. However, this could in no proper view be regarded as an unconstitutional or even unfair disability. As Justice Holmes said, in upholding the authority of government to insist that its employees not play politics: ". . . the petitioner may have a constitutional right to talk politics, but he has no constitutional right to be a policeman."

Be that as it may, civil servants have now for many years in most states had a right to join full-fledged trade unions without endangering their government employment. Indeed for the last six or seven years they have enjoyed such rights, under the U. S. Constitution, even in the few states which positively prohibited public employees from joining unions. This result was reached without the benefit of any statute, state or federal, protecting the jobs of civil servants who wished to join unions. That being the case, it is accurate to say that the associational rights of civil servants are greater than—not inferior to—those of private employees. For private employees acquired such rights only from labor statutes like the National Labor Relations Act. Prior to those labor relations statutes, private employers were privileged to refuse to employ persons who insisted upon joining unions.

Failure to Join

In view of these facts and developments, it seems fair to conclude that what bothers the unions is not that public servants are denied the rights of free association *but that too few have availed themselves of this "right."* The latest available figures indicate that of well over 11 million state and local civil servants only a little over one million have chosen to join unions, while another two million have preferred to join associations of other kinds, despite their universally prevailing right to join unions without fear of loss of employment.

One of the reasons, perhaps, for this failure of more civil servants to join unions is that in a substantial majority of the states right-to-work laws are in effect for civil servants, even when they are not in effect for private employees. In those states more employees have not joined, probably, simply because they have not been forced to join.

We are now in a position to understand why unions are so anxious to have the states and the federal government pass compulsory public-sector bargaining laws. Those laws, at least in the version pushed by the unions, usually provide for either permissive or mandatory "union shops"; that is, they contain provisions imposing union membership as a condition of employment. The insistence upon such laws demonstrates that unions are not really interested in extending the right of free association to public employment. That right is already there. What the unions want is to demolish the right; they want to be in a position to force union membership upon unwilling civil servants.

As yet only a minority of the states have passed full compulsory public-sector bargaining laws; and a still smaller minority (11 or 12) have passed laws under which union membership may be made a condition of public employment. This is the state of affairs which the public-sector unions find unsatisfactory. The contention that public servants are denied rights of free association is false—a smoke screen designed to conceal what is really going on.

Leaders Seek Power

To sum up: the union drive for compulsory public-sector bargaining laws has nothing to do with any desire to expand the rights of public servants. What it has to do with is the overweening lust for power which characterizes most union leaders, especially in the public sector. They want such laws because when they get them they will be in a position to arrogate to themselves, out of the fund of rights which now belongs to public servants, the power to compel all civil servants to accept them as exclusive bargaining representatives and then, on top of that, the additional power to make unwilling civil servants pay for the union services which they do not want.

Naturally, no public-sector union leader will admit to such impolitic objectives. He will move on, instead, to the second series of contentions which, he hopes, will convince legislators and an unwary public that compulsory public-sector bargaining laws are needed. Weeping copiously, he will lament the sad conditions in which public servants work, how terribly abused they are in terms of wages, hours, and other terms and conditions of employment. His contention will be that if only public servants have universally conferred upon them the blessings of collective bargaining all their complaints, all their troubles, will disappear.

Here again, what the public and the legislators need is a good strong dose of fact. The truth of the matter is that the wages of government employees have easily kept up with, when they have not materially surpassed, those of comparable private-sector employees. According to the U. S. Department of Commerce, while state and local government employment was rising by 151 percent between 1951 and 1972, their monthly payrolls increased by 596 percent.

The most detailed and authoritative private reporting service in the field, the Government Employee Relations Report, published by the Bureau of National Affairs, carries, almost each week, news items indicating that government employees are by no means coming out on the short end. There is no need here to place more emphasis upon such extraordinary phenomena as the $17,000 annual wage [1975] recently extracted from the taxpayers by San Francisco's street-sweepers. The average hourly wages of all civil servants for actual working hours are: in Ohio, $4.94; Minnesota, $5.13; Michigan, $6.67; Alaska, $9.53.

Federal Employees

As to employees of the federal government, a December 1974 article in *The Washington Monthly,* interestingly entitled "Government Unions: The New Bullies on the Block," tells an even more dramatic tale concerning the generosity with which public employees are treated. All government wage scales—federal, state, and local—are by law required to be comparable with those prevailing in the private sector. (Incidentally, they have to be if government is to attract employees.) Perhaps the most suggestive fact pointed out by *The Washington Monthly* article is that at least federal government employees are quite markedly outdistancing their colleagues in the private sector:

> ... [F]ederal employees are among the highest-paid workers in the country. One third of all federal workers on GS scale are paid more than $15,000, and receive supplemental benefits equal to a third of their salaries. Officially, federal white-collar employees are supposed to be paid salaries "comparable" to what they would earn in private industry. But in practice, many federal employees, especially those in the middle grades and those just below the highest paid "super grades," are paid significantly more than they would get on the open market. For example, the appropriate salary for all GS-13s is determined by examining only five professions—attorneys, chief accountants, chemists, personnel directors, and engineers. Each of these positions (with the exception of personnel directors) demands greater training and technical skill than most government GS-13s possess. And the federal government has become so top-heavy that, for example, 52 percent of the employees of the Department of Transportation are GS-12s or above. The starting salary for a GS-12 is $18,463.

The Question of Happiness

We hear a great deal about how gravely abused public employees are under the civil service merit system—and how much they would be benefited by replacing that system with union representation. Two comments should suffice here. In the first place, the civil service merit system, now in effect in all public employment, represents the most serious and most comprehensive attempt ever made *anywhere* to insure just treatment of employees on the job. In the second place, the assertion that union representation will insure better, fairer, more humane treatment for employees than the civil service merit system does is *only* assertion. All experience from the private sector seems to indicate that employees represented by unions are, to say the least, no happier or more contented than the vast majority of private-sector employees who have chosen to remain nonunion. By the latest count union members constitute considerably less than one-fourth of the private labor force. Moreover, it is reasonable to believe that a large number of that one-fourth belong to unions only because they must in order to keep their jobs. For something on the order of 80 percent of all collective agreements contain provisions requiring union membership as a condition of employment.

The state of soul or mind called "alienation" may exist in government employment, but it is certainly not confined uniquely to non-union civil servants. In all probability it is a permanent and ineradicable aspect of the human psyche. We live in a universe which we have not made and which we can remold nearer to our desires, apparently, to only a very small degree, if at all. The idea that the brutal, insensitive collectivism which animates unions will provide a cure for alienation is absurd and ridiculous. Alienation is a condition of the *individual* mind or soul; mass, collective action cannot cure it. By expanding the size and scope of the authority of large collectivities at the expense of individual autonomy, compulsory public-sector bargaining is more likely to increase alienation and individual discontent than to reduce it. One thing is certain: forcing civil servants to accept union representation when they do not wish to do so is not going to make them any happier.

Fallacious Premise: The "Private-Sector Analogy"

The factual misrepresentations, rank as they may be, are far less serious than the false premises and lame logic of the drive for compulsory public-sector bargaining laws. We must have such laws in government employment, we are told, because we have them in the private sector, because they have worked so well there to produce industrial peace and worker satisfaction (so they say), and because without them there will be great strife and unrest in government employment.

It is difficult to judge which is worse—the bold and brassy error in these contentions, or the profoundly significant omissions they tend to conceal.

Quite obviously it would not follow that we should have compulsory collective bargaining in the public sector merely because we have it in the private sector—even if the claims made for it in the private sector were true. One would have to establish (at least) that there are no material differences between the public sector and the private sector: no mean task, since, as we shall see, the public and private sectors are basically and radically different in all the ways that matter most.

Before going into that, however, I believe it desirable to make some brief observations about our private-sector labor policies. In the first place, as already noted, only a minor fraction of private-sector employment is subject to collective bargaining, despite the fact that for forty years now the federal government—and especially the National Labor Relations Board—has been doing its best to induce all private-sector employees to accept unionization. Year after year hundreds of thousands of private sector employees have spurned the NLRB's inducements. Moreover they have spurned them in the most definitive manner possible: in secret-ballot elections conducted by the NLRB itself under rules heavily weighted in favor of the unions.

One would need to be out of touch with reality to contend seriously that there is more strife, more labor unrest, or more alienation in the vastly preponderant non-unionized part of private employment than there is in the unionized quarter. In those sectors of private employment where they have taken hold, our compulsory collective bargaining laws have not produced labor peace and harmony, much less consumer-serving productivity. On the contrary, the results have been disastrous in at least six ways.

(1) Our private-sector compulsory collective bargaining policy has condemned countless thousands of working persons who actively oppose union representation to a condition of serfdom by forcing them to accept and to pay for union representation which they do not want.

(2) It has severely hampered and rigidified and thus made much less profitable and efficient many of our basic industries, to the enduring harm of the communities served by those industries.

(3) In the opinion of many if not most of the outstanding econo-mists of this country and of Europe, it has done great damage to the market economy in general and to the interests of workers and con-sumers in particular.

(4) The industries most subject to union control may be character-ized by high nominal wages, but, as in construction and the railroads, they are likewise characterized by extensive and apparently permanent under-employment. A bricklayer's scale of $15 per hour is not all that great if as a result bricklayers are unable to find work.

(5) Our private sector labor policies have placed in the leaders of the big unions enormous political power, power which is normally directed in vicious, antisocial ways. Examples are minimum-wage laws which make supernumeraries of our young people, especially young blacks; and the numerous types of interference with free trade which are pushed mainly by the big unions. In such instances—and in count-less others which could be listed—the leaders of the big unions created by our compulsory collective bargaining policies have set themselves boldly and arrogantly against the best and most humane interests of the community as a whole.

(6) Finally, it is simply untrue to say that the introduction of compulsory collective bargaining statutes in the private sector brought labor peace where strife existed before. Take a look any year at the *Handbook of Labor Statistics,* prepared by the U. S. Bureau of Labor Statistics. Strikes more than doubled the year after the National Labor Relations Act became fully effective. This had to happen. As we shall presently see in more detail, unions are nothing at all if they are not highly professional strike agencies. Encourage unionization and you encourage strikes. It is as simple as that. To believe that this universal truth would not apply in the public sector would be to deny the validity of all relevant experience and assert that reason has become obsolete.

Remove the Coercion

If my all too abbreviated critique of our private-sector experience has any merit at all, it suggests that we should repeal the statutes compelling collective bargaining in the private sector rather than ex-tend them to the public sector. However, even if we were to shut our eyes to that experience, even if we were inclined to agree that compulsory collective bargaining has "worked" in the private sector, it would remain true that universalizing compulsory collective bargaining in the public sector would be an extremely unwise and probably a fatally destructive move.

There is no proper analogy between the public sector and the private sector. Business is one thing. Government is, in every sense relevant to this discussion, entirely and categorically another. As Woodrow Wilson once said, "The business of government is to see that no other organization is as strong as itself; to see that no group of men, no matter what their private business is, may come into competition with the authority of society."

In his Farewell Address, George Washington said that, "The very idea of the right and power of the people to establish government presupposes the duty of every individual to obey the established government."

John Austin, one of the greatest jurists of the last two centuries, understood the concept *sovereignty* as few before or after him have understood it. His position was that "the all-powerful portion of the community which makes laws should not be divisible, that it should not share its power with anybody else."

What these great men were saying is that if government is to serve the role in society which must be served if there is to be *society*—civil order—it must have sovereign, supreme and undiluted, power: power greater than that possessed by any other person, or group, or group of groups.

Where the Analogy Fails

This is the fact which utterly demolishes the private-sector analogy. There is nothing basically destructive of private business in a law, however unwise that law may be, which forces employers to deal collectively with employee representatives on terms and conditions of employment. To repeat: it may be wrong to force dissident private employees to accept unions which they do not want and to compel private employers to bargain collectively with unions when they prefer to deal with their employees individually.

However, no social breakdown occurs as a consequence of compulsory private-sector bargaining. This is true in part because employers are compelled by the nature of things in a free society to bargain with their employees individually or collectively, anyway, if they wish to have employees; in part because few private employers, if any, are inclined to yield without resistance to extreme, anti-economic union demands; in part because private employers rarely if ever provide goods and services which cannot stand interruption for more or less sustained periods; and in part, finally and most importantly, because no private employer occupies a role so central and so indispensable to the survival of civilized society as all our governments—federal, state, and local—do.

Monopoly is normally a bad thing in the private sector. In the public sector undivided, monopoly, sovereign power is absolutely indispensable to any civilized social order. Law is either universal, supreme, and exclusive—or it is nothing. Imagine two competing police forces, two competing armies, two competing judicial systems! The name for such a state of affairs is anarchy, not civilized order.

Because government is and has to be monopolistic in character, it also must perforce stand outside the market. Political considerations, not economic considerations, must direct its activities. The consensus of the whole community, not the private interests of individual producers and consumers, must determine the way in which government operates.

Political Decisions

Government cannot, as private business does, allocate its resources and expenditures on the basis of balance sheet considerations of profit and loss. All its decisions—as to how many police or fire stations or schools or garbage trucks should be bought or employees hired—all such decisions are political decisions. Ludwig von Mises has made the point:

> The objectives of public administration cannot be measured in money terms and cannot be checked by accountancy methods. Take a nationwide police system like the F.B.I. There is no yardstick available that could establish whether the expenses incurred by one of its regional or local branches were not excessive.
>
> In public administration there is no market price for achievements. This makes it indispensable to operate public

offices according to principles entirely different from those applied under the profit motive.

... [The government] must define in a precise way the quality and the quantity of the services to be rendered and the commodities to be sold, it must issue detailed instructions concerning the methods to be applied in the purchase of material factors of production *and in hiring and rewarding labor* ... [Emphasis supplied.]

... It would be utterly impracticable to delegate to any individual or group of individuals the power to draw freely on public funds. It is necessary to curb the power of managers of nationalized or municipalized systems ... if they are not to be made irresponsible spenders of public money and if their management is not to disorganize the whole budget.

It should be obvious by now that—and why—government cannot share with unions its power over the public service and at the same time retain its character as government, responsible to the community consensus alone. Even if decisions concerning the course of government and of government employment could be made jointly by duly elected or appointed officials and union negotiators, there would be a dissolution of sovereignty and a dissipation if not destruction of popular government. But the unfortunate fact is that under compulsory public-sector bargaining there will not be merely a sharing of sovereignty; common sense and experience indicate that the sovereignty is bound to come to rest, ultimately, in the public-sector unions.

Strife Is Assured

I repeat: this is bound to happen. Proponents of compulsory public-sector bargaining contend that it is the only way to eliminate strife and unrest in public employment, but the fact of the matter is that such bargaining is a means of *insuring* strife and unrest, in the government service. From such strife and unrest the public-sector union leaders are bound to emerge in this country—as they already have in England and in Italy—as our ultimate rulers. For, as Henry C. Simons called them, unions are "battle agencies." They have to be. In order to get and keep members, they must continuously seek and bend every effort to get more than the employers of their members are willing to pay. By now, even the dullest observers of this field are aware that politicians and political officials tend to be far more generous with taxpayer money than private businessmen are with stockholders' money. Nevertheless, there comes a point, even in government, when the never-ending demands that unions are compelled to make must be met with a straightforward "No."

What happens then? Well, the history of the last decade is instructive. In order to keep their members, the unions must refuse to take "no" for an answer. Over the last decade the number of public-employee strikes has increased by well over 1100 percent. This is what refusing to take "no" for an answer means among the public sector unions: Striking. And the fact that until just the last year or so (and then in just a few states) public-employee strikes were (and are even now in most states) unlawful—this fact has neither discouraged the union leaders from calling strikes, nor made their members hesitate to participate in them.

If these facts prove anything, they prove that—not the law, not duty to the public, not respect for judicial orders—but union leaders have become for unionized public servants their sovereign liege lords. When I say that widespread adoption of compulsory public-sector bargaining laws will inevitably result in the destruction of popular sovereignty and in its replacement with the virtual anarchy of a sovereignty split among the leaders of the more critically placed public-sector unions, these are the facts and the common sense analyses upon which I rest the prediction.

It is strictly speaking absurd to suggest that compulsory public-sector bargaining laws are needed in order to eliminate strife and unrest in public employment. Before such laws were passed in the late fifties and the sixties, there were no strikes to speak of and no other significant forms of mass unrest in public employment. Before public agencies, especially in such places as New York City, began bargaining collectively with unions representing their employees—i.e., began recognizing unions as exclusive bargaining representatives and thus abdicating to unions the sovereign powers of government—there were no public-sector strikes, none to speak of anyway.

The strife and the unrest have come since unions have been recognized in some states and cities as exclusive bargaining representatives. Significantly, the strife and unrest have been localized in precisely those jurisdictions. It is largely absent in the localities which refuse to recog-

nize unions as exclusive bargaining representatives of public employees. And one may confidently conclude that it would be entirely absent
if militant trade unions were excluded from public sector employment—as a proper respect for the duties and powers of government
would require.

Such a state of affairs—leading to peace and harmony rather than
chaos and war between government and their employees—would not
require that the right of free association be denied to public employees.
Public employees might very well join or even be encouraged to join
associations confined to civil servants. Indeed, as we have seen, ever
since the first civil service laws were passed in this country (and they
are now universal), public servants have been free to form and join
their own civil service organizations.

A Dubious Progression: Chaos to Anarchy to Tyranny

In a drastic reversal of former opinion, state courts all over the
country have been upholding the constitutionality of recently passed
compulsory public-sector bargaining laws. Less than thirty years ago,
the consensus among judges was precisely to the contrary. All across
the land they had been holding that for a public agency to bargain
collectively on the terms and conditions of public employment would
involve an unconstitutional abdication and delegation of governmental
power and thus a betrayal of representative government.

Nowadays, however, we read repeatedly in judicial opinions that
there is nothing wrong in such laws. Some of the state courts have
gone so far as to uphold laws providing for compulsory arbitration of
public-sector labor disputes. Going even further, some have held that
public servants have a right to strike.

Despite these abrupt changes of opinion, however, a curious
movement is afoot among the judges. Several of the courts which have
gone furthest in welcoming the abdication of sovereign power implicit
in compulsory public-sector bargaining laws, have begun quietly and
unobtrusively to see to it that their sovereign powers remain unim-
paired! Some have been holding that court employees are excluded
from the compulsory bargaining laws. Others have been holding that
insofar as court employees are concerned, the proper party to do the
bargaining with them is not a state or local administrative officer, but
the presiding judge.

When the state or local administrative officers object to these decisions, contending, among other things, that they are scarcely likely to get fair hearings on the matter from judges who are themselves interested parties, the courts are brought face to face with the destructive and contradictory character of all compulsory public-sector bargaining laws. They are forced to see willy-nilly that such laws simply cannot be reconciled with any intelligible concept of sovereignty.

In one case the complaining county commissioner charged that the county was being denied due process of law and equal protection of the law because his opponent in the case was a member of the very judiciary which was deciding whether he, the county commissioner, or his opponent, the county judge, was the appropriate bargaining agent! The court could only reply, lamely, that it would do its best to insure a fair hearing.

Approaching a Critical Problem: Judicial Absolutism

Judicial absolutism has long been a problem in this country. Cases such as the ones we have just reviewed indicate that the problem is approaching a critical state. At the moment, the result of the compulsory public-sector bargaining laws prevailing in some of the states is that the ultimate power of government lies in the courts, the least representative branch of government. A number of considerations suggest, however, that this condition is strictly temporary: that before long the ultimate sovereignty will fall to the public-sector union leaders who, besides being representatives of only their own interests, not of the electorate, are not in the slightest degree a legitimate branch of government.

The authors of *The Federalist* knew what they were talking about when they referred to the judiciary as the weakest branch of the government. The judgments and decisions of the judiciary are meaningful only to the extent that the general public respects them and the executive branch of the government enforces them. What can judges do about public-sector strikes? If we are to take experience as our guide, the answer has to be: *nothing*.

To repeat, thousands of public-sector strikes have been called over the last decade—all illegally. However, the illegality made no difference: the unions called the strikes anyway, and, over the years, millions of police officers, firefighters, schoolteachers, garbage collectors, high-way-maintenance men (during blizzards, yet!) went out, apparently stirred only by contempt of the possible court actions against them. Indeed, when a New York court enjoined a garbagemen's strike, their union leader, John DeLury, instead of obeying the injunction, in the words of New York's highest court, "went to the other extreme, actually urged the men to make the strike 'effective 100%.'"

All competent scholars in the labor law field are aware that anti-strike injunctions are almost impossible to enforce, even in the private sector, where, at least, the forces of government are available to attempt to induce respect for the court orders. But what prospect is there for enforcement of a court order against a public-sector union when all civil servants are unionized, as they will be if compulsory collective bargaining laws prevail universally in this country? Who is going to enforce an injunction against a strike by a policeman? The National Guard? The Army?

The situation is even grimmer than the foregoing analysis suggests. In fact, public-sector strikes do such enormous harm in such a brief time that court actions aimed at enjoining them are usually an exercise in futility. Even before the legal papers are filed, the greater part of the damage done by a good many public-sector strikes is already done. The strikers have the community over a barrel. It has to give in. According to one study of events in the experimental laboratory of our subject, the City of New York, the vast preponderance of the public-sector strikes called there never reach the courts at all. The harm they do is so vicious that the striking unions are in a position to extort, as part of the price for going back to work, an agreement from the city authorities not to prosecute the strike, despite its illegality!

The only conclusion possible from the foregoing discussion is that compulsory public-sector bargaining is incompatible with both representative government and the kind of sovereign governmental power needed if we are to live in a free, peaceful, and decently ordered society. Under a universal regime of compulsory public-sector bargaining, the sovereign powers will belong neither to the people nor to their duly elected and appointed representatives. They will be fragmented and dispersed among the most power-hungry leaders of the public-sector unions. Those persons, not our elected representatives, will be our rulers.

Not all of us will be willing to accept them as rulers; indeed, no one in his right mind would accept any of the present leaders of the public-sector unions as his sovereign authority. This being true, the result will have to be, in order: chaos, the situation prevailing when sovereignty is divided among the public-sector union leaders; anarchy, the condition resulting from the refusal by all sensible persons to accept the feudal lordship of the public-sector union leaders; and finally, tyranny, the state of affairs which generally succeeds anarchy because of mankind's insuppressible and ineradicable need of order if life is to proceed at all satisfactorily.

Unemployment, Unions, and Inflation: Of Causation and Necessity

by Sylvester Petro

At a meeting of the Mont Pelerin Society a few years ago, a controversy arose over the inflationary role, if any, of unions. Among the celebrated free-market economists present, all members of the Society founded by Friedrich Hayek shortly after World War II, Milton Friedman led a group which contended that since inflation is strictly a monetary phenomenon, and since unions do not control the money or credit supply, there can be no sense in accusing the union leaders of bringing about inflation, no matter what other sin they might be guilty of. Lawrence Fertig took the other side, with an assist from the English economists present, who pointed out that unions, especially in England, are considerably more than merely worker-representatives in disputes with employers, and.that they have a great deal of influence one way or another, directly or indirectly, over the monetary policies of government.

I contend here that Mr. Fertig and the Englishmen were correct—in fact far more correct than they themselves believed. I will show that unions not only can bring about inflation, but that they absolutely must do so in order to survive in the present context of policy and law, at least in the United States, if not everywhere in the western world.

The Role of Unions

We are hearing a great deal these days from such union leaders as George Meany and Leonard Woodcock of the vicious inhumanity of current monetary and fiscal policy, which, according to them, is dooming millions of Americans to the sterile lives which mass unemploy-

Dr. Petro is the Director of the Institute for Law and Policy Analysis. This article, which appeared in the July 1976 issue of *The Freeman*, has been reprinted with permission from a paper delivered at Arden House in Harriman, New York, at the Fourth Annual Conference of The Committee for Monetary Research and Education, Inc.

ment creates. These men and hosts of other union leaders and supporting politicians and intellectuals blame "greedy" businessmen for inflation and an "insensitive" administration and Federal Reserve Board
for unemployment. Everybody is to blame, it seems, but the unions.
In my opinion there is no hope of a solution of the unemployment-
inflation problem till ruling opinion understands that it is brought
about largely by our labor policies and the power and the predicament
they have created for the big unions.

Admittedly, unions *alone* cannot cause inflation, and if unions dis-
banded, inflation might still occur. Nevertheless, I will show that right
here and now—current national labor policy being what it is—unions
are driven by the instinct of self-preservation to join with other forces
to bring about inflation and that, moreover, they rank today among
the most powerful and pervasive of all the inflationary agencies in the
country.

In a different setting, some other impulse may take over the inflationary role that circumstance, policy, and law presently assign to unions. For so long as we have fiat money and legal-tender laws we shall
have inflation. Politicians and bureaucrats, in office or aspiring, will
never be able to resist the temptations extended by the exciting possibilities inherent in what amounts to a license to engage in counterfeiting. Who could?

But while another agency may in another time provide the impetus—or flick the inflationary switch—unions at present fill the role.
They constitute the pre-eminent political pressure group in the country, and all their pressures coalesce to produce conditions in which the
inflationary measures so congenial to power-hungry bureaucrats and
demagogic politicians become politically propitious if not mandatory.

I. Inflation Defined in Search for Its Causes

Certain aspects of the controversy concerning unions and inflation
trace to unnecessary terminological difficulties and to confusion over
the causation question.

Some define "inflation" as a general increase in price levels, others
as any increase in the money supply, whether or not such an increase
results in generally higher prices. Let us call the first usage "price-
inflationism" and the second "money-inflationism."

In this paper I adopt the "money-inflationist" definition, and I do so because it advances and clarifies analysis—a plenty good reason for preferring one definition over another—while the price-inflationist usage fails to do so, or to do so as well. Thus a price-inflationist is likely to believe that he has exhausted inquiry when he discovers (if he ever does) that a necessary pre-condition to a rise in the general level of prices is an increase in the quantity of money (in the broad sense) greater than the concurrent increase in productivity. He is likely to announce that *the cause* of inflation has been located and that the cure lies simply in keeping the money machine from cranking out *excessive* increases in the money supply.

There is a fine and perhaps even appealing technical rigor to the analysis, but it is nevertheless seriously deficient, and if one adopts the money-inflationist definition, this deficiency appears immediately. Whereas the price-inflationist may say that inflation is *caused* by an abnormal increase in the money supply, the money-inflationist says that inflation is an abnormal increase in the money supply. Thus, whereas the price-inflationist's causal search ends quickly, the money-inflationist's only begins with his definition. The price-inflationist stops thinking when he concludes that abnormal increases in the money supply cause prices to rise generally. The money-inflationist, on the contrary, is compelled to begin thinking at the point where the price-inflationist stops.

The money-inflationist must ask himself: what is it that induces a nation to want—or even merely to accept—a policy of deliberately tampering with the quantity and hence the objective exchange value of money (in the broad sense which includes all fiduciary media)? Surely the laws against counterfeiting bespeak a general understanding among the citizenry of the seriousness of counterfeiting as a species of theft. Consider the comments of Tom Buell, the Tory counterfeiter in Kenneth Roberts' novel, *Oliver Wiswell*, written about the Revolutionary War from the point of view of American loyalists. Completely contemptuous of the rebels and of the mob rule and demagogy favored by many of them, Buell sneered at the near-worthlessness of their fiat currency and considered the dollar bills he produced on his own press in every significant respect as good as those which Congress forced people to accept as legal tender. Said Buell of the Continental forty-dollar bill:

That's all it's worth now. . . . That's all it'll ever be worth, after a few more people find out what it's worth, meaning nothing. My forty-dollar bills are just as good as Congress' forty-dollar bills, neither me nor Congress having anything to make 'em good with, so I got just as much right to issue 'em as Congress has. The rebels called themselves a government, didn't they, even though you and I and a million other Americans didn't want 'em to do it, and knew they hadn't any business to? All right: I'm a government, too, Oliver! I'm the government of New India, up on Passamaquoddy Bay! This money of mine, it's the legal currency of New India, and I raised it by taxing myself. If I was a private individual, I'd be more careful; but being as I'm a government, I'm privileged to make a God-damned fool of myself in any way I choose, especially by spending a lot more money than I've got or ever will have, and promising to do things that I ain't got a chance of doing.

Neither politicians, nor bureaucrats, nor citizens are about to accept Buell's position and allow free printing of dollar bills. While that much is obvious, its implications and the questions they raise are not. Why do we all approve of the laws prohibiting counterfeiting while the vast majority of Americans—including distinguished economists—continue to approve the activities of the Federal Reserve Board, even though, from the point of view of economic law, there is no difference between an increase in the monetary supply brought about by discreet counterfeiting and one brought about by the Federal Reserve Board. (I would go further and say there is no difference from the point of view of sound law, either, but that is another subject.)

Flicking the Switch

The explanation lies in a set of facts from an examination of which the inflationary character of our current unionism clearly emerges. Before we go into detail, however, it seems useful to say something about causation for the benefit of those who believe that only the activities of the legal monetary authority—the Federal Reserve System and its satellite banks—can cause inflation.

If, when I flick the switch, the light goes on, is it not meaningful and, in a certain sense at least, correct to say that I have caused the light to go on? I have not been the sole and sufficient cause; there have been many others: the architect, the building contractor, the electrician, the scientists who learned something about the natural forces which we call electrical, the natural forces themselves, and on and on to the impenetrable and inexplicable mystery which the ancients called the unmoved mover.

Yet it remains true that I have been the specific cause in the particular case. For despite their significance and the indispensable character of their contributions, the other elements in the causal chain did not produce the result; but for my willed and deliberate action the light would not have come on. I, therefore, have been *the cause that matters;* they, relative to me, have been only the *conditions* within which my causal impulse has been operative.

In the same way, unions are among the causes that matter in producing inflation. To repeat, if we were to abandon fiat-money policies, unions could not bring about inflation; but then nothing else could, either—except reinstatement of the fiat-money system. In the kind of fiat-money system we have, the Federal Reserve Board, the printers it employs, the paper manufacturers, and the other means by which it transmits its money-and-credit-increasing policies—they all occupy the same position that the architects, electricians, natural laws, and so forth occupy in the production of light when the switch is flicked.

Let us call them *conditions* in which causes may be operative, rather than causes themselves. The term "cause" we shall reserve for teleological agents—persons who bring about certain results because those results are congruent with or necessary to their purposes.

Who Activates the Presses?

In an inquiry of the present nature, this is the only kind of causal analysis which makes any sense. We are not concerned particularly to discover laws of nature or of economics; we don't care about printing technology. What we want to do, if possible, is to eliminate inflation because it threatens the survival of society; and in order to eliminate it we know that we must fix responsibility with precision among the human actors involved—simply because that is the only area susceptible to the kind of corrective available to us. For example we should find the problem insoluble if, by some perversity, nature inflicted upon every commodity which we adopted as a medium of exchange the same disease of uncontrollable proliferation which afflicts fiat money.

Instead of stopping with the Federal Reserve Board and its quasi-counterfeiting capacities, then, we must ask: who or what turns the Federal Reserve Board on? When we have answered that question we shall have fixed responsibility for the inflation we are suffering now.

The ultimate cause—the prime mover—is, speaking comprehensively, the desire to have a booming economy, in which there are high wages, high profits, and no unemployment, combined with the belief that poverty and unemployment must be combatted by easy money, or by deficit spending which amounts to the same thing.

* * * * *

To sum up the discussion thus far: in the fiat-money system now operative in the United States, increases in the money supply may be the immediate "material cause" of inflation, *but the ultimate causes lie in those agencies whose activities bring about states of affairs which prevailing opinion believes can be cured only or best by inflationary increases in the money supply.*

II. Enter, the Unions

Unions fit into this scheme of things as the actors who do and must bring about the conditions which, in the current state of opinion, can be cured only by easy money. As the chief (though by no means unique) producers and promoters of industrial and financial stagnation and hence of unemployment and misery and poverty; as the most tireless advocates of trade-restrictionism and governmental-expansionism, especially by way of deficit-spending; and finally, as the most powerful, arrogant, and aggressive political force in the country—our trade unions are easily entitled to be called the pre-eminent teleological agents of the inflation now loose in the country. For their prime directive, the chief purpose of their actions—their own survival and aggrandizement—forces them to hit the inflationary switches constantly. In a more sensible frame of labor law and labor policy, unions would have no more power to bring about inflation than any other private agency; but as matters now stand, they are forced by their determination to survive as the beneficiaries of extensive special privilege to bring about states of affairs which produce inflationary increases in the money supply more or less directly.

In order to make the analysis reasonably complete and convincing, I must establish (1) that unions have the power to bring about the conditions which current opinion is determined to remedy by inflationary measures, and (2) that in the current structure of law and policy unions *must* create those conditions, if they wish to survive. When these things are established we shall understand (3) why unions as political agencies engage in inflationary activities and promote inflationary policies.

Compulsory Collective Bargaining

Taken all in all, the current structure of labor law and labor policy is a vast and infernally complex machine for eliminating all competition in labor markets by promoting compulsory and monopolistic collective bargaining. The ultimate objectives are variously stated—to produce "industrial peace," to eliminate "commerce-impairing strikes," to equalize bargaining power between powerful employers and powerless employees, or, by "taking wages out of competition," to get for workers higher wages and better working conditions than they are able to get by individual bargaining on free labor markets.

This is not the place for a detailed description of the many ways in which prevailing law and policy create in unions the power to secure for their members wages and other labor returns higher than those which would prevail in free labor markets. A brief account of two of the most significant features will have to suffice as illustrations.

The first and in my opinion the most significant source of monopolistic union power derives from the virtually universal failure of governments in the United States to prevent unionists from violently excluding competitive workers. A great deal of nonsense is heard on this subject. It has been fashionable, for example, to say that "labor violence" is now a thing of the past, and that such violence as existed in the past was mainly the doing of vicious anti-union employers. Both assertions are sheer fabrications.

There is at least as much violence going on now in labor relations as there ever has been, maybe more—and this in spite of the fact that relatively few employers, having learned the sad lessons of the past, dare come to a confrontation by operating plants during strikes. If they do, you can win money betting that there will be violent attempts by the strikers to keep the plants from operating. And in the past, exactly as now, the aggressors have always been the strikers and their union leaders. Consider the fate of the "liberal," pro-union, pro-collective bargaining *Washington Post* in its recent dispute with its printers.

Such occasional employer violence as has existed has always been in the nature of self-defense, a fact which emerges from even the many biased histories of labor violence, if closely read. For the authors of such works are really saying that employers are in the wrong when they "provoke" union violence by rejecting demands for a "living wage," or when they hire private police to protect their plants against violent strike aggression.

Employers would be guilty of the aggressive kinds of violence common to unions only if they went forward violently to compel strikers to return to work. This they have never done, and have never even been accused of doing.

Monopolistic Wages

Strike violence produces monopolistic wage structures—wage rates higher than would otherwise prevail—by denying competitive workers access to the labor markets in question. It analyzes out as no different from any other exclusive franchise or monopoly grant. The same is true of the other basic and equally destructive special privilege that unions possess—this one granted them by contemporary labor relations legislation: *exclusive representative status*. If a union gains the support of a majority of employees in an appropriate bargaining unit, that union becomes the exclusive bargaining representative of all employees in the unit, no matter how small and contrived the majority may be, no matter how egregiously the NLRB may rig the election, no matter how outrageously the bargaining unit may be gerrymandered.

As exclusive bargaining representative, the union is, so long as it retains such status (an important qualification, as we shall see), what may be called an intra-unit monopolist. It is the only agency that the employer may legally deal with over wages, hours, and other terms and conditions of employment. The employer may not even discuss with dissident employees in the unit any subject which comes within the legally mandatory bargaining range.

If the collective bargaining comes to a bona fide "impasse" (a literally indefinable condition) the employer is privileged technically to offer directly to the employees the same wages and other terms and conditions which the union has rejected, but if he departs from them at all he is certain to be held guilty of an unfair practice and ordered to resume bargaining with the union. Probably other more or less serious penalties will be imposed.

If he is guilty of no unfair practice during or after the impasse, he is privileged to lock out the unionists, and they are privileged to strike. However, if there is a strike, and if the employer attempts to keep the business going during the strike by offering striker-replacements terms of employment which the union has rejected, in 99 cases out of a hundred there will be vandalism and violence—which the police will in more cases than not be either unwilling or unable to prevent or control.

Of the numerous cases I have read about or observed first hand, I can say with confidence that in not a single one has a resisted strike been free of violence and intimidation, overt or covert. By necessary inference, the terms and conditions of employment negotiated under the regime of the exclusive representation principle, complemented by the virtual legitimization of union violence in bargaining impasses, must therefore be regarded as containing a monopoly premium. Labor costs under such a system *must* be higher than they would be in freely competitive labor markets.

Collective bargaining must not only produce a monopoly premium in the form of labor returns higher than those which would have been forthcoming from individual bargaining. Much more importantly, from the point of view of the union leadership, the existing union members must be convinced that they have made such a monopoly gain. Otherwise they will leave the union, and the union leadership would, by virtue of the laws which gave it to them, lose their status and power.

Leaders Must Convince Members Concerning Monopoly Gains

We reach here a critical point. If they wish to retain power, union leaders must convince their members that they have been the beneficiaries of monopoly gains. But such gains carry with them as an inseparable cost that which is implicit in every significant monopoly: namely, a reduction in the production which would have occurred but for the monopoly condition. The necessary consequence of monopolistic la-

bor returns is relative unemployment. The cost of compulsory, monopolistic collective bargaining is continuous and progressive unemployment. No union leader can stop with one monopoly gain. His
members are not content to continue paying dues forever on the
strength of one large increase in the past. Each union member is always
asking of his leadership: "What have you done for me *lately?*"

Hence union leaders under current labor law and policy are driven
to a never-ending career of monopolistic wage-setting. This is another
way of saying that they are doomed eternally to use every political,
economic, and physical measure available which will tend to (a) produce as many employment opportunities for their members as possible
and (b) to eliminate as many contenders for those employment opportunities as possible. Like all monopolists, unions must be interested
equally in the shape of their demand and supply curves.

Besides their vital interest in eliminating as much competitive labor
as possible and expanding job opportunities to the greatest possible
extent for their own members, union leaders are driven by one more
unremitting goad: they must keep alive the destructive myths and
superstitions upon which class-warfare thrives.

If the union leaders for one moment admitted to their members
the obvious truth that employers and employees are bound together
by the strongest bonds of mutual and reciprocal self-interest known
to mankind—perhaps exceeding even the family bond—the party
would be over as far as the union leaders were concerned. They might
continue to exist in certain special cases, but as founts of the kind of
glory, power, opulence, and influence which they now enjoy, they
would be ciphers.

Once employees learned that they have deeper and more permanent common interests with their employers than they do with their
union leaders, unions as we now know them would be no more.
Hence, the third of the ineluctable necessities which account for the
inflationary activities of unions is the necessity to discredit and to
undercut the business community and to deride the rights and privileges indispensable to the survival of the enterprise system.

III. Political Action of Unions

Having now examined the imperatives at work in the quest among
labor leaders for survival and power, let us observe the union leaders

in political action. For in doing so we shall be able to doublecheck the analysis thus far. If we find that their political activities fall dominantly in the categories of (1) elimination of competitive labor, (2) creation of as many jobs as possible, useless or not, for their own members, and (3) advancement of measures designed to debilitate the enterprise system, we can be fairly confident that we have been correct. Furthermore, if we find that all their activities add up to conditions in which inflationary measures are made politically irresistible, then we can be sure that we have been correct on that score, too.

A standard economic analysis holds that unions cannot be responsible for inflation because if they push labor costs and hence prices above market levels in the sectors where they have monopoly power, the ensuing unemployment, owing to labor mobility, tends to push wages and hence prices *down* in the competitive sectors. Thus no *general* increase in wages and prices (and no "inflation" as that term is often defined) occurs. As Albert Rees put it, unionism "alters the wage structure in a way that, impedes the growth of employment in sectors of the economy where productivity and income are naturally high and that leaves too much labor in low-income sectors of the economy."

All right as far as it goes, the analysis does not go far enough. The economics are sound, but the more significant political analysis is nonexistent. Unions are not content to let the unhampered market take care of the unemployment they have created. They are not content to do so because they cannot afford to do so. Experience and common-sense economics have taught them that their positions are fatally threatened whenever and wherever they leave labor markets free.

Unions cannot afford to have vast numbers of unemployed overhanging the labor market, even if they are able to erect impenetrable monopolistic walls around the sectors of the labor market that they wish to control. The free enterprise system is too flexible, too resilient, too adaptable, too mobile. If they leave freedom anywhere, the stultified, monopolized areas will soon die, as the textile industry has died in New England only to emerge more productive than ever in the still nonunion South. The only way they can retain their monopolies, the union leaders have found, is by destroying these characteristics of the system, and hence the system itself. Never take the anti-Communist, anti-fascist protestations of the union leaders and their economic advisers and apologists seriously. They may not know what kind of a system they are building, but disinterested observation should certainly be able to see how their efforts, intentionally or not, are destroying the enterprise system.

Eliminate Competition

Unions are preoccupied first and foremost to eliminate entirely from all labor markets any competition that would endanger their monopoly positions. This motivation explains the overwhelming energies they expend in promoting laws forbidding child labor and fixing minimum wages high enough to reduce white teenage labor and virtually to nullify black teenage labor. It also explains the otherwise inexplicable union pressure for welfare payments so high that they create a permanent corps of unemployed. And there is no need to say much here about union efforts to eliminate competition from imports, for these are a way to eliminate competition from foreign workers, just as high minimum-wage laws eliminate competition from marginal domestic workers. Everyone should be able to think of other such competition-excluding political pressures by unions.

What has to be grasped here is that if unions do not in one way or another either exclude people entirely from labor markets or bribe them to quit looking for work, the enterprise system is bound to put them to work, provided the private sector is allowed to retain some of the capital it creates. One might think that unions would find it desirable to promote all political measures designed to provide ever-increasing private-sector employment: reduction of corporate taxes, elimination of capital-gains taxes, allowance of realistic accounting, removal of nonsensical and debilitating regulatory schemes, and so on. The only possible reason for their thus far successful opposition to such obviously beneficial policies is that they cannot afford either to let the enterprise system run loose or to admit that capitalists and entrepreneurs are by far the best if not indeed the only members of society who can be called uniquely consumer-servants. If they allowed the enterprise system to run loose, it would soon seal them off, leaving them in little pockets of scar tissue, and the action would move to the areas in which they lacked monopoly power.

In fact, something like that is going on right now. In spite of our determined efforts over the last generation to destroy the enterprise system, it is still producing and, closer to our purpose, it is simply going around the unions. Consider companies such as I.B.M. with no unions at all; G.E., no more than half-unionized; the construction industry, where unions are losing ground day by day; the printing industry, likewise. Consider also the flight of the textile industry to the nonunion South, already mentioned. Consider finally that even in the representation elections often rigged by the National Labor Relations Board in favor of unions, year after year at least one-half of the votes, and usually more, are against union representation.

Yes, indeed, union leaders, like all legally sheltered monopolists, have much to fear from the unhampered market economy.

Preserve Jobs for Members

Besides the necessity of ousting as much competitive labor as possible, unions are faced with the need of preserving as many jobs for their own members as they can. If they do not, they cannot hope to keep the power-base so vital to the political influence and the economic affluence which they cherish. This inexorable drive also must be channeled along destructive ways. Their class-warfare anti-capitalism and their promises of labor returns higher than those produced by competitive labor markets prevent them from encouraging the growth of employment in constructive and productive ways. So how do they direct their awesome political influence?

While innumerable examples of destructive political action by unions are available, let us focus attention on only two of their most recent endeavors. The first is the common-situs picketing bill. Readily available facts demonstrate that the unions spent enormous sums in the form of political contributions to get the bill passed. Its obvious purpose was to preserve as many jobs as possible for unionized construction workers—jobs which the unions themselves had helped to destroy directly by the monopolistic wage structures in construction that they have created and indirectly by the many measures they have supported which have contributed to the general debility of the economy.

Persons unfamiliar with the field might find it hard to believe that unions should be interested in pushing a bill which, but for the President's veto, was bound in the long run to hurt rather than help the construction industry. The explanation is simple. The unions are not interested in the health of the construction industry—or for that matter any other industry; despite their protestations, they are not interested in full employment. They are interested only in such employment as strengthens or preserves their power base. And that is why they pushed so hard for the common-situs picketing bill. It would have reduced private construction employment, but, and this is the only thing the union leadership cared about, it would have reinforced their monopolistic control of such employment as remained. And they would resort to further political action to soak up the unemployment attendant upon the situs picketing bill.

The six-billion-dollar public works bill, also passed overwhelmingly by a union-dominated Congress but vetoed, provides an example of the way in which unions thus act to soak up by political means the unemployment they play a critical role in creating by the exercise of legislatively granted monopoly powers. There can be no doubt about the fact that the unions were the most powerful and persistent lobbyists for this measure, for again available records attest to the influence they exerted. And again there can be no question but that the unions pushed for this bill because it promised to relieve some of the unemployment among union members that the unions have themselves created.

Promote Inflationary Measures

The six-billion-dollar public works bill is extremely significant to our present inquiry. Besides showing how unions are compelled somehow to compensate for the unemployment they create, if they are to preserve their power base, it shows also how the unions are compelled to compensate by inflationary measures, not by measures which would at once combat inflation and contribute to the health of the economy.

Observe the political trap. On the one hand, unions cannot possibly push for measures which would encourage the growth of private capital without exposing the myth by which they survive—the myth, that is, that workers and employers are natural antagonists, that the "trickle-down" theory of universal prosperity is a cruel hoax. On the other hand, they cannot push for public works and other governmental spending programs financed only by taxation, because in order to keep their bamboozled members, already overtaxed as they are, they must resist higher taxation of the "middle class," and they know that the rich, no matter what union demagogues say on the subject, are already taxed to the limit.

Albert Shanker, president of the American Federation of Teachers, documented this point in a recent news release in which he expressed "strong support" for a bill in Congress which would provide emergency aid to local school districts facing severe budget crises[1]. Everybody knows that the teachers' unions are mainly responsible for the budgetary crises of the schools. Everybody also knows that local taxation has about reached the limit and that everywhere local communities are voting down bond referenda designed to produce public-school financing. In these conditions, Shanker had no alternative but to support legislation which would provide federal government financing of the local public-school deficits.

And where is the federal government to get the funds with which to finance all the unemployment which the unions are compelled to create if they wish to retain power? Let us review the ground we have covered, adopting the point of view of a union leader who is naturally concerned to preserve the economic and political powers which have accrued to him:

- a. He has a monopoly position from which he derives satisfying economic affluence and heady political influence.
- b. This monopoly position absolutely depends upon a conviction among the workers he represents that they derive greater returns from collective bargaining than they would from individual bargaining.
- c. Such a conviction can be preserved only by persuading workers (i) that employers and free labor markets are their natural antagonists and (ii) that militant unionism is the only possible means of achieving higher than market wages.
- d. Higher-than-market wages cannot possibly be gained without creating significant unemployment.
- e. The workers unemployed by monopolistic wage structures cannot be left free to overhang the market, for if they are it will be impossible for unions to produce monopolistic wage settlements. In short, the union leaders must strive endlessly to immobilize the competitive or potentially competitive workers, and they must do this by governmental subsidies and proscriptions, not by measures which encourage the growth of private capital.
- f. Thus unions must push endlessly for minimum-wage laws, tariffs, ever-increasing unemployment compensation, high and early pensions, profligate welfare programs, and all

other conceivable devices for keeping potentially competitive workers out of labor markets.

- g. At the same time, they must find some way to maximize the employment of the number of members they need in order to preserve a credible economic and political power base.
- h. Since state, local, and federal tax sources are now for all practical purposes exhausted, only one source of funding remains: federal deficit-spending financed by inflationary increases in the money supply.

IV. A Case in Point: The Humphrey-Hawkins Bill

I believe I have made my point: unions not only do but must cause inflation; indeed, in the current structure of labor law and policy they are absolutely constrained to do so if they wish to survive.

It will be useful, I believe, to conclude with a discussion of a union-backed measure which ties the unions even more closely to the inflationary process. I refer to the Humphrey-Hawkins Full Employment Bill. A recent story in *The New York Times* about this bill shows how it provides us with a perfect paradigm. *The Times*[2] said that:

> Representatives of three centers of influence in the Democratic Party—the A.F.L.-C.I.O., the Congressional Black Caucus, and Senator Hubert H. Humphrey of Minnesota—have been quietly negotiating for weeks in an effort to draft legislation that would commit the Government to create a job for everyone who wants to work.

The obvious purpose of the bill, as it seems to me, is to rid the unions forever of any fear that they will be held responsible for the unemployment they create. An equally obvious purpose, though not yet completely worked out, is to eliminate any possibility that the Federal Reserve Board will ever pursue deflationary policies, or even merely anti-inflationary policies. As *The Times* story has it, the bill:

> would augment the Employment Act of 1946 ... by requiring the President to propose and Congress to pass, each year,

specific numerical goals for employment, economic growth, and changes in the price level. . . .

The subjects to be covered by the annual economic policy resolution would include the monetary policy to be followed by the Federal Reserve System.

There you have it. The Federal Reserve Board has been called an engine of inflation. Because of union sponsorship of the Humphrey-Hawkins Bill, the *Times* story suggests that there is no hope of getting the AFL-CIO. "to agree to any provisions . . . that appear to be imposing restrictions on the ability of unions to seek higher wages for their members." So if the Federal Reserve Board is an engine of inflation, we know who the engineer will be. And this should put an end to debate over the causation issue.

One of the more repugnant features of these unlovely times is that the union leaders who have succeeded in selling so many intellectuals a bill of goods are in their petty pursuit of affluence and influence getting away with measures which not only abuse simple workingmen but also are likely to destroy the economy. A particularly ugly touch is added to this repulsive picture by the cooperation of the Black Congressional Caucus. There can be no doubt that the big monopolistic unions have been the worst enemy that American blacks as a whole have had since 1865. If the Humphrey-Hawkins Bill is passed and enforced, the condition of American blacks is likely to be even worse than it was before 1865. They are likely to become permanent wards of the State, and it won't make things any better that we'll all be in the same position.

---

1. American Federation of Teachers, News Release, February 3, 1976.
2. *The New York Times,* p. 1, February 16, 1976.

Employee Ownership: A Rapidly Growing Threat to a Free Market

by Dwight D. Murphey

In the first nine months of 1989, nearly 80 of the "Fortune 500" companies established Employee Stock Ownership Plans (ESOPs) involving shares worth more than $15 billion. Prompted by a decision of the Delaware Supreme Court that ESOPs can be used to forestall hostile takeovers, the massive growth of employee ownership in 1989 accelerated what already had been a rapid rate of growth.[1] In one of the fastest structural changes that has ever occurred in the American economy, the move toward employee ownership had by 1987 resulted in between 7,000 and 8,000 ESOP companies, involving between 11 and 13 million workers.[2] There were virtually no ESOPs before the push for employee ownership began in 1974.

With such a start, employee ownership will soon become a major economic constituency in the United States—and, as we shall see, an ideological and political constituency as well. Each ESOP is an institutionalized framework for a continuing increase in the amount of employee ownership. If the trend continues, the near future will see the creation of ESOPs at tens of thousands of companies. Each will lead to a growing presence of employee ownership.

The mechanics of an ESOP are simple. It begins with a business firm's creating a trust. The firm transfers stock in itself to the trust, with the company's own employees as the beneficiaries. In a "leveraged" ESOP, the trust obtains the shares by borrowing from a bank and using the money to pay the company for the stock. The company serves as guarantor on the bank loan. As an important part of all this, federal law gives major tax breaks both to the company and to the bank.

What has caused this phenomenon? Three related factors: massive government intervention to prefer ESOPs with billions of dollars in

Dwight D. Murphey is editor of *Universitas,* the journal of University Professors for Academic Order and author of several books on social and political philosophy. This article appeared in the July 1990 issue of *The Freeman.*

tax breaks; the desire of the business community to emulate the Japanese through greater employee participation and company loyalty, as well as to use ESOPs for their tax advantages and as a way to fight takeovers; and a good deal of feverish effort by the media, the academic community, and the American Left to popularize employee ownership at a time when there has been virtually no awareness of danger among free market proponents.

Sixteen major pieces of federal legislation since 1974 have created tax breaks and other preferential treatment for employee ownership. State legislatures have joined in by declaring public policies in favor of employee ownership and creating other preferences and tax incentives.

The rush toward employee ownership is part of a worldwide phenomenon. The world Left pushes it as part of its renewed interest in "workers' control" as the centerpiece of democratic socialism. Employee ownership is important to socialist policies both in Western Europe and in the countries emerging from the Soviet cocoon.

At the same time, ironically, many leaders of American conservatism have spoken up for employee ownership. Unaware of the dangers, they see it as a way to "involve employees in capitalism" and also to "privatize" governmentally owned enterprises both inside and outside the United States.

The purpose of this article is to sound an alarm. Employee ownership poses a serious and expanding threat to a free market.

"Workers' Control"

Since the danger emanates from the Left, it cannot be fully appreciated without understanding the role that "workers' control" has played in a century and a half of socialist thought.

The various forms of "decentralized socialism" proposed by nineteenth-century socialist thinkers are relevant today because the decline of Soviet prestige in the world intellectual community since World War II has resulted in a renewal of those earlier socialist models. During the period between the Bolshevik Revolution in 1917 and approximately 1947, those earlier models were eclipsed in the imaginations of most socialists by a highly idealized perception of the Soviet example, which involved a centralized state socialism under the dictatorship of the Communist party.

The inspiration for most models of "decentralized" socialism came from the French socialist Pierre Joseph Proudhon (1809–1865). Proudhon, famous for his statement that "property is theft," advocated organizing the economy around "mutualist associations." The associations were to be funded by low-interest government loans ("social credit").

Among the followers of Proudhon was the Russian socialist N. G. Chernyshevsky (1828–1889). In his famous novel *What Is to Be Done?* (a title later copied by Lenin), Chernyshevsky idealized the image of a workshop that its owner had turned over to its employees. Again, "social credit" was to provide the funds.

In France prior to the revolutionary tumult in 1848, Louis Blanc called for worker-owned producers' cooperatives called "social workshops." He, too, wanted them financed by the state through social credit. Later in France, Georges Sorel, a syndicalist, wanted French society run by confederation of trade union associations.

Perhaps most important, certainly so far as its impact on socialist and liberal thought in the United States was concerned, was the British Guild Socialist movement early in the twentieth century. Foremost among its popularizers was G. D. H. Cole. Guild Socialists wanted each industry organized into a "guild." These in turn would form a confederation of industries. There would be two parliaments—one representing people in their capacity as producers, the other as consumers.

We should note that each of these types of "decentralized" socialism isn't really decentralized at all—but is rather a blueprint for centralized power. While calling for local collectives under one name or another, proponents want the collectives brought together into industry-wide, and then national, networks. Mussolini did precisely that with his "Corporazioni." The network then provides what is, in essence even if not in name, a state. The "rational planning" that socialists crave is done through the confederation.

It was Guild Socialism that led to the great "Industrial Democracy" vogue within American "liberalism" between 1910 and approximately 1925. The journal *The New Republic* was established in late 1914 and for several years was the principal sounding board for Guild Socialism. Although *The Nation* focused mostly on international issues, it, too, promoted Guild Socialism after Oswald Garrison Villard became its owner and editor in 1918.

The Soviet example absorbed the attention of the world Left after 1917, although it took until about 1925 for Guild Socialism to go fully out of fashion. Since World War II, however, there has been a major socialist literature both in Western Europe and the United States making workers' control a principal element.

One socialist author wrote in 1968 that "for socialists and radicals who mean business, workers' control has already become the central strategic axis. . . ."[3] In 1973, another spoke of "the growing worldwide movement for workers' control" and called it "the central issue of class struggle in our generation."[4] A book by Christopher Gunn in 1984 treats "workers' self-management" as a way "of linking ideological, grass-roots, and spontaneous resistance to capitalism." He expressed the hope that "it may offer the potential for creation of a new socialist politics. . . ."[5]

Distinctions Without a Difference

Confusion often arises between "employee ownership," "workers' control," and "workers' self-management." Though related, these aren't identical. What should be emphasized, however, is that it is largely a matter of "distinctions without a difference."

Conceptually, it is possible for employees to own a company while not controlling it. Here, they would acquiesce in continuing control by, perhaps, the prior management. Although it is often assumed that employee ownership won't displace existing management, there are compelling reasons to think that the employees eventually will assert control. The very existence of majority ownership creates a moral, as well as a legal, right to control. There is an articulate pressure from the Left for employees to exercise that right. "Workers' control" will no doubt become a major factor in the American economy once the thousands of ESOP firms reach the "tipping point" at which the employees own a majority interest.

Whether the employees will then delegate management functions to directors of their own choosing or will undertake to manage themselves by committee or by some other form of "participatory democracy" depends upon the choices the employees make after they have control.

Oddly enough, employee ownership and the workers' control that results are compatible, at least in theory, with all three economic models: a market economy, state interventionism, and socialism.

The theoretical model of a free market certainly doesn't bar firms that are owned and run by the same people. Sole proprietorships, partnerships, and many small corporations already meet that description.

This compatibility assumes, however, that certain distorting factors won't be present. It assumes that the worker-owned firms will have come about freely through market choices and freedom of contract, not through massive state intervention.

It presupposes also that the worker-owned firms won't harbor an ideological virus that will make them a transitional vehicle to socialism or to further interventionism. It would not be compatible with a free market for them ideologically to invoke "labor solidarity" and to demand the abolition of the type of firms where owners hire employees. Socialists have long attacked such businesses, which involve the much-hated "wage relation," "absentee ownership," and "making of 'surplus value'" (the socialist name for an employer's profit).

But the question of purely theoretical compatibility isn't the major issue to pose about workers' control today. The more important query is: What are the realistic prospects, given the world we live in today? Is there any reasonable expectation that employee ownership, leading to workers' control, will really serve free market purposes?

The answer, unfortunately, must be that, "no, there is none." This is true both outside and inside the United States.

1. Outside the United States. Workers' control isn't a feasible transition to a market economy in Eastern Europe or the Third World. It merely substitutes one form of socialism—the misnamed "decentralized socialist" models we have just examined—for another. Given the predominance of the Left in much of the world, workers' control will take its place as a form of "democratic socialism."

If under present circumstances it proves to be a more humane type of socialism—one that actually has "a human face"—that is to be desired, so far as it goes. But it is a tragedy for the peoples of the Third World or those emerging from Soviet domination to become enmeshed in yet another round of the economic wastefulness and inefficiency that long and painful experience shows typify every sort of socialism.

Workers' control is inefficient to the extent that it is socialist. If "privatization" occurs through a movement into workers' control, entrepreneurs will continue to be victims of ideological hostility and state blockage if they go outside the "workers' control" model. And the "rational planning" that even a democratic socialism will employ will interpose all sorts of obstacles to free market activity.

How much better it will be if "privatization" can be of a sort that will move Eastern Europe and the Third World into a true free market system! It will avoid millions of people's having to go through yet another painful cycle during which the lessons of economics—hammered home forcefully to the world recently by the utter failure of the Soviet economy—have to be learned all over again.

2. In the United States. It is unlikely that the rush into employee ownership will actually lead to socialism in this country. Despite everything that the American Left will foreseeably do to bring that about, the inefficiencies of workers' control almost certainly will prevent it from displacing the customary forms of enterprise.

Disappointment comes when workers have reached majority ownership but then delegate management functions to others. They have found in the past that "we haven't really gained anything, since one boss is pretty much like another."

Inefficiency comes when workers seek to self-manage the company "by committee" or through the chaos of "democratic participation." Factionalism, the tedium of decision-through-infinite-discussion, and in-house politics have been found to destroy the viability of many such enterprises in the past.[6]

Danger Ahead

If a socialist victory doesn't threaten us, what, then, is the danger? The answer is twofold:

Even though the Left won't be able to use workers' control to displace other forms of enterprise, it will be able to work constantly to mold employee ownership into an ideologized constituency. The past half-century has seen the secular decline of labor unions as a hostile institution within a free market. Now, however, we are threatened with a movement for "industrial democracy" that will be potentially even more hostile. Do we really want to see that happen?

To the extent that the Left imbues employee ownership with its ideology, an extra dimension will have been added to a movement that already will have become, for other reasons, a powerful economic and political constituency in the interventionist system we have today.

206 / Dwight D. Murphey

Even without ideological content, ESOPs are quickly creating one of our larger interest groups. When tens of millions of people come to be encompassed within "employee ownership," the movement will possess vast political power.

The intervention that is most immediately foreseeable is one that is utterly incompatible with a free market: that the government will no longer be able to allow any of the thousands of employee-owned firms to fail (or will have to compensate the employees in each firm for the enterprise's failure). Why? Because by subsidizing and encouraging a type of employee "fringe benefit" that lacks diversification, the government has since 1974 caused millions of people to rely upon a precarious form of asset for their ultimate security in retirement. An irresistible moral claim will be made that the government cannot then allow the failure of an employee-owned firm to cause the employees to lose the value of the assets they've been relying upon. The government will have to either guarantee the viability of thousands of firms or provide transfer payments to make up each individual's loss.

The intervention can hardly be counted upon to stop there. Such a constituency, when organized as all interest groups are today, will predictably call for interventions that we can only speculate about now. Employee ownership may well become the constituency that the American Left has long yearned for, one that will undergird the Left's entire welfare-state program.

Conclusion

The time for response is short. Underwritten by billions of dollars of tax-preferences, and thus far having faced no opposition from market advocates, ESOPs are ushering in a new age for the American economy in which employee ownership will be a dominant factor. Thus, just when we least expect it, we find we are in a time of crisis for a free market economy.

---

1. Sylvia Nasar, "The Foolish Rush to ESOPs," *Fortune*, September 25, 1989, pp. 141–50.

2. Joseph Raphael Blasi, *Employee Ownership Through ESOPs: Implications for the Public Corporation* (New York: Pergamon Press, 1987), p. 13.

3. Ken Coates, ed., *Can the Workers Run Industry?* (London: Sphere Books Ltd., 1968), p. 12.

4. Gerry Hunnius, G. David Garson, and John Case, eds., *Workers' Control: A Reader on Labor and Social Change* (New York: Random House, 1973), p. 469.

5. Christopher Eaton Gunn, *Workers' Self-Management in the United States* (Ithaca: Cornell University Press, 1984), p. 201.

6. See the case studies of chaotic inefficiency cited in Daniel Zwerdling's *Workplace Democracy: A Guide to Workplace Ownership, Participation, and Self-Management Experiments in the United States and Europe* (New York: Harper Colophon Books 1978), pp. 91, 117, 127, 128.

Government's Assault on Freedom to Work

by Thomas J. DiLorenzo

This essay suggests ways of thinking about one of the most important economic freedoms—the freedom to earn a living. Economic freedom may be defined generally as the freedom to trade or to engage in any consensual economic activity.[1] In the context of the labor market, economic freedom means the freedom of an employee or a group of employees to "trade" labor services in return for remuneration.

Since free trade in the labor market is mutually advantageous, it benefits both parties. Moreover, labor market freedom entails many other freedoms, such as freedom of contract, of choice, and of association. To maximize their own well-being, workers and employers must be free to contract with whomever they want, to associate with whomever they want, and to have as wide a choice of labor market options as possible, so long as they don't interfere with the equal rights of others. Thus, an unregulated labor market is most conducive to individual workers' (and employers') pursuit of happiness and economic well-being as they subjectively value it.

Government can play two different roles regarding the labor market. One role is to serve as a "referee" by enforcing voluntary contracts, protecting private property rights, and generally maintaining the rule of law. Government, in other words, can enforce the rules of the game without directly determining the outcome.

The second role of government is to make rules that determine the outcome by passing legislation and issuing regulations that affect wages, working conditions, and other aspects of labor markets. This second role is the predominant objective of governmental labor policy in democratic countries, and it conflicts with the objective of economic freedom. Rather than protecting private contracts and private property, government all too often attenuates the rights of both individual workers and employers.

Dr. DiLorenzo, a contributing editor of *The Freeman,* is Professor of Economics in the Sellinger School of Business and Management at Loyola College in Baltimore. This article originally appeared in the September 1991 issue of *The Freeman*.

The reason governments do a poor job of protecting these rights is the basic asymmetry in political decision-making in democratic countries. Generally speaking, governments pass legislation to benefit relatively small, well-organized, and well-financed interest groups. The costs of the legislation are usually hidden and widely dispersed among the general public. To promise voters well-defined and exaggerated benefits, and to hide the costs, is the route to a successful political career.

Thus, labor legislation is typically (but not always) intended to improve the economic well-being of one group by diminishing another's. Such laws infringe on the economic liberties of individuals and groups that are less politically effective.[2] Most labor legislation, in other words, amounts to protectionism—it tries to protect the jobs and incomes of one group of employees by restricting the opportunities of others. Like protectionist trade policies, such laws tend to impoverish an entire nation while providing benefits to a relatively small, politically active minority.

The types of legislation (and their economic effects) to be discussed are: 1) union legislation, 2) domestic labor legislation, and 3) immigration legislation. Given that there are literally thousands of labor laws and regulations, the following analysis is at best a preliminary assessment of economic freedom in the labor market. Only the most severe labor market interventions are considered.

Although preliminary, such an analysis is important because labor market freedom is arguably the most important economic freedom of all. Without the freedom to earn a living, citizens are bound to become ever more subservient to the state.

I. Union Legislation

Much labor legislation deals with the relationships between unions and employers. From the perspective of economic freedom—especially freedom of association—there is nothing particularly objectionable about "combinations of labor" any more than there is about any other combination of individuals for whatever purpose, so long as the group does not interfere with the equal rights of others. A government that respects economic freedom will not restrict the rights of individuals to associate freely with one another, nor will it restrict the rights of individuals who choose *not* to be associated with any such groups.

Labor law in democratic countries contains much rhetoric about protecting freedom of association, but in reality it does a poor job of it. Governments interfere or meddle with private contractual relationships between workers (or their unions) and employers on a massive scale. Most union legislation attempts to replace private, voluntary labor contracts and agreements with governmental edicts. In essence, it socializes labor relations. Furthermore, much legislation confers special privileges on labor *unions* often to the detriment of individual workers and employers.

Compulsory Unionism. One example of such legislation is laws that encourage or even mandate unionization. In the United States, for example, labor legislation discusses the importance of freedom of association, but then it talks of such freedom in terms of freedoms "to form, join, or assist labor *organizations*"[3] for the purpose of *collective* bargaining. Many of the employee "rights" protected by U.S. labor law are ones that can be advanced only through unionization.

Thus, an important measure of labor market freedom is the degree to which labor law protects *individual workers* rather than unions as organizations. Since the interests of individual workers are quite often in conflict with the interests of union officials, a legal framework that encourages or mandates unionization diminishes individual economic freedom. Laws that mandate collective bargaining, for example, are a restriction of workers' (and employers') freedom. A worker may prefer to bargain individually, and an employer may prefer to ignore a union.

The benefits of individual, rather than collective, bargaining are clear. Research in labor economics has shown that collective bargaining tends to reduce the dispersion of wages. More specifically, more productive workers are usually paid less than they could have earned had they bargained individually, whereas less productive workers often earn more, as union wages are set at something close to the median wage within a bargaining unit. Thus, if collective bargaining *imposes* an outcome on all employees, it is bound to make some of them— usually the most productive ones—worse off.

Despite the fact that some workers are made worse off, it is illegal for workers in a unionized industry in the United States and many other countries to bargain individually. Such bargaining is deemed an "unfair labor practice" and is a punishable offense.

Yellow-Dog Contracts. With regard to employers' rights, it is illegal in many countries for an employer to refuse to bargain with a union. In the United States it is a per se violation of the National Labor Relations Act to refuse to bargain with a union, but it is not illegal for a union to refuse to bargain with an employer. So-called "yellow-dog" contracts—agreements between employers and employees not to have a union—have been illegal in the United States and many other countries for decades.

Labor historians have found that one of the reasons for such contracts (which, it is worth stressing, were voluntary) was the desire by *workers* to avoid the work disruptions and loss of wages during strikes that characterize unionized industries.[4] Moreover, since such agreements were voluntary, they must have benefited employers and employees, just as all voluntary free market agreements do. Either party was free to end the employment relationship "at will" if dissatisfied.

The only way that such agreements could persist in a free marketplace is if they were "efficient" in the sense that they enhanced the welfare of both parties—the anti-union employees and employers who must have believed that unionization would not be in their best interest. Thus, legislation that outlaws such contracts must necessarily make some workers and employers worse off.

Exclusivity. Another aspect of labor legislation that grants special privileges to unions at the expense of economic freedom for workers is so-called exclusive representation. Exclusivity gives a union, once it has been certified, the legal right to be the *exclusive* bargaining agent for all workers in a bargaining unit, whether they wish to be represented or not. Any attempt by employers or workers to bargain individually—even over the most mundane things—is illegal.

Exclusivity gives unions a legal monopoly in the employee representation business. It not only is illegal for workers to bargain individually with their employers; exclusive representation legislation also prohibits bargaining through another, competing union, or any other agent.[5]

Protected from competition by exclusive representation laws, unions act like all other monopolists: they restrict their "output" and raise their prices. Because unions face no competition in the employee representation business, they are less constrained than they otherwise would be from charging excessive dues and also are likely to provide fewer services to their members.

Evidence of the latter type of behavior abounds. In the United States, unions are major participants in all sorts of political causes that are unrelated to labor relations or to the economic welfare of their members. Unions have been active in the pro-abortion movement; they have spent considerable resources in support of left-wing authoritarian governments in Central America, Africa, and elsewhere; they are part of the anti-nuclear power movement; they have lobbied for sanctions against the South African government; and they actively lobby for socialistic economic policies (i.e., price controls and nationalization of some industries) that, by hampering economic growth, are not in the best interests of the workers they represent.[6]

Exclusivity allows unions to shirk some of their basic responsibilities, such as contract administration, bargaining, and grievance handling, in order to pursue political causes that are irrelevant or even harmful to the economic welfare of workers. An indication of how far afield American unions have strayed from their basic responsibilities is a 1989 Supreme Court decision that it is unconstitutional to compel workers to pay union dues to finance activities that are not directly related to bargaining, contract administration, and grievance procedures. In the case of *Beck* v. *Communication Workers of America,* the Court found that the union spent less than 20 percent of its dues revenues on appropriate expenses. The other 80 percent was spent on politics. Other cases have found that as little as 10 percent of dues revenues are spent on legitimate purposes. The Supreme Court ruling will likely weaken the monopolistic grip that unions have over their members, but exclusivity continues to entrench much of their monopoly power.

Because of the monopoly powers granted to them by exclusivity legislation, unions may also be unresponsive to their members' demands for changes in collective bargaining strategies. There have been many cases in the United States, for example, where workers were convinced that they would have to make concessions if they wanted to remain employed. Union officials, however, often have refused to heed the preferences of their members, sometimes causing the members to lose their jobs. Unions would be more likely to cater to their members' preferences if there were competitors in the employee representation business, but such freedom of choice is precluded by law.

Agency Shop. A further infringement on the economic liberties of workers is the so-called agency shop, whereby workers who do not belong to a union must nevertheless pay union dues. The rationale for the agency shop is derived from exclusivity. Since unions are required to bargain for all workers (union and nonunion) in a bargaining unit, it is supposedly necessary to compel all workers to pay for bargaining services.

In the terminology of economics, collective bargaining is said to provide workers with "public goods," and compulsory union dues supposedly are necessary to prohibit free riding. But since government created the situation where all workers are forced to submit to a single monopoly bargaining agent, a better phrase than "free riders" would be "forced riders." Workers are forced to accept the results of union bargaining and, where an agency shop exists, also are forced to support the union financially. To workers who are worse off because of this arrangement, exclusivity creates a "public bad," not a public good: workers are forced to pay dues for the "privilege" of being made worse off. An agency shop literally constitutes taxation without representation and is a serious encroachment on economic freedom.

Union Violence. The long history of union violence can be readily explained by economic theory. In order to push wages above competitive levels, unions must restrict the supply of labor services on the market. They strike or threaten to strike in order to do this, and strikes are often more effective if workers who choose not to strike can be intimidated by violence. Employers also can be subjected to violence, threats of violence, and the destruction of property unless they acquiesce to union demands.

II. Domestic Labor Legislation

Governments also deprive workers of economic freedom through laws and regulations that affect wages and working conditions. Although these restrictions vary greatly, they all share the common element that they substitute governmental for individual (or market) decision-making. They all are carried out under the pretense that government somehow has better knowledge of the "best" wages, hours of work, types of jobs, and so on, than individual workers and employers have. This type of thinking is what F. A. Hayek calls "the fatal conceit" because of the dire economic consequences to which it lends intellectual support.

Minimum-Wage Legislation. Most democratic countries have a minimum-wage law that raises wages of low-skilled workers above going market rates. Virtually any economics text explains that mandating above-market rates causes unemployment by pricing low-skilled workers out of jobs. There is no better example of a law that hurts those whom it purports to help or that constitutes a clearer infringement on economic liberties. As Adam Smith said in *The Wealth of Nations*, "The patrimony of a poor man lies in the strength and dexterity of his hands," and to deprive him of this through restrictive labor legislation "is a manifest encroachment upon the just liberty both of the workman, and of those who might be disposed to employ him."

The minimum-wage law even harms workers who are not priced out of the market by it. If employers are forced to pay higher wages, they either will lay off some workers or cut back on other fringe benefits so that the total compensation package doesn't exceed each worker's marginal productivity. Thus, freedom of choice is diminished for workers who may prefer a different mix of wages and fringe benefits.

The minimum-wage law is inefficient and inequitable, but it persists for several political reasons. First, it lends itself to demagoguery better than most government policies. It is natural for politicians to claim to be able to solve social problems by simply passing a law, and what nicer law than one mandating higher wages for the poor?

A second reason is that unions want to price unskilled nonunion labor, which competes with more skilled, union labor, out of the market. In the name of compassion for the poor, unions lobby for legislation that makes the poor even poorer. The minimum wage is a device through which the poor are used as political pawns to the benefit of demagogic politicians and politically active unions seeking protectionist legislation.

Maximum-Hour Legislation. Another infringement on economic liberties is maximum-hour legislation which, in general, limits the number of hours that workers can work and/or mandates that higher wages must be paid for any work hours over a specified amount. Since overtime pay provisions increase labor costs, the effect is to reduce the level of production and, consequently, the number of hours worked. Individuals who prefer to work more hours or to vary their work hours over the course of a week may be precluded from doing so.

Davis-Bacon Laws. Another related measure of labor market intervention is the existence of laws, such as the Davis-Bacon Act in the United States, which mandate that government-specified wages be paid. In the case of Davis-Bacon, the government-specified "prevailing wage" in an area must be paid on all federally supported construction projects, even if the federal support is less than 1 percent of the cost of the project. The "prevailing" wage is almost always the union wage, and the effect of the Act is to drive lower-wage, nonunion labor from the market. Making wages artificially high restricts competition from lower-wage firms, depriving their owners, managers, and employees of economic opportunities.

Restrictions on Child and Female Labor. For over a century various countries have prohibited or limited child and female labor. The rationale behind the restrictions is that they supposedly are needed to protect women and children from being exploited by employers.

Even though this rationale for regulation is widely accepted by the general public, the regulations are not likely to protect the intended beneficiaries. It is difficult to perceive that regulations prohibiting such work would benefit those individuals who *voluntarily* chose to work. If they felt they were being made worse off by their employment situation, they would simply quit.

There is evidence, moreover, that when such regulation originally was being proposed in England there was fierce opposition to it *by the woman whom the regulation was supposed to help*. It is likely, therefore, that such regulation may always have been designed to protect incumbent workers from competition.

Occupational Licensing Laws. Occupational licensing laws have been shown to create barriers to entry in literally hundreds of professions in the United States and many other countries.[7] The restrictions come in many forms, such as license fees, educational requirements, and regional or national examinations.

Licensing has been defended on the grounds that it assures professional competence and protects consumers from lower-quality products and services. These arguments may or may not have merit, and they will not be discussed in detail here. But regardless of the motivation for the laws, their effect is to make it more difficult to enter regulated professions. Consequently, many individuals are deprived of employment opportunities.

This licensing-induced reduction of employment opportunities likely imposes a greater burden on lower-income individuals rather than on higher-income people since it often deprives the former group of valuable opportunities to accumulate human capital—opportunities they may not otherwise be able to obtain.

Again, there is much evidence that occupational licensing is often a *political* response to pressures from incumbent practitioners who want protection from competition. An anecdote will illustrate what I believe to be typical of the politics of occupational licensure.

Economist Walter Williams recently appeared on a televised debate with Congressman Charles Rangel. Williams, who is black, made the point that the licensing of hairdressers in Rangel's home state of New York discriminates against blacks. It does so, said Williams, because to become certified as a hairdresser one must pass a practical exam as well as a more academic one that includes math problems. (The relationship between the ability to coif hair and the ability to do mathematics is, to say the least, dubious.) Williams pointed out that an equivalent percentage of blacks passed the practical exam as whites, but the failure rate of blacks on the academic exam was several times higher than the whites. Williams blamed the discrepancy on inferior government schools that so many black New Yorkers are compelled to attend.

Congressman Rangel, who also is black, did not dispute the test results and did not deny that the system kept many of his constituents unemployed. But he nevertheless supported the licensing system. His preferred "remedy" for urban unemployment was not to eliminate the sources of unemployment, such as occupational licensing laws, but to increase welfare spending.

This type of behavior is readily explained by elementary public-choice logic. On the "demand side," the unionized practitioners are well organized and well financed politically, and are able to use the political process to protect themselves from competition with occupational licensing regulations. Those who are harmed by the regulations are not well organized and, hence, are less politically effective.

From a "supply side" perspective, politicians can win votes from the incumbents by supporting licensing, and they can also win votes from those who are denied employment opportunities because of licensing by offering them welfare payments or government patronage jobs.

In this instance the citizens whose liberties are abridged are made effective wards of the state either as welfare recipients or by relying on another form of handout—a government job—for their livelihood. Thus, occupational licensing is yet another way in which the poor are used as mere political pawns by cynical political opportunists.

Equal Pay for Equal Work Laws. These laws are intended to protect certain groups, particularly women, from wage discrimination by mandating that employers pay equal wages for the "same" work performed by workers of different sex and race. The irony is that these laws result in reduced employment opportunities for those who are supposedly helped.

If an employer pays females less than males, for example, it is because he subjectively values female labor less highly. He may genuinely believe that his female employees are less productive and less capable, or he may simply be discriminating against them because they are women. In either case, equal pay for equal work laws will induce the employer to hire fewer female workers. If forced to pay equal wages, the employer will prefer male workers. Thus, women who are willing to work at least temporarily for lower wages in order to prove that they can do the job are denied the opportunity.

In other words, women can provide employers with *economic* incentives to hire them, despite discrimination, but are not permitted to do so because of "equal pay" laws. Thus, equal pay for equal work rules, which are supposed to reduce discrimination, actually increase it.

That these laws harm the groups they are supposed to help is made clear by the fact that in some countries, such as South Africa, there is no pretense that the laws are supposed to protect people who are discriminated against. In South Africa, white racist labor unions lobbied for "equal pay" laws for black workers because they knew the laws would protect white employees from competition by relatively less skilled black workers. Since most blacks were less experienced, forcing employers to pay them wages that exceeded their marginal productivity would price them out of jobs.[8] In other countries the motivation behind the laws may be well-intentioned, but the effects are the same.

Equal pay for equal work laws reduce economic freedom, but "equal pay for work of comparable value" legislation would be even worse. This is a proposed system of governmental wage determination whereby government bureaucrats, rather than the marketplace, would set wages. I will not say anything more about this other than it's already been tried—in the Soviet Union, China, and Eastern Europe—and it doesn't work. History shows that such governmental control over wages is grossly inefficient and inequitable.

Employment Quotas. Most democratic governments have policies that require employers to make some of their hiring and promotional decisions solely on the basis of non-economic factors, such as race or sex. Obviously, this denies individuals the freedom to seek employment or career advancement based on merit.

In the United States, employment quotas originally were enacted with the promise that they would *not* be used to force employers to make decisions based solely on race. The late Senator Hubert Humphrey promised that the Civil Rights Act of 1964 "does not require an employer to achieve any kind of racial balance in his work force by giving preferential treatment to any individual or group." The phrase "affirmative action" was coined by President Kennedy in his executive order that "affirmative action" should be taken to assure that federal contractors *do not* make employment decisions based on race, creed, color, or national origin.[9]

In practice, so-called affirmative action policies do exactly the opposite of what their proponents claimed they would. They *require* that employment decisions be made specifically according to employees' race, creed, color, or national origin. Consequently, "non-preferred" individuals who may be more qualified are passed over by employers who must satisfy the *government's* preferences for discrimination in the workplace. There is mounting evidence, moreover, that even many of the "protected" minorities are denied economic opportunities because of affirmative action policies.

Economist Thomas Sowell has found that the relative economic position of "protected" minority groups in the United States actually *fell* after employment quotas were instituted. "In 1969, *before* the federal imposition of numerical 'goals and timetables,' Puerto Rican family income was 63 percent of the national average. By 1977, it was down to 50 percent. In 1969, Mexican-American family income was 76 percent of the national average. By 1977 it was down to 73 percent. Black family income fell from 62 percent of the national average to 60 percent over the same span."[10]

Sowell also found that blacks with less education and job experience have fallen farther behind, while blacks with more education and experience have been advancing even faster than their white counterparts. He offers a clear explanation of this phenomenon:

Affirmative action hiring pressures make it costly to have no minority employees, but continuing affirmative action pressures at the promotion and discharge phases also make it costly to have minority employees who do not work out well. The net effect is to increase the demand for highly qualified minority employees while decreasing the demand for less qualified minority employees or for those without a sufficient track record to reassure employers. Those who are most vocal about the need for affirmative action are of course the more articulate minority members—the advantaged who speak in the name of the disadvantaged. Their position on the issue may accord with their own personal experience, as well as their own self-interest.[11]

Thus, like the minimum wage and occupational licensing laws, employment quotas deny employment opportunities to those who need them the most—relatively unskilled and uneducated minorities who are "targeted" for help by the government.

Government "Jobs" Programs. All democratic governments have long been involved in employment or job training programs. Despite their popularity, however, they *reduce* economic liberties and employment opportunities.

It is impossible for government to "create" jobs because of the law of opportunity cost. Government may "create" some jobs with such programs, but it necessarily destroys other private-sector jobs by diverting financial resources from the private sector (through taxes, government borrowing, or inflationary money creation) to pay for the government jobs. At best, government "jobs" programs alter the *composition* of employment, but not the aggregate level.

Furthermore, many government jobs are wasteful because they don't meet legitimate consumer demands. The history of government jobs programs is filled with examples of "make work" jobs that seem to emphasize political patronage more than employment opportunity.[12]

The reason government jobs programs remain popular despite their failure to stimulate employment (or training, for that matter) is that the benefits are well defined—job recipients know where the jobs came from and whom to thank (or vote for)—whereas the costs are hidden. Those unemployed because of the crowding-out effect of these programs have no idea of the cause of their unemployment.

This is one way—generating unemployment—that government

jobs programs diminish economic freedom. They also impair economic freedom and opportunity because the *kinds* of jobs and training determined by government bureaucrats are not necessarily those that people would freely choose in the private sector. This allows government bureaucrats to exert a degree of control over what types of jobs will exist and what types of skills people will possess. Giving government such powers opens the door for ever-expanding governmental control of the allocation of labor. In totalitarian regimes such as the Soviet Union there is a nearly complete domination of the labor market by government. Its "jobs programs" are so extensive that everyone works for the state. The only "real" jobs in the Soviet Union are ones held by black marketeers.

In Nazi Germany, government officials were allowed to monitor and control every proposed job change, thereby directing workers into those endeavors the bureaucrats thought served "national interests" regardless of the interests of individuals who comprised the nation.

Of course, modern democratic governments don't possess anything like the powers over labor markets that the Soviet Union does or Nazi Germany did. But the differences are only a matter of degree (albeit a large degree). Along with extensive employment programs, all democratic countries keep extremely detailed personal information on workers and labor markets, and they use that information to shape government policy.

Government employment programs threaten economic freedom in a very general sense in that consumer sovereignty is replaced by bureaucratic sovereignty. In a free market the types of jobs created are those that serve the desires of consumers. Government jobs, on the other hand, usually are designed to serve the whims of political authorities, which often are in conflict with consumers. After all, if there is a legitimate consumer demand, there is an incentive for a private entrepreneur to meet it and to hire workers to assist him in doing so. Thus, to a large extent, government jobs are created to provide goods or services that consumers either have not expressed a preference for or, if they have expressed a preference, it was a negative one.

Mandatory Government Arbitration. All the labor market interventions discussed thus far involve government's attempt to intervene in private contractual relations between workers (or their unions) and employers by setting wages, establishing bargaining procedures, and so forth. In addition, governments also intervene in the *arbitration* of labor disputes. The U.S. government, for example, has a "Federal Mediation and Conciliation Service" that cajoles negotiating parties into "voluntarily" cooperating in order to end a labor dispute. The federal government has only limited power to mandate a settlement for most workers (with the exception of those covered by the Railway Labor Act), but it can apply significant political pressures to achieve that end in virtually any industry. The effect of this intervention is that disagreements between workers (or their unions) and employers often are settled according to criteria established by the Federal Mediation and Conciliation Service, not by the negotiating parties.

Although there is no formal power to force such agreements on most industries, the federal government's ability to "induce" an agreement should not be underestimated. American industry is so heavily regulated, and so many businesses accept government subsidies, that government has a tremendous amount of leverage over the private sector. Government has a long list of "carrots and sticks" it can use to affect private bargaining outcomes. It can threaten regulation and the withdrawal of subsidies, or it can bribe the bargaining firms and unions with promises of subsidies and other governmental favors.

Occupational Safety and Health Regulation. Modern democracies also heavily regulate "occupational safety and health." This intervention gives government enormous powers over private labor relations because an argument can be made that almost any aspect of a business operation is at least tangentially related to safety and health. Governments have taken advantage of these broad powers to regulate everything from the construction of ladders to the shape of toilet seats.

Research has shown, however, that occupational safety and health regulation is not likely to improve workplace safety, despite massive expenditures.[13] Furthermore, the regulation has interfered with market forces, which "address" the problem through compensating wage differential That is, in a free market, employees in more dangerous jobs will be paid higher wages, all other things equal. Employers must pay higher wages to attract workers to more dangerous jobs. This won't necessarily eliminate or even reduce the incidence of workplace accidents but, then, neither does regulation. Furthermore, reliance on compensating wage differentials, rather than regulation, would avoid the loss of jobs associated with the heavy costs of occupational safety and health regulation. It also would give workers and employers more freedom in determining how to improve workplace safety, rather than relying on bureaucratic edicts.

There is much to commend this market approach, for no one has stronger incentives to assure a safe workplace than employees themselves. Regardless of how well-intentioned the safety regulators may be, they just don't have the incentive or the detailed knowledge required.

It should be kept in mind that there are economic (and common-sense) incentives to reduce workplace accidents, for accidents are costly to employers and especially to workers. And it should be remembered that governmental "safety" regulation can provide a false sense of security. Job safety depends ultimately on how careful and responsible individual workers are. If they are told by governmental safety inspectors that their workplace is "safe," they may be less inclined to take their own precautions. The end result may be a *less* safe workplace.

Employer Payroll Taxes. All democratic countries have mandatory employer payroll taxes, the most significant of which are taxes for unemployment insurance and old-age pensions, or social security. A detailed examination of the economic effects of such programs is beyond the scope of this essay, but several aspects of them are particularly relevant to economic freedom.

First, these programs constitute what might be called "mandated benefits," whereby governments compel employers to finance certain benefits on behalf of their employees. One implication of this is that employees consequently have less freedom of choice to determine their own mix of wage and non-wage remuneration. Furthermore, even though the taxes are at least partly paid by employers, they are passed on to employees in the form of lower wages or other benefits, thereby constituting a hidden tax on workers. Because the tax is hidden, workers are less able to make well-informed choices regarding their own compensation mix.

Government-operated unemployment insurance and social security programs often allow governments to become monopolists in the provision of those services. There are many actual and potential substitutes for these government-controlled programs but it is difficult, if not impossible, for them to compete with government. For example, individual retirement accounts (IRAs) compete with the Social Security system in the United States, but since the system drains so much income from workers through mandatory payments, there is much less available for private retirement plans.

It also would be possible for individual workers to contribute to an IRA-type account to be used as unemployment insurance, but governments usually prohibit such options. This is especially unfortunate in light of the many failures of governmental unemployment insurance, which essentially pays people not to work by offering unemployed workers "replacement income" as a percentage—sometimes close to 100 percent—of their prior wages.

By reducing the cost to workers of being unemployed, unemployment insurance lengthens the duration of unemployment. It also increases unemployment by indirectly subsidizing industries that experience seasonal or cyclical variations in employment.

For example, without unemployment insurance a firm with an unstable employment pattern would have to pay higher wages to attract workers. The higher wage would be necessary to compensate workers for the risk of becoming unemployed. But with unemployment insurance the *government* compensates workers for becoming unemployed.

This in turn makes unstable employment more attractive to workers than it otherwise would be. The increased supply of labor in those industries will reduce wage rates, which in turn diminish the incentive for firms to do anything about unstable employment patterns. Thus, unemployment insurance encourages unstable sectors of the economy to expand, resulting in higher overall unemployment.

Both unemployment insurance and social security taxes are major infringements on the economic liberties of workers and employers, because they place severe limitations on freedom of choice, freedom of exchange, freedom of contract, and freedom of association. Because government controls a significant portion of workers' income through these programs, and because the programs crowd out private-sector alternatives—if the law permits alternatives at all—individuals are denied all these freedoms.

Peter Ferrara describes how the Social Security system infringes upon individual economic liberties. Government-controlled social security, he writes,

> . . . forces individuals to enter into contracts, exchanges, and associations with the government that they should have the

right to refuse. It prohibits individuals from entering into alternative contracts, exchanges, and associations with others concerning the portion of their incomes that social security consumes. It prevents individuals from choosing courses of action other than participation in social security, although these courses of action will hurt no one. It prevents individuals from enjoying the fruits of their own labor by taking control of a major portion of each individual's income. The program prevents individuals from arranging their own affairs and controlling their own lives. It operates by the use of force and coercion against individuals rather than through voluntary consent. The social security program thus restricts individual liberty in major and significant ways, violating rights that are worthy of great respect.[14]

The same can be said for any government-mandated benefit program.

Taxes on Labor Income. Perhaps the most important interference with an individual worker's economic freedom is the income tax. The income tax denies a worker the ability to keep the fruits of his or her own labor, and is truly a way in which workers are exploited—by government.

Karl Marx's labor exploitation thesis was half right. He complained that labor was unfairly exploited because it supposedly produced all value—an incredibly naive and simplistic assumption—yet it received only a small part of it in the form of wages. Marx was correct about labor being exploited, but he was wrong about who the exploiters were. By blaming capitalists, he ignored the productive contributions of capital and entrepreneurs. He also ignored the fact that government is the major source of worker exploitation by expropriating income to which government itself has no legitimate claim. Ironically, Marx was a strong proponent of progressive income taxation, which exploits workers even more than proportional taxation.

Income taxation is, in effect, a form of slavery or forced labor. It forces individuals to pay taxes so that part of their income is given away to someone else—farmers, corporations, welfare recipients, defense contractors, unions, and thousands of other well-organized special interest groups—who did nothing to earn or deserve it. H. L.

Mencken's dictum that an election is an advance auction in stolen property is as true as it is trite.

Of course, not all income that is taxed is necessarily used for government-mandated income transfers. To the extent that some of it is used to finance a criminal justice system, national defense, and in generally maintaining the rule of law, it enhances rather than diminishes economic freedoms. However, these functions are a relatively minor aspect of the modern welfare state. The modern state is a vast income redistribution machine that shuffles wealth around *within* the middle class.

Mandating Job Security. Many countries have various laws and regulations that supposedly guarantee "job security" by restricting the flow of capital. Laws that make it more costly or prohibitive to close down a plant are examples. Such laws may be well-intentioned, but they deprive workers and business owners of economic freedom and are undeniably harmful to a nation's economy. By hampering economic growth, they ultimately impoverish the workers in whose name the laws are enacted. Job security laws, in other words, reduce job security.

Advocates of such legislation usually ignore the fact that workers and employers often negotiate various types of "job security" provisions in their contracts. It must be realized that if, for example, a union wants a contract that includes severance pay if the plant closes down, that provision will be "paid" for by a negotiated reduction in wages or other fringe benefits. There is no free lunch; acquiring such benefits requires trade-offs. That's why laws that mandate job security provisions reduce economic freedom. They deprive workers of freedom of choice by forcing them to accept one particular benefit—a benefit they may not want if they know how much it costs them in terms of forgone wages. So-called job security legislation also deprives employers and business owners (shareholders) of economic freedom. It prohibits them from making the best use of their resources, which can only be impoverishing.

III. Immigration

Freedom of migration is a basic human right that is essential if individuals are to be free from governmental oppression. The ability to change employment or to seek employment elsewhere even in another country—is a hallmark of economic freedom. Thus, free immigration and emigration is most conducive to economic freedom and opportunity.

No country in the world has perfectly free immigration. The United States is generally regarded as among the most free—there are about twice as many immigrants entering the United States each year as there are in all the rest of the world combined. Yet America does place restrictions on immigration.

Since all countries place some limits on immigration, one method of comparing them is by calculating the allowable number of immigrants as a percentage of the nation's population.

Taxes on Immigration. Some countries charge immigrants fees or taxes. In such cases large statutory numbers of allowable immigrants may not be very meaningful if the charges are so high as to exclude large numbers of people. Therefore, the existence of "entrance fees" into a country is another criterion that may be used. The amount of the fee may be standardized as a percentage of average annual income in the country receiving the immigrants.

Enforcement. Many countries are concerned about illegal immigrants. From the perspective of labor market freedom, however, the more illegals the better. The fact that the United States finds that its enforcement of illegal immigration is weak, and that its borders are "out of control," is a plus. Consequently, another measure of labor market freedom is the budget of the appropriate immigration enforcement agency as a percentage of the nation's total governmental budget. The higher the budget allocation, the stronger the enforcement and the lesser the degree of economic freedom.

Labor Market Tests and Lists of "Undesirables." In some countries, laws specifically outlaw immigration if the immigration enhances a free market in labor. In the United States, immigrants are required to prove that their employment won't displace an American worker *and* that their presence won't reduce wages. This is clearly a protectionist law instigated by organized labor. Some countries limit immigration according to racial or ethnic criteria. America has a long history of discriminating against Chinese and Japanese immigrants in this way, although such discrimination was outlawed in 1965.

Amnesty. Granting amnesty to illegal immigrants who over a period of years have established "roots" in a country dilutes immigration restrictions and, consequently, enhances economic freedom.

Temporary Workers. Since a half a loaf is better than none, countries that allow temporary "guest workers" exhibit a higher degree of economic freedom, all other things equal, than those that don't.

Concluding Thought

Government at all levels spends hundreds of billions of dollars each year ostensibly to help the unemployed and others living in or near poverty. Despite these massive expenditures, however, the welfare state is a failure. Paying people not to work only fosters perpetual dependency.

Rather than continuing to fund a counterproductive welfare system, a more direct means of reducing poverty would be the deregulation of labor markets. As this essay has shown, the major forms of government intervention in labor markets serve only to "protect" certain groups of workers from competition by denying job opportunities to others. More often than not, those workers who are denied job opportunities because of government intervention are those most in need: the least skilled, least educated, and least affluent.

---

1. Economic freedom requires a set of customs, moral constraints, or laws that prevent individuals or groups from committing violent or coercive acts against others. Thus, mutual consent between two burglars plotting a robbery, for example, is not an example of economic freedom in the sense we are discussing.

2. See Bernard Siegan, *Economic Liberties and the Constitution* (Chicago: University of Chicago Press, 1980); Richard Epstein, *Takings* (Cambridge, Mass.: Harvard University Press, 1985); and Terry L. Anderson and Peter J. Hill, *The Birth of a Transfer Society* (Stanford, Calif.: Hoover Institution Press, 1980).

3. National Labor Relations Act, Section 7 (emphasis added). Quoted in James T. Bennett, Dan C. Heldman, and Manuel H. Johnson, *Deregulating Labor Relations* (Dallas: Fisher Institute, 1981), p. 50.

4. Morgan O. Reynolds, *Power and Privilege: Labor Unions in America* (New York: Universe Books, 1984), p. 98.

5. Thomas J. DiLorenzo, "Exclusive Representation in Public Employment: A Public Choice Perspective," *Journal of Labor Research*, Fall 1984, pp. 371–90.

6. For a detailed discussion of the political agenda of organized labor in the United States see James T. Bennett and Thomas J. DiLorenzo, *Destroying Democracy: How Government Funds Partisan Politics* (Washington, D.C.: Cato Institute, 1985), chapter 13.

7. A thorough discussion of the economics of occupational licensing is found in S. David Young, *The Rule of Experts: Occupational Licensing in America* (Washington, D.C.: Cato Institute, 1987). See also R. D. Blair and S. Rubin, *Regulating the Professions* (Lexing-

ton, Mass.: Lexington Books, 1980); and Timothy R. Muzondo and Bohumir Pazderka, "Occupational Licensing and Professional Incomes in Canada," *Canadian Journal of Economics,* November 1980, pp. 659–67.

8. Walter E. Williams, *South Africa's War Against Capitalism* (New York: Praeger, 1989).

9. Thomas Sowell, *Civil Rights: Rhetoric or Reality?* (New York: William Morrow & Co., 1984), p. 39.

10. *Ibid.,* p. 51.

11. *Ibid.,* p. 53.

12. Thomas J. DiLorenzo, "The Myth of Government Job Creation," Cato Institute *Policy Analysis,* February 1984.

13. W. Kip Viscusi, "The Impact of Occupational Safety and Health Regulation," *Bell Journal of Economics,* Spring 1979.

14. Peter J. Ferrara, *Social Security: The Inherent Contradiction* (Washington, D.C.: Cato Institute, 1980), pp. 275–76.

Do Unions Have a Death Wish?

by Sven Rydenfelt

Hans Vaihinger, known for his "as-if" philosophy, stated that researchers and philosophers sometimes have to work with "crazy" assumptions. Thus, Copernicus assumed that the earth is a sphere, although almost everyone living at the time was convinced that the world is flat. In a similar fashion, Sigmund Freud concluded that the behavior of certain people could be explained only by assuming that they have a death wish, contrary to the common assumption of a general instinct for self-preservation.

In recent years, many labor unions have behaved in a manner which can only be described as self-destructive. Can it be that unions, which have attained special privileges through the political process, are abusing their privileges to the point that they are destroying the public confidence and legislative support which have been the source of their power?

Let us consider three episodes of union behavior which seem to exhibit a death wish.

Unions and the Swedish Shipping Industry

According to the American economist, Mancur Olson (*The Rise and Decline of Nations,* 1982), powerful organizations in unholy alliances with strong governments have been the primary cause of the economic stagnation which has gripped the Western World during the last fifteen years. There is no better example than the strangulation of Swedish shipping .

Since the mid-1970s, shippers all over the world have suffered from an overcapacity which has idled vessels and depressed shipping rates. If the market had been allowed to adjust, overproduction would have been eliminated quickly. In free markets private firms have to adapt supply to demand, because overproduction means losses. But

---

Dr. Rydenfelt is a professor of economics at the University of Lund in Sweden. This article is reprinted from the October 1987 issue of *The Freeman.*

the unions were able to extort large subsidies from the different Swedish governments—socialist as well as non-socialist—to preserve employment in the shipyards. Of course, they realized that production had to be cut, but they hoped that those burdens would be borne by other nations.

As orders for Swedish ships declined, more and more state subsidies were granted. Orders that didn't cover half the building costs were accepted, and finally, ships were produced without any orders at all. Despite the huge subsidies, all Swedish shipyards eventually had to be shut down.

With other countries subsidizing their own ship-building industries, the oversupply of ships grew worse. Freight rates plunged and the Swedish shipping industry called upon Swedish maritime unions to cooperate in cutting costs. The unions, however, with support from the Swedish government, were able to block meaningful cuts.

The ship owners soon realized that sailing under so-called convenience flags (Liberia, Panama, etc.) was their only hope for survival. The Swedish sailors were offered the same net wages, after taxes, that they would have received in ships under Swedish flags. However, they would have lost their government-guaranteed privileges—minimum crews, extra holidays, etc.—losses they refused to accept. Instead, they extorted from the government another privilege, a law prohibiting ships owned by Swedes to sail under convenience flags.

The only resource for the ship owners, threatened by bankruptcy, was a gradual sale of their ships to companies in other countries—a forced sale in a depressed market. The Swedish merchant marine, which ten years ago measured 13 million deadweight-tons, is now reduced to 2.5 million tons.

In *Human Action* (1949), Ludwig von Mises maintains that government-granted special privileges, designed to favor certain groups, often wind up hurting the groups they are supposed to help. The Swedish regulations which prohibited Swedish ships from sailing under convenience flags are an obvious example. Designed to aid the Swedish maritime unions, they combined with other regulations to destroy the very jobs they were supposed to save. The unions, who agitated for these regulations, acted in a manner which is perhaps best characterized as displaying an economic death wish.

Unions and the British Printing Industry

The British printing industry offers another example of the self-destructive behavior of unions in defending the privileges of their members. The printers always were an aristocracy among workers, so well organized and prepared to fight for their interests that the employers were forced to buy production peace at very high prices.

Their unions fought a last and bitter battle for their privileges in 1986–1987—privileges including automatic life tenure, job-assignment rights, and wage scales higher than those for most reporters. The basic issue was the introduction of labor-saving technology. The printers refused to use the new technology, and claimed the exclusive right to continue to work with the outdated technology that had granted them a key position in the newspaper industry.

The outcome of the fight meant life or death for several large British newspapers, that had suffered losses for many years and were near bankruptcy. The new technology was their only chance for survival.

After years of vain negotiations, Rupert Murdoch, who published four large newspapers, had to sidestep the unions. At Wapping in the harbor district of eastern London he had a new printing office built, and in January 1986 he moved with his newspaper production (34 million copies a week) from Fleet Street to Wapping. At the same time he fired 5,500 striking print workers, whom he replaced with workers from the less militant electricians' union. The printers had been offered a generous economic package, which they refused to accept. The chairman of their union federation, Brenda Dean, realized that this offer was their last chance for an acceptable agreement, but a majority of union hawks chose to continue to strike.

British union members have always had the special privilege — unlike other citizens—to apply physical force against non-strikers and other adversaries in labor conflicts. Although not formally legal, the right functioned in practice as a legal right, accepted by the police and the courts. Of course, this was a very remarkable privilege, fully comparable to the privileges of the old European nobility.

The Thatcher government, however, abolished this privilege by means of laws prohibiting all physical force in labor conflicts—"violent picketing" included. According to union tradition, strike-breakers are to be treated like outlaws without legal rights. But only in fascist states can such legal discrimination exist. In a law-governed society all citizens should be protected by law.

When the fired printers—in spite of the new laws—attacked non-strikers as well as the Wapping office, the government ordered police to stop the attacks. The conflict, including a siege of the Wapping office, continued for more than a year. With empty strike funds and threatened with high compensation claims against law-breaking members, the printers and their union had to surrender unconditionally in February 1987.

Unions and the British Mining Industry

Still another illustration of union behavior patterns can be found in the strike of 120,000 British coal miners—out of a total number of 180,000—between March 1984 and March 1985. The strikers did not fight for higher wages. Their strike was a last desperate effort to stop the gradual closing down of the coal mining industry. At the nationalization in 1947, roughly 1,000 mines were being worked, a number that had shrunk to 170 by 1984. Simultaneously, the number of miners had decreased from 600,000 to 180,000.

The principal cause of the decline was the emergence of oil as a cheaper and better substitute for coal. When the British government tried to slow the substitution of oil for coal in industry by means of tariffs, taxes, and prohibitions on oil, energy prices in British industry rose above the prices in competing countries. This had a devastating impact on Britain's ability to compete.

The mines that remained open were sustaining heavy losses which had to be made up by massive subsidies. But the striking miners insisted that mine closings be stopped and current production levels maintained. What they sought, in fact, were new privileges at the expense of the coal industry and the British taxpayers.

When the striking British miners, after a year-long conflict, abandoned their strike in March 1985, this was perhaps the greatest union defeat in British history. This defeat together with the defeat of the printers in February 1987 meant, in fact, a turn of the tide. The British union movement may never recover.

With strong organizations and government granted privileges, the unions in their heydays had functioned like power blocs—states within states. But power leads to abuse, and the more power the more abuse. As a general rule, the privileged classes indulge in wishful thinking and interpret their acts of abuse as wise and just policies. But more and more people have been shocked by the union abuse of power. And in a democratic society, the turn of public opinion is bound to have consequences.

Boulwarism: Ideas Have Consequences

by William H. Peterson

"What's in a name?" asked Shakespeare's star-crossed Juliet. "That, which we call a rose/By any other name would smell as sweet."

Boulwarism. An idea. Sweet or sour? Description or invective? The death of Lemuel R. Boulware (1895–1990) in Florida in November of 1990 recalls the controversy over his name as embodied in a General Electric employee strategy that prevailed for some 15 years after World War II. The controversy is seen in a 1969 U.S. Second Circuit Court of Appeals decision upholding a National Labor Relations Board (NLRB) ruling that GE had committed an "unfair labor practice" via Boulwarism. Asserted the Court in passing: "We do not think that [National Labor Relations] Board Member Fanning's use of the term 'Boulwarism' was indicative of bias; the term is more description than invective."

Certainly America's unions sought to make Boulwarism into invective, to undo Lemuel Boulware's lifelong idea of avoiding force, public or private, by "trying to do right voluntarily." He held that labor and capital, employees and managers, wages and profits, are allies and not enemies in production. His ideas help explain GE's innovative employee policy following a rough seven-week strike in 1946 that saw acts of sabotage at various plants.

The strike shocked the company, which had long voluntarily installed such forward-looking employee programs as a suggestion system (1906), pensions (1912), and insurance (1920). Employee disapproval and distrust of the company, fanned by union hype, were widespread. GE charged Lemuel Boulware to correct the situation.

So began "Boulwarism," the GE program that can be reviewed in his book, *The Truth About Boulwarism* (Bureau of National Affairs, 1969), written eight years after he retired from GE. Boulware tackled his charge first through job research, applying merchandising techniques that had been successful with GE's consumer products. He

Dr. Peterson, Heritage Foundation adjunct scholar, is a contributing editor of *The Freeman*. This article originally appeared in the April 1991 issue of *The Freeman*.

interviewed employees, for example, to find out what they knew about economics including the origin of jobs and wages. His finding: Not much. His solution: employee economic education on a massive scale.

For starters, he borrowed Du Pont's flannelboard economic study course entitled "How Our Business System Operates," and gained full participation of every GE employee (then 190,000 of them) "from top management to the last nonsupervisory worker." The course involved three 90-minute sessions on company time. He also distributed thousands of copies of New York University economist Lewis H. Haney's book, *How You Really Earn Your Living,* to supervisors and other sponsors of study and discussion groups in GE plants, offices, and plant communities.

In addition, in sustained employee communications Boulware hammered on the theme that market competitiveness was decisive, that the GE customer was the ultimate employer and paymaster, that quality and cost control were crucial to GE jobs. As GE's vice president for employee and public relations, he explained that at bottom industrial harmony springs from employee attitudes and perceptions.

Later on he hired a Hollywood actor named Ronald Reagan to heighten the popularity of GE's TV show. To bring about that goal, Reagan toured GE plants where he found that "we didn't chain the workers to the machines." The GE assignment apparently helped sell free enterprise to the future President.

Breaking Pattern Wage Settlements

The immediate point of Boulwarism, however, was the break with pattern wage settlements that especially had rippled out from auto and steel negotiations. To Boulware that pattern had elements of theatrics in the postwar era when employers felt they had to go through the motions of first offering essentially nothing when the real plan all along was, say, an increase of five cents an hour. As he put the rest of the scenario in his book: "Then, under public strike-threat pressure, about half would be offered. Then, after all the union representatives had been called in from the plants and the resulting vote for a strike had been well aired in a receptive press, management would 'capitulate' by upping the offer to the full five cents per hour."

Argued Boulware: Pattern settlements played into the hands of union officials who portrayed an employee need to "triumph over greedy and vicious management," and who accordingly had to drag an unwilling company into doing the right thing by its employees. Boulware believed that such tactics discredited both capitalism and the company in the eyes of employees. He further believed that those tactics nurtured employee resentment and hurt productivity by appearing to give credit to the unions for wringing from the company what it had been willing to give at the very outset of negotiations.

Accordingly Boulware abandoned the pattern idea. Instead he painstakingly researched each opening GE offer. Soon after that he presented an up-front fleshed-out competitive "product" that he termed "fair but firm"—an offer he felt would be at once attractive to the employees and within the limited means of the company and its customers.

Union officials bristled at this new management approach and argued that the offer was but a rigid "take-it-or-leave-it" stand, that for all its talk of "balanced best interests" GE was "playing God," that the company was simply not bargaining "in good faith," that it could have offered GE employees lots more out of its "swollen" profits without having to raise prices. As Boulware rebutted this soon-standard union rhetoric in his book: "The trouble with our country's so-called 'free collective bargaining' in those days was that it too often turned out to be not free, not collective, and, in fact, too one-sided to be real bargaining at all." So what often passed for bargaining, he went on, was but the imposition of a settlement that some union officials had already unilaterally decided, even though for public consumption they might later cut their initially too high demands by as much as half in order to look reasonable.

Too, Boulware maintained that he was not inflexible, that only one of his opening proposals wound up without amendment in the GE union contract, that he was always receptive to the idea of letting the unions provide "any old or new information proving changes would be in the balanced best interests of all." The ongoing Boulware-union officials battle of ideas became public knowledge, and the media had a field day, with politicians, commentators, and editorialists taking sides.

But GE's 1960 negotiations with the International Union of Electrical, Radio, and Machine Workers, AFL-CIO, misfired, leading to a three-week strike and the NLRB ruling that through Boulwarism General Electric had committed an "unfair labor practice." For, according to that 1969 U.S. Second Court of Appeals decision sustaining the ruling, GE had allegedly used "sham discussions" instead of "genuine arguments"; too, GE supposedly conducted a communications program that emphasized "both powerlessness and uselessness of union to its members" and that "pictured employer as true defender of interest of employees, further denigrating union, and sharply curbing employer's ability to change its own position."

Boulware retired from GE in 1961, and Boulwarism as an idea and policy passed into history. Yet so too did the heyday of adversarial unionism and the tide of union membership, with both the nation's and GE's labor force becoming sharply de-unionized in the new age of information and global competitiveness.

Ideas have consequences. Lemuel R. Boulware's prescient long-run employee economic education program, anticipating today's quality circles, T-groups, and closer employer-employee rapport, may have triumphed in the end.

Index

Abramson, Irving, 105
AFL, 25, 156
AFL-CIO, 9, 58, 118, 198–199, 236
Agency shop, 212–213
Air Associates Strikes (1941), 100–
    115
Amalgamated Transit Union, 58, 116–
    117
American Economic Association,
    41
*American Idea of Industrial Democracy,
    The* (Derber), 66
American Revolution, 32
American Steel Foundries v. *Tri City
    Trades Council* (1921), 59, 61, 64,
    117
Amnesty for immigrants, 226–227
Anarchism, 82, 179–182
Anderson, Benjamin, 135
Anderson, Robert G., 143–155
Antitrust and Monopoly (Armentano),
    66
Apex Hosiery (1940), 117
Arbitration, 95, 220–221
Armentano, Dominick, 66
Austin, John, 175

Baird, Charles W., 57–64, 100–115,
    116–120
Barbaro, Frank J., 119
Barbash, Jack, 137
Beasley, Major Peter, 112
Bechara, Dennis, 156–166
Beck v. *Communication Workers of Amer-
    ica,* 212
Belknap v. *Hale* (1938), 62
Bellamy, Edward, 71
Bendix, *see* Air Associates Strikes
Bidinotto, Robert James, 65–72

Blacks, effect of labor legislation on,
    21, 199
Blanc, Louis, 71, 202
Boston police strike (1919), 156–157
Boulware, Lemuel, 234–237
Boycott, 24–25
Brandeis, Louis, 59
British printing and mining industries,
    231–232
Browne, Sheriff William, 104, 105,
    108, 109, 113
Bywater, William, 57

Cambridge School, 41
Capital formation, 45–46
Carnegie Steel Company, 119
Carson, Clarence B., 13–27, 29–34.
    129–142
Cartels, cartel theory, 35, 88–89, 95,
    150
Chalaire, Walter, 100, 105, 106, 107,
    108, 110
Chartist movement, 8
Chase, Stuart, 130–132
Chernyshevsky, N.G., 202
Chesapeake and Ohio Canal, 17
Child labor, restrictions on, 138, 194,
    215
Chinese Exclusion Act, 21
Chrysler, 78
CIO, 109, 134; *see also* AFL-CIO,
    UAW-CIO
Civil Rights Act (1964), 218
Civil Service Reform Act (1978), 158
Civil Service system, 171–172
Class warfare, 20
Clayton Antitrust Act, 16
Coal Strike (1902), 4
Coburn, Frederic, 113, 114

Coercion, 77, 87

Cole, G.D.H., 202

Collective bargaining, 6, 37, 45, 67, 123, 161, 164, 167–182, 189–191

"Common law of the shop," 95

Commons, John R., 130, 131

Communications Workers v. *Beck* (1988), 63

Communism, 201

Competition, 93, 124–125, 144

"Competitive disadvantage," 68

Compulsory public-sector bargaining, 124, 162–165, 167–182, 189

Connecticut Civil Rights Commission, 17

Consumption economics, 132

Coolidge, Calvin, 151, 156

Copernicus, 229

Craftsmen vs. unskilled workers, 19

"Cutting," "nibbling," 49–50

Davis-Bacon Act, 214–215

Dean, Brenda, 231

DeBeers oligopoly, 73

Decertification elections, 37

Decline of American Liberalism (Ekirch), 66

DeLury, John, 181

Derber, Milton, 66

Dickman, Howard (*Industrial Democracy in America*), 65–72

DiLorenzo, Thomas J., 208–228

Diocletian, 97

Eastern Airlines strike, 57, 58

Eastern Europe, 203–205

Economic freedom, 208

Economics of Welfare (Pigou), 45

Economist, 116

Edison, Charles, 104–105, 110

Ekirch, Arthur, 66

Elrod v. *Burns,* 161

Employee ownership, 200–207

Employer

  as consumer, 151

constitutional rights of, 79

relations with employees, 14, 18, 68, 84–85, 192

Employment, monopoly of, 19, 35

Employment quotas, 217–219

Encyclopedia Britannica, 137

Engels, Friedrich, 130

Equal pay for equal work, 217

ESOPs, 200–207

Executive Order 10988 (1962), 91, 158

Exploitation theory, 4–5, 49–50, 145

Fair Labor Standards Act (1938), 135

Fascist Labor Charter (1927), 72

Featherbedding, 30

Federal Mediation and Conciliation Service, 221

Federal Reserve System, 186–187, 188, 199

Federal Shipbuilding and Dry Dock Company, 103, 111

Federalist, The, 180

Ferrara, Peter, 223–224

Fertig, Lawrence, 183

Fiat money, 187–188

Fichte, Johann Gottlieb, 70–71

Fine, Sidney, 66

First Amendment, 32

Fisher, Antony G.A., 97–99

France, 98

Frankensteen, Richard T., 111, 112

Frankfurter, Felix, 59

Fraser, Douglas, 78

Free trade in labor markets, 208

Freedom of association, 168

Freedom of contract, 40

Freedom to work, government's assault on, 208–228

Freud, Sigmund, 229

Frick, Henry, 119

Friedman, Milton, 183

Fringe benefits, 136

Galbraith, John Kenneth, 130

Garfield, James A., 160

Gartner, Michael, 118
General Electric, 234–237
George, Henry, 90
Golden Rule, 30
Gompers, Samuel, 70, 156
Government employees, unionization of, 79–82, 85, 124ff, 156–166, 167–182
Government "jobs" programs, 219–220
Graham, Frank P., 107
Great Depression, 31, 134, 157
Great Britain, 8, 97, 98, 99, 231–232
Great Railroad Strikes (1877), 4
Greaves, Percy L., Jr., 28–34
Greyhound strike, 57, 58, 117
Grimaldi, Anthony, 106, 110, 112, 113, 114
Guild socialism, 202–203
Gunn, Christopher, 203

Haggard, Thomas R., 117
Hairdressing, licensing of, 216
Haney, Lewis H., 235
Harding, Earl, 100, 103, 108, 110
Hayek, Friedrich, 66, 140, 183, 213
Haymarket Riot (1886), 4
Health care, 5
Herrin Mines (1922), 22–23
Hessen, Robert, 66
Hill, F. Leroy, 100–115
Hill, Mrs. F. Leroy, 100
History textbooks, treatment of labor unions in, 13
Hoge, James, 118
Holmes, Oliver Wendell, Jr., 59, 168
Home workshops, 137, 138
Homestead strike (1892), 4, 119–120
Houser, Loren, 106
How You Really Earn Your Living (Haney), 235
Human Action (Mises), 230
Humphrey, Hubert, 198, 218
Humphrey-Hawkins Full Employment Bill, 198–199

Hutcheson, William L., 25
Hutt, W.H., 66

Immigrant workers, 21, 226
In Defense of the Corporation (Hessen), 66
"Inability-to-wait" doctrine, 48, 49
Income taxes, 224–225
Industrial Democracy in America: Ideological Origins of National Labor Relations Policy (Dickman), 65–72
Industrial Revolution, 52
Inflation, 98, 140, 183–199
International Association of Machinists, 58
International Brotherhood of Electrical Workers, 17, 24–25
Intimidation, 90

Jefferson, Thomas, 61
Job, proprietary interest in one's, 67–68, 164
Job security mandates, 225
Jones, Roy M., 112, 113
Judicial absolutism, 180

Kennedy, John F., 91, 158
Keynes, John Maynard, 44
Kirkland, Lane, 118
Knights of Labor, 25
Knights of St. Crispin, 21
Knudsen, William S., 110, 111
Kohler strike, 122

Labor
  "disadvantage" of, 43–44
  as a factor of production, 146
  free market in jobs, 29
  labor/capital conflict theory, 146
  market tests, 226
  monopoly, 31, 35, 39
  "perishability" of, 50
  role of sentiment, sympathy , 51
  supply of, government intervention in, 15, 23–24, 138–140
  surplus versus scarcity, 132–133

Labor policies, intellectual influences, 66
Labor theory of value, 68, 129–130, 145
Labor unions
  adversary nature of unionism, 78–86
  Christian view of, 73–77
  competition and, 4
  as educational institutions, 2
  exclusive powers of, 36–37, 211–212
  free rider arguments, 39
  as gangs, 121–122
  and government employment, 156–166
  ideology, 1–10, 26, 41–54
  inflation, 183–199
  myths surrounding, 1–10, 65
  as non-market entities, 36
  origins of American unions, 13–27
  privilege, 148–149
  religious character of, 33, 129
  unemployment, 134–135, 183–199
  and violence, 87–96, 116–120, 213
Laissez Faire and the General Welfare State (Fine), 66
Landrum-Griffin Act (1959), 57, 72, 118
Law of market competition, 75–76
Leadville Miner's Union Strike (1880), 22
Leef, George C., 35–40
Legal positivism, 59
Legislation
  domestic labor, 213–215
  immigration, 225–227
  union, 209–213
Lewis, John L., 17, 23, 101, 111, 134
London, Jack, 61
Longshoremen's Union, 25
Looking Backward (Bellamy), 71
"Ludlow Massacre" (1914), 4

Malthus, Thomas Robert, 48–49
Margin of "indeterminateness," 45
Marginal utility theory, 135, 145

Marshall, Alfred, 1, 41, 43, 44, 50
Marx, Karl, ideas of, 66, 78, 98, 130, 145
Marxism (Sowell), 66
Maximum-hour legislation, 214
McCulloch, J. R., 1, 41, 42, 68
Meany, George, 183
Medieval guild system, 67
Mencken, H.L., 224–225
Mill, John Stuart, 1, 41, 42, 43, 44, 69
Minimum-wage laws, 2, 6, 29, 75, 135–136, 174, 213–214
Mises, Ludwig von, 66, 159–160, 176–177, 230
Monopoly gains, 191–193
Monopoly pricing, 74, 89–90
Monopoly representation, 31, 175
Morton, W.C., 112
Murdoch, Rupert, 231
Murphey, Dwight D., 200–207
Mussolini, Benito, 202

Nation, The, 202
National Defense Mediation Board, 100–101, 105, 106, 107, 108, 110
National Industrial Policy Board, 9
National Labor Relations Act (NLRA), 32, 38, 39, 57, 59, 60–61, 64, 71, 74, 78, 91, 101, 102, 104, 118, 134, 135, 147, 157, 211
National Labor Relations Board (NLRB), 36, 74, 101, 102, 173, 190, 236
National Recovery Act (1933), 157
Nazi Germany, 220
Nelson, John O., 78–86
New Castle (Pa.) *News,* 65
New Deal, 117
New Jersey Chamber of Commerce, 110
New Republic, The, 202
New York *Daily News* strike, 116, 117, 118, 119
New York Federation of Labor, 137

New York Police Department, 118
New York Times, The, 100, 108, 109, 110, 111, 112, 113, 114, 198–199
NLRB v. *Mackay Radio & Telegraph Company* (1938), 61, 62, 64, 107
Norris-La Guardia Act, 118, 147, 157
North American Aviation Company, 103
North, Gary, 73–77

Occupational licensing, 215–216
Occupational safety and health regulation, 221–222
Office of Production Management, 105
Oliver Wiswell (Roberts), 185–186
Olson, Mancur, 229
Ordinance of Labourers (1349), 72
Organized Against Whom? (Carson), 13–27, 28–34 (review), 129–142
Over-production, 130–131
Overtime, 136
"Owning" one's job, 67–68

Packard, Vance, 131
PATCO strike, 57, 163
Pattern Makers League v. *NLRB* (1985), 63
Pattern wage settlements, 235–236
Patterson, Robert, 110, 111–112, 113
Pattison, Governor Robert E., 120
Payroll taxes, 222
Pearl Harbor, 100
Pendleton Act (1883), 160
Perry v. *Sinderman,* 164
Peterson, William H., 234–237
Petro, Sylvester, 65–66, 162, 165, 167–182, 183–199
Pigou, Arthur Cecil, 1, 41, 44–45
Pinkerton agents, 119
Pittston Coal strike, 57, 58, 61, 116
Pluralism, 70
Population, growth of, 48–49
Pound, Roscoe, 59
Prices, price system, 133, 143

Principles of Political Economy (Mill), 43
Private sector vs. government behavior, 159
Procrustes, fable of, 136
Productivity of labor, 3, 10
Profit, 146
Protestant Ethic and the Spirit of Capitalism (Weber), 73
Proudhon, Pierre Joseph, 202
"Public interest" laws, 38
Public-employee unions, 162–163
Public-sector bargaining, 154, 163, 165, 167–182
Pullman Strike (1894), 4

Railway Labor Act, 221
Rand, Ayn, 66
Rangel, Charles, 216
Rawls, John, 71
Reagan, Ronald, 57, 92, 235
Redistribution of wealth, 143–155
Reynolds, Morgan O., 87–96
Right of contract, individual, 83
Right to strike, 57–64
Right to a job, 60
Rise and Decline of Nations, The (Olson), 229
Roberts, Kenneth, 185
Roosevelt, Franklin Delano, 92, 100, 103, 105, 109, 111, 112, 113, 114, 135
Roosevelt, Theodore, 160
Russia, 123
Rydenfelt, Sven, 229–233

Saturday Evening Post, 100
Say, Jean-Baptiste, 1, 41, 42, 48, 51
"Scabs," 13, 20, 22, 61, 74, 149
Scarcity, 130, 132
Sennholz, Hans F., 1–10, 41–54
Shanker, Albert, 196–197
Shipping industry in Sweden, 229–230
Shulman, Harry P., 106, 107
Simons, Henry C., 177

Smith, Adam, 1, 41–42, 43, 44, 45, 46, 48, 68, 69
Social order, threat of compulsory collective public-sector bargaining to, 167–182
Social Security, 223–224
Socialism, 70, 130, 201–202, 203
Socialism (Mises), 66
Sorel, Georges, 202
South Africa, 217
Southern Illinois Coal Company, 23
Sovereignty, 175, 176
Sowell, Thomas, 66, 218–219
"Stasis" in society, 97
Strikes, 57–64, 76–77, 92, 98, 100–115, 174, 178, 180–181, 189, 190
Surplus versus scarcity, 133
"Sweating system," "sweatshops," 137
Sweden, 229–230

Taft-Hartley Labor Act (1947), 57, 72, 78, 118
Theory of Unemployment (Pigou), 44–45
Thieblot, Armand J., Jr., 117
Third World, 204–205
Thornton, W.T., 43, 44
Treatise On the Circumstances which Determine The Rate of Wages (McCulloch), 42
Tribune Company, 116
Trumka, Richard, 61
Truth About Boulwarism, The (Boulware), 234
Tugwell, Rexford G., 131
TWA v. Flight Attendants (1989), 63

UAW-CIO, 101, 102, 103, 104, 106, 111, 114
Unemployment, 28, 31, 141–142, 152
Union Violence: The Record and the Response by Courts, Legislatures, and the NLRB, 117
United Auto Workers Union, 78
United Brotherhood of Carpenters and Joiners of America, 25

United Mine Workers, 23, 58, 61, 101, 116
U.S. Congress, 31, 32, 33, 57, 59
U.S. Constitution, 168
U.S. Supreme Court, 25, 32, 37, 57, 59, 61, 62, 63, 64, 117, 160–161, 164, 212

Vaihinger, Hans, 229
Veblen, Thorstein, 130
Villard, Oswald Garrison, 202
Violence, 31, 47–48, 112, 148–149
Voluntary way, free market for labor and, 30

Wage rates, determination of, 42, 46–47, 140–141, 150–151, 155, 171, 174
Wages Question, The (Walker), 43
Wagner Act, *see* National Labor Relations Act
Walker, Francis A., 41, 43–44, 51–52
War Department, 113–114
War Labor Board, 157
Washington, George, 175
Washington Monthly, 171
Wat Tyler's Rebellion, 97
Wealth of Nations (Smith), 41, 43
Weber, Max, 73
Webster, Pelatiah, 98
What Is to Be Done? (Chernyshevsky), 202
"Wildcat strike," 14
Wiles, Peter, 96
Wilke, Joan, 121–125
Williams, Walter, 216
Wilson, Woodrow, 175
Women workers, 20, 215
Woodcock, Leonard, 183
Work, biblical view of, 76
Workers' control, 203
Workers' Self-Management in the United States (Gunn), 203
WPA, 135

Yellow-dog contracts, 210–211

PRICE LIST
American Unionism: Fallacies and Follies

Quantity	Price Each
1 copy	$14.95
2-4 copies	12.00
5-49 copies	9.00
50-499 copies	7.50
500 copies	6.00

Please add $3.00 per order for shipping and handling. Send your order, with accompanying check or money order, to The Foundation for Economic Education, 30 South Broadway, Irvington-on-Hudson, New York 10533. Visa and MasterCard telephone and fax orders are welcome; call (914) 591-7230 weekdays or fax (914) 591-8910 anytime.

About The Foundation for Economic Education

The Foundation for Economic Education (FEE) is a "home" for the friends of freedom everywhere. Its spirit is uplifting, reassuring, contagious: FEE has inspired the creation of numerous similar organizations at home and abroad.

FEE is the oldest conservative research organization dedicated to the presentation of individual freedom and the private-property order. It was established in 1946 by Leonard E. Read, and guided by its adviser, the eminent Austrian economist, Ludwig von Mises. Both served FEE until their deaths in 1983 and 1973, respectively.

Throughout the years the mission of FEE has remained unchanged: to study the moral and intellectual foundation of a free society and share its knowledge with individuals everywhere. It avoids getting embroiled in heated political controversies raging in Washington, D.C. Located in Irvington-on-Hudson, New York, FEE has remained a purely educational organization.

Since 1956, FEE has published *The Freeman,* an award-winning monthly journal with a long and noble lineage. Under the profound editorship of Paul Poirot it rose to great heights, always fighting for the timeless principles of the free society.

The *Freeman Classics* series of books reflects these heights, consisting of topical collections of great essays and articles published throughout the years. *American Unionism* is the ninth volume in the series. Also available: *The Morality of Capitalism, Private Property and Political Control, Prices and Price Controls, Public Education and Indoctrination, Politicized Medicine, Man and Nature, Taxation and Confiscation,* and *Bankers and Regulators.*

—Hans F. Sennholz